BEACHWAY*press*

VERMONT

Maps designed and produced by Beachway Press
Photographs by Jen Mynter, Charles Samuels
Illustrations by Michael Drake
Mountain Bike America Design by Gilles Collette

Printed in the United States of America by
Automated Graphic Systems, Inc.

Published by Beachway Press
9201 Beachway Lane
Springfield, VA 22153-1441

10 9 8 7 6 5 4 3 2 1

ISBN 1-882997-07-7

Library of Congress Cataloguing-in-Publication Data
        Mynter, Jen
        Mountain Bike America: Vermont
        An Atlas of Vermont's
        Greatest Off-Road Bicycle Rides / by Jen Mynter
        1st ed. Springfield, VA: Beachway Press, ©1997.
192 pages: Illustrations, Photographs, Maps, Graphics
1. All-terrain cycling–Vermont–Guidebooks.
Vermont–Guidebooks.
97-071748
CIP

BEACHWAY*press*

VERMONT

An Atlas of Vermont's Greatest
Off-Road Bicycle Rides
By Jen Mynter
Introduction by Scott Adams, Series Editor

Beachway Press
An addition to
Beachway Press' Mountain Bike America Series

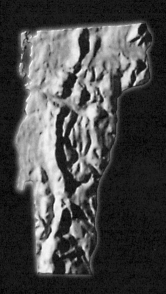

I dreamed that I went to the City of Gold,
To Heaven resplendent and fair,
And after I entered that beautiful fold
By One in authority there I was told
That not a Vermonter was there.

We give them the best the Kingdom provides;
They have everything here that they want,
But not a Vermonter in Heaven abides;
A very brief period here he resides,
Then he rides his horse swiftly back to Vermont.

Ernest Fenwick Johnstone
1867 – 1938

Dear Readers:
Every effort was made to make
this the most accurate, informative,
and easy-to-use guidebook on the
planet. Any comments, suggestions,
and corrections regarding this guide
are welcome and should be sent to:
Beachway Press
c/o Editorial Dept.
9201 Beachway Lane
Springfield, VA 22153

We'd love to hear from you so we
can make future editions and future
guides even better.

Thanks and happy trails!

Beachway Press

Contents

Other Places To Ride

Appendix

Preface

My first real experience leaving Vermont came when I was 18. I had lived in the same house in a small Vermont village for many years, on a side street my father had named himself. I remember vividly that day I left for college. I'd never been more nervous in my life. The feelings of anxiety and fear I had were not just about heading off to school, but of leaving the comforting security of the green hills that surrounded me. Those hills had always been my source of strength and inspiration.

Once at college in New York state, I quickly befriended several other homesick Vermont girls, and we spent many evenings in our rooms together listening to Jon Gailmor's "For the Love of Vermont," talking wistfully of our rolling Green Mountains. As the years passed, we grew to enjoy college life, but the yearning to return home to Vermont never vanished. Today, we have all settled back in Vermont; some of us raising families, some milking cows, and some riding mountain bikes in the hills and valleys of our homeland.

Growing up in Vermont was one of those things I took for granted as a youngster. It wasn't until high school that I began to realize there was something incredibly special in the hills around me. My passion in those days was alpine skiing, and like many Vermont kids, I was lucky enough to have a small ski area practically in my back yard. Every winter afternoon, as soon as school let out, I would grab my backpack and run the mile between school and ski area. Then I'd strap on my skis and, for an hour or so, race down the hillsides with utter abandon. Most days, at the end of the afternoon, I would ski down my favorite trail on the northwest side of the mountain and catch the glorious colors from the sun as it slowly faded behind clouds and hilltops. I would then ski home from the slopes, not removing my skis until I was literally in my own back yard.

This connection with the natural wonder and beauty of Vermont has remained sacred in my existence since this young age. A walk in the woods or a drive down an untraveled dirt road always elicits a response of appreciation from my senses. My love for skiing has since carried over to other forms of recreating in Vermont's woodlands. Snowshoeing, hiking, running, cross-country skiing, swimming, and mountain biking have all given me new ways to observe and explore this wonderful backcountry.

But it is mountain biking that has given me the most ultimate connection with the true personality of homeland. Over the last 10 years I have ridden in every corner of Vermont with friends who have shown me secret places that I would never have seen but on a mountain bike. Mossy caves, sparkling waterfalls, crystal-clear swimming holes filled with frigid water, and windy mountain summits were all best experienced on my bike. My love for the sport has since taken me exploring on a 10,000-mile mountain bike voyage through Southeast Asia, New Zealand, Australia, and Europe. And over the last 10 years I have raced my bike all over this country. But as always, I have come home to ride in Vermont.

Vermont's incredible network of backroads and trails is unmatched for its challenging variety of terrain, conditions, and scenery. Although Vermont riding is renowned for its technical single-track, there is plenty of riding that rolls along smooth forest paths or down quiet dirt roads. In fact, there seems to be a lot of everything in what Vermont offers us fat-tire fanatics. And to top it off, most of the riding is accessible from one Vermont village or another, each complete with thriving general stores and vibrant downtowns still exciting for visitors to explore.

No matter where I have roamed, it is Vermont's spirit that always draws me back. It is a spirit that is evident in both the land and the extraordinary people who live here and who make it the independent and determined little state that it is. As far back as Vermont's earliest beginnings Vermont has been a place resounding with strong, creative ideas, so much so that it declared itself the "Republic of Vermont" when it was initially denied statehood. It isn't just this feistiness that creates Vermont's spirit, but also an inherent feeling of appreciation for the fertile valleys and green highlands Vermont is so famous for. Vermont's strict codes for development and strong feelings toward environmentalism make it unique in an age of furious development.

My hope with this book is that you will have an opportunity to share a very special place by extraordinary means—your mountain bike. I wish that you too might catch the last rays of sun from a highland meadow, or the first burst of color from a solid sugar maple. I imagine you might also enjoy the taste of warm maple syrup poured over a bowl of fresh snow, or perhaps a sharp slice of Vermont cheddar cheese on a home-baked slice of bread.

I also hope that the spirit of Vermont will inspire you to tread lightly upon the paths you find mapped in this book, and encourage the kind of mountain biking that makes the farmer who owns the land happy to see you each time you ride through. As the Abenaki Indians—*Vermont's first residents*—might have said if early settlers had arrived on mountain bikes: "Leave only tire tracks, take only pictures."

Enjoy the Green Mountains!

Jen Mynter

Acknowledgment

A heartfelt thanks to my family for encouraging me to enjoy Vermont's Green Mountains from a very young age, and a special thanks to my mom for letting me go on those long hikes alone in the surrounding hills when I was in high school. I know they made you nervous.

I couldn't have completed this project without the incredible support of my husband, Tom Masterson, who kept my bike in shape, cooked many dinners as I worked late on the computer, and poured over maps looking for rides with me. Thank you for your support and enthusiasm.

I am grateful to the cycling community in Vermont for their help over the years with both my racing career and this writing endeavor. The West Hill Shop and Onion River Sports have been especially generous. Without their help, I'd probably still be riding the 35-pound bike I started on 10 years ago! Several New England bike companies also deserve a thank you, most recently, Independent Fabrications, for their belief in me.

Thanks to all the folks who put up with my picture taking and talking into my recorder after inviting you to join me on one of the many rides. These folks include Alexander Johnston, Betsy Geraghty, Tiffany Mann, Kirsten Jeppesen, Jan Bolland, Robin and John Miller, Win Kelly, Penny Griggs, Ben Hewitt—and of course Tom! A big hug goes to my dog Charlie, who was my most frequent riding companion, and was always happy regardless of the conditions or weather.

Finally, a special thanks to Pam Hockenbury, one of my high school English teachers. Your positive support of my early writing efforts has always stayed with me

Introduction

Introduction

Welcome to the new generation of bicycling! Indeed, the sport has evolved dramatically from the thin-tired, featherweight-frame days of old. The sleek geometry and lightweight frames of racing bicycles, still the heart and soul of bicycling worldwide, have lost much ground in recent years, unpaving the way for the mountain bike, which now accounts for the majority of all bicycle sales in the U.S. And with this change comes a new breed of cyclist, less concerned with smooth roads and long rides, who thrives in places once inaccessible to the mortal road bike.

The mountain bike, with its knobby tread and reinforced frame, takes cyclists to places once unheard of—down rugged mountain trails, through streams of rushing water and thick mud, across the frozen Alaskan tundra, and even to work in the city. There seem to be few limits on what this fat-tired beast can do and where it can take us. Few obstacles stand in its way, few boundaries slow its progress. Except for one—its own success. If trail closure means little to you now, read on and discover how a trail can be here today and gone tomorrow. With so many new off-road cyclists taking to the trails each year, it's no wonder trail access hinges precariously between universal acceptance and complete termination. But a little work on your part can go a long way to preserving trail access for future use. Nothing is more crucial to the survival of mountain biking itself than to read the examples set forth in the following pages and practice their message. Then turn to the maps, pick out your favorite ride, and hit the dirt!

WHAT THIS BOOK IS ABOUT

Within these pages you will find everything you need to know about off-road bicycling in Vermont. This guidebook begins by exploring the fascinating history of the mountain bike itself, then goes on to discuss everything from the health benefits of off-road cycling to tips and techniques for bicycling over logs and up hills. Also included are the types of clothing to keep you comfortable and in style, essential equipment ideas to keep your rides smooth and trouble-free, and descriptions of off-road terrain to prepare you for the kinds of bumps and bounces you can expect to encounter. The two major provisions of this book, though, are its unique and detailed maps and relentless dedication to trail preservation.

Each of the 34 rides included in this book is accompanied by four very different maps. A *location map* shows where each ride is in relation to the rest of the region; the *profile map* displays an accurate view of each ride's ups and downs, the *route map* leads you through each ride and is accompanied by detailed directions, and a *three-dimensional surface area map* provides a fascinating view of the surrounding topography and landscape.

Without open trails, the maps in this book are virtually useless. Cyclists must learn to be responsible for the trails they use and to share these trails with others. This guidebook addresses such issues as why trail use has become so controversial, what can be done to improve the image of mountain biking, how to have fun and ride responsibly, on-the-spot trail repair techniques, trail maintenance hotlines for each trail, and the worldwide-standard Rules of the Trail.

Each of the 34 rides is complete with maps, trail descriptions and directions, local history, and a quick-reference ride information board including such items as trail-maintenance hotlines, park schedules, costs, and alternative maps. Also included at the end of the book is an "Honorable Mentions" list of alternative off-road rides.

It's important to note that mountain bike rides tend to take longer than road rides because the average speed is often much slower. Average speeds can vary from a climbing pace of three to four miles per hour to 12 to 13 miles per hour on flatter roads and trails. Keep this in mind when planning your trip.

MOUNTAIN BIKE BEGINNINGS

It seems the mountain bike, originally designed for lunatic adventurists bored with straight lines, clean clothes, and smooth tires, has become globally popular in as short a time as it would take to race down a mountain trail.

Like many things of a revolutionary nature, the mountain bike was born on the west coast. But unlike Rollerblades, purple hair, and the peace sign, the concept of the off-road bike cannot be credited solely to the imaginative Californians—they were just the first to make waves.

The design of the first off-road specific bike was based on the geometry of the old Schwinn Excelsior, a one-speed, camel-back cruiser with balloon tires. Joe Breeze was the creator behind it, and in 1977 he built 10 of these "Breezers" for himself and his Marin County, California, friends at $750 apiece—a bargain.

Breeze was a serious competitor in bicycle racing, placing 13th in the 1977 U.S. Road Racing National Championships. After races, he and friends would scour local bike shops hoping to find old bikes they could then restore.

It was the 1941 Schwinn Excelsior, for which Breeze paid just five dollars, that began to shape and change bicycling history forever. After taking the bike home, removing the fenders, oiling the chain, and pumping up the tires, Breeze hit the dirt. He loved it.

His inspiration, while forerunning, was not altogether unique. On the opposite end of the country, nearly 2,500 miles from Marin County, east coast bike bums were also growing restless. More and more old, beat-up clunkers were being restored and modified. These behemoths often weighed as much as 80 pounds and were so reinforced they seemed virtually indestructible. But rides that take just 40 minutes on today's 25-pound featherweights took the steel-toed-boot-and-blue-jean-clad bikers of the late 1970s and early 1980s nearly four hours to complete.

Not until 1981 was it possible to purchase a production mountain bike, but local retailers found these ungainly bicycles difficult to sell and rarely kept them in stock. By 1983, however, mountain bikes were no longer such a fringe item, and large bike manufacturers quickly jumped into the action, producing their own versions of the off-road bike. By the 1990s, the mountain bike had firmly established its place with bicyclists of nearly all ages and abilities, and now command nearly 90 percent of the U.S. bike market.

There are many reasons for the mountain bike's success in becoming the hottest two-wheeled vehicle in the nation. They are much friendlier to the cyclist than traditional road bikes because of

Beachway Press

their comfortable upright position and shock-absorbing fat tires. And because of the health-conscious, environmentalist movement of the late 1980s and 1990s, people are more activity minded and seek nature on a closer front than paved roads can allow. The mountain bike gives you these things and takes you far away from the daily grind—even if you're only minutes from the city.

MOUNTAIN BIKING INTO SHAPE

If your objective is to get in shape and lose weight, then you're on the right track, because mountain biking is one of the best ways to get started.

One way many of us have lost weight in this sport is the crash-and-burn-it-off method. Picture this: you're speeding uncontrollably down a vertical drop that you realize you shouldn't be on—only after it is too late. Your front wheel lodges into a rut and launches you through endless weeds, trees, and pointy rocks before coming to an abrupt halt in a puddle of thick mud. Surveying the damage, you discover, with the layers of skin, body parts, and lost confidence littering the trail above, that those unwanted pounds have been shed-permanently. Instant weight loss.

There is, of course, a more conventional (and quite a bit less painful) approach to losing weight and gaining fitness on a mountain bike. It's called the workout, and bicycles provide an ideal way to get physical. Take a look at some of the benefits associated with cycling.

Cycling helps you shed pounds without gimmicky diet fads or weight-loss programs. You can explore the countryside and burn nearly 10 to 16 calories per minute or close to 600 to 1,000 calories per hour. Moreover, it's a great way to spend an afternoon.

No less significant than the external and cosmetic changes of your body from riding are the internal changes taking place. Over time, cycling regularly will strengthen your heart as your body grows vast networks of new capillaries to carry blood to all those working muscles. This will, in turn, give your skin a healthier glow. The capacity of your lungs may increase up to 20 percent, and your resting heart rate will drop significantly. The Stanford University School of Medicine reports to the American Heart Association that people can reduce their risk of heart attack by nearly 64 percent if they can burn up to 2,000 calories per week. This is only two to three hours of bike riding!

Recommended for insomnia, hypertension, indigestion, anxiety, and even for recuperation from major heart attacks, bicycling can be an excellent cure-all as well as a great preventive. Cycling just a few hours per week can improve your figure and sleeping habits, give you greater resistance to illness, increase your energy levels, and provide feelings of accomplishment and heightened self-esteem.

BE SAFE—KNOW THE LAW

Occasionally, even the hard-core off-road cyclists will find they have no choice but to ride the pavement. When you are forced to hit the road, it's important for you to know and understand the rules.

Outlined below are a few of the common laws found in Vermont's Vehicle Code book.

- *Bicycles are legally classified as vehicles in Vermont.* This means that as a bicyclist, you are responsible for obeying the same rules of the road as a driver of a motor vehicle.

- *Bicyclists must ride with the traffic—NOT AGAINST IT!* Because bicycles are considered vehicles, you must ride your bicycle just as you would drive a car—with traffic. Only pedestrians should travel against the flow of traffic.
- *You must obey all traffic signs.* This includes stop signs and stoplights.
- *Always signal your turns.* Most drivers aren't expecting bicyclists to be on the roads, and many drivers would prefer that cyclists stay off the roads altogether. It's important, therefore, to clearly signal your intentions to motorists both in front and behind you.
- *Bicyclists are entitled to the same roads as cars (except controlled-access highways).* Unfortunately, cyclists are rarely given this consideration.
- *Be a responsible cyclist.* Do not abuse your rights to ride on open roads. Follow the rules and set a good example for all of us as you roll along.

THE MOUNTAIN BIKE CONTROVERSY

Are Mountain Bicyclists Environmental Outlaws?
Do We have the Right to Use Public Trails?

Mountain bikers have long endured the animosity of folks in the back-country who complain about the consequences of off-road bicycling. Many people believe that the fat tires and knobby tread do unacceptable environmental damage and that our uncontrollable riding habits are a danger to animals and to other trail users. To the contrary, mountain bikes have no more environmental impact than hiking boots or horseshoes. This does not mean, however, that mountain bikes leave no imprint at all. Wherever man treads, there is an impact. By riding responsibly, though, it is possible to leave only a minimum impact—something we all must take care to achieve.

Unfortunately, it is often people of great influence who view the mountain bike as the environment's worst enemy. Consequently, we as mountain bike riders and environmentally concerned citizens must be educators, impressing upon others that we also deserve the right to use these trails. Our responsibilities as bicyclists are no more and no less than any other trail user. We must all take the soft-cycling approach and show that mountain bicyclists are not environmental outlaws.

ETIQUETTE OF MOUNTAIN BIKING

Moving softly across the land means leaving no more than an echo.

Hank Barlow

When discussing mountain biking etiquette, we are in essence discussing the soft-cycling approach. This term, as mentioned previously, describes the art of minimum-impact bicycling and should apply to both the physical and social dimensions of the sport. But make no mistake—it is possible to ride fast and furiously while maintaining the balance of soft-cycling. Here first are a few ways to minimize the physical impact of mountain bike riding.

- *Stay on the trail.* Don't ride around fallen trees or mud holes that block your path. Stop and cross over them. When you come to a vista overlooking a deep valley, don't ride off the trail for a better vantage point. Instead, leave the bike and walk to see the view. Riding off the trail may seem inconsequential when done only once, but soon someone else will follow, then

Beachway Press

others, and the cumulative results can be catastrophic. Each time you wander from the trail you begin creating a new path, adding one more scar to the earth's surface.

- *Do not disturb the soil.* Follow a line within the trail that will not disturb or damage the soil.
- *Do not ride over soft or wet trails.* After a rain shower or during the thawing season, trails will often resemble muddy, oozing swampland. The best thing to do is stay off the trails altogether. Realistically, however, we're all going to come across some muddy trails we cannot anticipate. Instead of blasting through each section of mud, which may seem both easier and more fun, lift the bike and walk past. Each time a cyclist rides through a soft or muddy section of trail, that part of the trail is permanently damaged. Regardless of the trail's conditions, though, remember always to go over the obstacles across the path, not around them. Stay on the trail.
- *Avoid trails that, for all but God, are considered impassable and impossible.* Don't take a leap of faith down a kamikaze descent on which you will be forced to lock your brakes and skid to the bottom, ripping the ground apart as you go.

Soft-cycling should apply to the social dimensions of the sport as well, since mountain bikers are not the only folks who use the trails. Hikers, equestrians, cross-country skiers, and other outdoors people use many of the same trails and can be easily spooked by a marauding mountain biker tearing through the trees. Be friendly in the forest and give ample warning of your approach.

- *Take out what you bring in.* Don't leave broken bike pieces and banana peels scattered along the trail.
- *Be aware of your surroundings.* Don't use popular hiking trails for race training.
- *Slow down!* Rocketing around blind corners is a sure way to ruin an unsuspecting hiker's day. Consider this—If you fly down a quick singletrack descent at 20 mph, then hit the brakes and slow down to only six mph to pass someone, you're still moving twice as fast as they are!

Like the trails we ride on, the social dimension of mountain biking is very fragile and must be cared for responsibly. We should not want to destroy another person's enjoyment of the outdoors. By riding in the backcountry with caution, control, and responsibility, our presence should be felt positively by other trail users. By adhering to these rules, trail riding—a privilege that can quickly be taken away—will continue to be ours to share.

TRAIL MAINTENANCE

Unfortunately, despite all of the preventive measures taken to avoid trail damage, we're still going to run into many trails requiring attention. Simply put, a lot of hikers, equestrians, and cyclists alike use the same trails—some wear and tear is unavoidable. But like your bike, if you want to use these trails for a long time to come, you must also maintain them.

Trail maintenance and restoration can be accomplished in a variety of ways. One way is for mountain bike clubs to combine efforts with other trail users (i.e. hikers and equestrians) and work closely with land managers to cut new trails or repair existing ones. This not only reinforces to others the commitment cyclists have in caring for and maintaining the land, but also breaks the ice that often separates cyclists from their fellow trailmates. Another good way to help out is to show up on a Saturday morning with a few riding buddies at your favorite off-road domain ready to work. With a good attitude, thick gloves, and the local land manager's supervision, trail repair is fun and very rewarding. It's important, of course, that you arrange a trail-repair outing with the local land manager before you start pounding shovels into the dirt. They can lead you to the most needy sections of trail and instruct you on what repairs should be done and how best to accomplish the task. Perhaps the most effective means of trail maintenance, though, can be done by yourself and while you're riding. Read on.

ON-THE-SPOT QUICK FIX

Most of us, when we're riding, have at one time or another come upon muddy trails or fallen trees blocking our path. We notice that over time the mud gets deeper and the trail gets wider as people go through or around the obstacles. We worry that the problem will become so severe and repairs too difficult that the trail's access may be threatened. We also know that our ambition to do anything about it is greatest at that moment, not after a hot shower and a plate of spaghetti. Here are a few on-the-spot quick fixes you can do that will hopefully correct a problem before it gets out of hand and get you back on your bike within minutes.

• **MUDDY TRAILS.** What do you do when trails develop huge mud holes destined for the EPA's Superfund status? The technique is called corduroying, and it works much like building a pontoon over the mud to support bikes, horses, or hikers as they cross. Corduroy (not the pants) is the term for roads made of logs laid down crosswise. Use small-and medium-sized sticks and lay them side by side across the trail until they cover the length of the muddy section (break the sticks to fit the width of the trail). Press them into the mud with your feet, then lay more on top if needed. Keep adding sticks until the trail is firm. Not only will you stay clean as you cross, but the sticks may soak up some of the water and help the puddle dry. This quick fix may last as long as one month before needing to be redone. And as time goes on, with new layers added to the trail, the soil will grow stronger, thicker, and more resistant to erosion. This whole process may take fewer than five minutes, and you can be on your way, knowing the trail behind you is in good repair.

• **LEAVING THE TRAIL.** What do you do to keep cyclists from cutting corners and leaving the designated trail? The solution is much simpler than you may think. (No, don't hire an off-road police force.) Notice where people are leaving the trail and throw a pile of thick branches or brush along the path, or place logs across the opening to block the way through. There are probably dozens of subtle tricks like these that will manipulate people into staying on the designated trail. If executed well, no one will even notice that the thick branches scattered along the ground in the woods weren't always there. And most folks would probably rather take a moment to hop a log in the trail than get tangled in a web of branches.

• **OBSTACLES IN THE WAY.** If there are large obstacles blocking the trail, try and remove them or push them aside. If you cannot do this by yourself, call the trail maintenance hotline to speak with the land manager of that particular trail and see what can be done.

We must be willing to *sweat for* our trails in order to *sweat on* them. Police yourself and point out to others the significance of trail maintenance. "Sweat Equity," the rewards of continued land use won with a fair share of sweat, pays off when the trail is "up for review" by the land manager and he or she remembers the efforts made by trail-conscious mountain bikers.

RULES OF THE TRAIL

The International Mountain Bicycling Association (IMBA) has developed these guidelines to trail riding. These "Rules of the Trail" are accepted worldwide and will go a long way in keeping trails open. Please respect and follow these rules for everyone's sake.

1. *Ride only on open trails.* Respect trail and road closures (if you're not sure, ask a park or state official first), do not trespass on private property, and obtain permits or authorization if required. Federal and state wilderness areas are off-limits to cycling. Parks and state forests may also have certain trails closed to cycling.

2. *Leave no trace.* Be sensitive to the dirt beneath you. Even on open trails, you should not ride under conditions by which you will leave evidence of your passing, such as on certain soils or shortly after a rainfall. Be sure to observe the different types of soils and trails you're riding on, practicing minimum-impact cycling. Never ride off the trail, don't skid your tires, and be sure to bring out at least as much as you bring in.

3. *Control your bicycle!* Inattention for even one second can cause disaster for yourself or for others. Excessive speed frightens and can injure people, gives mountain biking a bad name, and can result in trail closures.

4. *Always yield.* Let others know you're coming well in advance (a friendly greeting is always good and often appreciated). Show your respect when passing others by slowing to walking speed or stopping altogether, especially in the presence of horses. Horses can be unpredictable, so be very careful. Anticipate that other trail users may be around corners or in blind spots.

5. *Never spook animals.* All animals are spooked by sudden movements, unannounced approaches, or loud noises. Give the animals extra room and time so they can adjust to you. Move slowly or dismount around animals. Running cattle and disturbing wild animals are serious offenses. Leave gates as you find them, or as marked.

6. *Plan ahead.* Know your equipment, your ability, and the area in which you are riding, and plan your trip accordingly. Be self-sufficient at all times, keep your bike in good repair, and carry necessary supplies for changes in weather or other conditions. You can help keep trails open by setting an example of responsible, courteous, and controlled mountain bike riding.

7. *Always wear a helmet when you ride.* For your own safety and protection, a helmet should be worn whenever you are riding your bike. You never know when a tree root or small rock will throw you the wrong way and send you tumbling.

According to Responsible Organized Mountain Pedalers (ROMP) of Campbell, California, "thousands of miles of dirt trails have been closed to mountain bicycling because of the irresponsible riding habits of just a few riders." Don't follow the example of these offending riders. Don't take away trail privileges from thousands of others who work hard each year to keep the backcountry avenues open to us all.

THE NECESSITIES OF CYCLING

When discussing the most important items to have on a bike ride, cyclists generally agree on the following four items.

- **HELMET.** The reasons to wear a helmet should be obvious. Helmets are discussed in more detail in the Be Safe—Wear Your Armor section.
- **WATER.** Without it, cyclists may face dehydration, which may result in dizziness and fatigue. On a warm day, cyclists should drink at least one full bottle during every hour of riding. Remember, it's always good to drink before you feel thirsty—otherwise, it may be too late.
- **CYCLING SHORTS.** These are necessary if you plan to ride your bike more than 20 to 30 minutes. Padded cycling shorts may be the only thing preventing your derriere from serious saddle soreness by ride's end. There are two types of cycling shorts you can buy. Touring shorts are good for people who don't want to look like they're wearing anatomically correct cellophane. These look like regular athletic shorts with pockets, but have built-in padding in the crotch area for protection from chafing and saddle sores. The more popular, traditional cycling shorts are made of skin-tight material, also with a padded crotch. Whichever style you find most comfortable, cycling shorts are a necessity for long rides.
- **FOOD.** This essential item will keep you rolling. Cycling burns up a lot of calories and is among the few sports in which no one is safe from the "Bonk." Bonking feels like it sounds. Without food in your system, your blood sugar level collapses, and there is no longer any energy in your body. This instantly results in total fatigue and light-headedness. So when you're filling your water bottle, remember to bring along some food. Fruit, energy bars, or some other forms of high-energy food are highly recommended. Candy bars are not, however, because they will deliver a sudden burst of high energy, then let you down soon after, causing you to feel worse than before. Energy bars are available at most bike stores and are similar to candy bars, but provide complex carbohydrate energy and high nutrition rather than the fast-burning simple sugars of candy bars.

BE PREPARED OR DIE

Essential equipment that will keep you from dying alone in the woods:
- **SPARE TUBE**
- **TIRE IRONS**—See the Appendix for instructions on fixing flat tires.
- **PATCH KIT**
- **PUMP**
- **MONEY**—Spare change for emergency calls.
- **SPOKE WRENCH**
- **SPARE SPOKES**—To fit your wheel. Tape these to the chain stay.

- **CHAIN TOOL**
- **ALLEN KEYS**—Bring appropriate sizes to fit your bike.
- **COMPASS**
- **FIRST AID KIT**
- **MATCHES**
- **GUIDEBOOK**—In case all else fails and you must start a fire to survive, this guidebook will serve as excellent fire starter!

To carry these items, you may need a bike bag. A bag mounted in front of the handlebars provides quick access to your belongings, whereas a saddle bag fitted underneath the saddle keeps things out of your way. If you're carrying lots of equipment, you may want to consider a set of panniers. These are much larger and mount on either side of each wheel. Many cyclists, though, prefer not to use a bag at all. They just slip all they need into their jersey pockets, and off they go.

BE SAFE—WEAR YOUR ARMOR

While on the subject of jerseys, it's crucial to discuss the clothing you must wear to be safe, practical, and—if you prefer—stylish. The following is a list of items that will save you from disaster, outfit you comfortably, and most important, keep you looking cool.

- **HELMET**. A helmet is an absolute necessity because it protects your head from complete annihilation. It is the only thing that will not dis-integrate into a million pieces after a wicked crash on a descent you shouldn't have been on in the first place. A helmet with a solid exteri-or shell will also protect your head from sharp or protruding objects. Of course, with a hard-shelled helmet, you can paste several stickers of your favorite bicycle manufacturers all over the outer shell, giving com-panies even more free advertising for your dollar.
- **SHORTS**. Let's just say Lycra cycling shorts are considered a major safety item if you plan to ride for more than 20 or 30 minutes at a time. As men-tioned in The Necessities of Cycling section, cycling shorts are well regarded as the leading cure-all for chafing and saddle sores. The most preventive cycling shorts have padded "chamois" (most chamois is synthetic nowadays) in the crotch area. Of course, if you choose to wear these traditional cycling shorts, it's imperative that they look as if someone spray painted them onto your body.
- **GLOVES**. You may find well-padded cycling gloves invaluable when traveling over rocky trails and gravelly roads for hours on end. Long-fingered gloves may also be useful, as branches, trees, assorted hard objects, and, occasionally, small animals will reach out and whack your knuckles.
- **GLASSES**. Not only do sunglasses give you an imposing presence and make you look cool (both are extremely important), they also protect your eyes from harmful ultraviolet rays, invisible branches, creepy bugs, dirt, and may prevent you from being caught sneaking glances at riders of the opposite sex also wearing skintight, revealing Lycra.
- **SHOES**. Mountain bike shoes should have stiff soles to help make pedaling easier and pro-vide better traction when walking your bike up a trail becomes necessary. Virtually any kind of good outdoor hiking footwear will work, but specific mountain bike shoes (especially those

with inset cleats) are best. It is vital that these shoes look as ugly as humanly possible. Those closest in style to bowling shoes are, of course, the most popular.

- **JERSEY or SHIRT**. Bicycling jerseys are popular because of their snug fit and back pockets. When purchasing a jersey, look for ones that are loaded with bright, blinding, neon logos and manufacturers' names. These loudly decorated billboards are also good for drawing unnecessary attention to yourself just before taking a mean spill while trying to hop a curb. A cotton T-shirt is a good alternative in warm weather, but when the weather turns cold, cotton becomes a chilling substitute for the jersey. Cotton retains moisture and sweat against your body, which may cause you to get the chills and ills on those cold-weather rides.

OH, THOSE COLD VERMONT DAYS

If the weather chooses not to cooperate on the day you've set aside for a bike ride, it's helpful to be prepared.

- *Tights or leg warmers.* These are best in temperatures below 55 degrees. Knees are sensitive and can develop all kinds of problems if they get cold. Common problems include tendinitis, bursitis, and arthritis.
  - *Plenty of layers on your upper body.* When the air has a nip in it, layers of clothing will keep the chill away from your chest and help prevent the development of bronchitis. If the air is cool, a polypropylene long-sleeved shirt is best to wear against the skin beneath other layers of clothing. Polypropylene, like wool, wicks away moisture from your skin to keep your body dry. Try to avoid wearing cotton or baggy clothing when the temperature falls. Cotton, as mentioned before, holds moisture like a sponge, and baggy clothing catches cold air and swirls it around your body. Good cold-weather clothing should fit snugly against your body, but not be restrictive.
  - *Wool socks.* Don't pack too many layers under those shoes, though. You may stand the chance of restricting circulation, and your feet will get real cold, real fast.
  - *Thinsulate or Gortex gloves.* We may all agree that there is nothing worse than frozen feet—unless your hands are frozen. A good pair of Thinsulate or Gortex gloves should keep your hands toasty and warm.
- *Hat or helmet on cold days?* Sometimes, when the weather gets really cold and you still want to hit the trails, it's tough to stay warm. We all know that 130 percent of the body's heat escapes through the head (overactive brains, I imagine), so it's important to keep the cranium warm. Ventilated helmets are designed to keep heads cool in the summer heat, but they do little to help keep heads warm during rides in sub-zero temperatures. Cyclists should consider wearing a hat on extremely cold days. Polypropylene Skullcaps are great head and ear warmers that snugly fit over your head beneath the helmet. Head protection is not lost. Another option is a helmet cover that covers those ventilating gaps and helps keep the body heat in. These do not, however, keep your ears warm. Some cyclists will opt for a simple knit cycling cap *sans* the helmet, but these have never been shown to be very good cranium protectors.

All of this clothing can be found at your local bike store, where the staff should be happy to help fit you into the seasons of the year.

Beachway Press

TO HAVE OR NOT TO HAVE...

(Other Very Useful Items)

Though mountain biking is relatively new to the cycling scene, there is no shortage of items for you and your bike to make riding better, safer, and easier. I have rummaged through the unending lists and separated the gadgets from the good stuff, coming up with what I believe are items certain to make mountain bike riding easier and more enjoyable.

- **TIRES.** Buying yourself a good pair of knobby tires is the quickest way to enhance the off-road handling capabilities of your bike. There are many types of mountain bike tires on the market. Some are made exclusively for very rugged off-road terrain. These big-knobbed, soft rubber tires virtually stick to the ground with unforgiving traction, but tend to deteriorate quickly on pavement. There are other tires made exclusively for the road. These are called "slicks" and have no tread at all. For the average cyclist, though, a good tire somewhere in the middle of these two extremes should do the trick.

- **TOE CLIPS or CLIPLESS PEDALS.** With these, you will ride with more power. Toe clips attach to your pedals and strap your feet firmly in place, allowing you to exert pressure on the pedals on both the downstroke and the upstroke. They will increase your pedaling efficiency by 30 percent to 50 percent. Clipless pedals, which liberate your feet from the traditional straps and clips, have made toe clips virtually obsolete. Like ski bindings, they attach your shoe directly to the pedal. They are, however, much more expensive than toe clips.

- **BAR ENDS.** These great clamp-on additions to your original straight bar will provide more leverage, an excellent grip for climbing, and a more natural position for your hands. Be aware, however, of the bar end's propensity for hooking trees on fast descents, sending you, the cyclist, airborne.

- **FANNY PACK.** These bags are ideal for carrying keys, extra food, guidebooks, tools, spare tubes, and a cellular phone, in case you need to call for help.

- **SUSPENSION FORKS.** For the more serious off-roaders who want nothing to impede their speed on the trails, investing in a pair of suspension forks is a good idea. Like tires, there are plenty of brands to choose from, and they all do the same thing—absorb the brutal beatings of a rough trail. The cost of these forks, however, is sometimes more brutal than the trail itself.

- **BIKE COMPUTERS.** These are fun gadgets to own and are much less expensive than in years past. They have such features as trip distance, speedometer, odometer, time of day, altitude, alarm, average speed, maximum speed, heart rate, global satellite positioning, etc. Bike computers will come in handy when following these maps or to know just how far you've ridden in the wrong direction.

TYPES OF OFF-ROAD TERRAIN

Before roughing it off road, we may first have to ride the pavement to get to our destination. Please, don't be dismayed. Some of the country's best rides are on the road. Once we get past these smooth-surfaced pathways, though, adventures in dirt await us.

- **RAILS-TO-TRAILS.** Abandoned rail lines are converted into usable public resources for exercising, commuting, or just enjoying nature. Old rails and ties are torn up and a trail, paved or unpaved, is laid along the existing corridor. This completes the cycle from ancient Indian trading routes to railroad corridors and back again to hiking and cycling trails.
- **UNPAVED ROADS.** These are typically found in rural areas and are most often public roads. Be careful when exploring, though, not to ride on someone's unpaved private drive.
  - **FOREST ROADS.** These dirt and gravel roads are used primarily as access to forest land and are kept in good condition. They are almost always open to public use.
    - **SINGLETRACK.** Singletrack can be the most fun on a mountain bike. These trails, with only one track to follow, are often narrow, challenging pathways through the woods. Remember to make sure these trails are open before zipping into the woods. (At the time of this printing, all trails and roads in this guidebook were open to mountain bikes.)
      - **OPEN LAND.** Unless there is a marked trail through a field or open space, you should not plan to ride here. Once one person cuts his or her wheels through a field or meadow, many more are sure to follow, causing irreparable damage to the landscape. "Human tracks are like cancer cells; they spread very quickly."

TECHNIQUES TO SHARPEN YOUR SKILLS

Many of us see ourselves as pure athletes—blessed with power, strength, and endless endurance. However, it may be those with finesse, balance, agility, and grace that get around most quickly on a mountain bike. Although power, strength, and endurance do have their places in mountain biking, these elements don't necessarily form the framework for a champion mountain biker.

The bike should become an extension of your body. Slight shifts in your hips or knees can have remarkable results. Experienced bike handlers seem to flash down technical descents, dashing over obstacles in a smooth and graceful effort as if pirouetting in Swan Lake.

Here are some tips and techniques to help you connect with your bike and float gracefully over the dirt.

Braking

Using your brakes requires using your head, especially when descending. This doesn't mean using your head as a stopping block, but rather to think intelligently. Use your best judgment in terms of how much or how little to squeeze those brake levers.

The more weight a tire is carrying, the more braking power it has. When you're going downhill, your front wheel carries more weight than the rear. Braking with the front brake will help keep you in control without going into a skid. Be careful, though, not to overdo it with the front brakes and accidentally toss yourself over the handlebars. And don't neglect your rear brake!

When descending, shift your weight back over the rear wheel, thus increasing your rear braking power as well. This will balance the power of both brakes and give you maximum control.

Good riders learn just how much of their weight to shift over each wheel and how to apply just enough braking power to each brake, so not to "endo" over the handlebars or skid down a trail.

GOING UPHILL—Climbing Those Treacherous Hills

- *Shift into a low gear (push the thumb shifter away from you).* Before shifting, be sure to ease up on your pedaling so there is not too much pressure on the chain. Find the gear best for you that matches the terrain and steepness of each climb.
- *Stay seated.* Standing out of the saddle is often helpful when climbing steep hills with a road bike, but you may find that on dirt, standing may cause your rear tire to lose its grip and spin out. Climbing requires traction. Stay seated as long as you can, and keep the rear tire digging into the ground. Ascending skyward may prove to be much easier in the saddle.
- *Lean forward.* On very steep hills, the front end may feel unweighted and suddenly pop up. Slide forward on the saddle and lean over the handlebars. This will add more weight to the front wheel and should keep you grounded.
- *Keep pedaling.* On rocky climbs, be sure to keep the pressure on, and don't let up on those pedals! The slower you go through rough trail sections, the harder you will work.

GOING DOWNHILL—
The Real Reason We Get Up in the Morning

- *Shift into the big chainring.* Shifting into the big ring before a bumpy descent will help keep the chain from bouncing off. And should you crash or disengage your leg from the pedal, the chain will cover the teeth of the big ring so they don't bite into your leg.
- *Relax.* Stay loose on the bike, and don't lock your elbows or clench your grip. Your elbows need to bend with the bumps and absorb the shock, while your hands should have a firm but controlled grip on the bars to keep things steady. Steer with your body, allowing your shoulders to guide you through each turn and around each obstacle.
- *Don't oversteer or lose control.* Mountain biking is much like downhill skiing, since you must shift your weight from side to side down narrow, bumpy descents. Your bike will have the tendency to track in the direction you look and follow the slight shifts and leans of your body. You should not think so much about steering, but rather in what direction you wish to go.
- *Rise above the saddle.* When racing down bumpy, technical descents, you should not be sitting on the saddle, but standing on the pedals, allowing your legs and knees to absorb the rocky trail instead of your rear.
- *Drop your saddle.* For steep, technical descents, you may want to drop your saddle three or four inches. This lowers your center of gravity, giving you much more room to bounce around.

- *Keep your pedals parallel to the ground.* The front pedal should be slightly higher so that it doesn't catch on small rocks or logs.
- *Stay focused.* Many descents require your utmost concentration and focus just to reach the bottom. You must notice every groove, every root, every rock, every hole, every bump. You, the bike, and the trail should all become one as you seek singletrack nirvana on your way down the mountain. But if your thoughts wander, however, then so may your bike, and you may instead become one with the trees!

WATCH OUT!
Back-road Obstacles

- **LOGS.** When you want to hop a log, throw your body back, yank up on the handlebars, and pedal forward in one swift motion. This clears the front end of the bike. Then quickly scoot forward and pedal the rear wheel up and over. Keep the forward momentum until you've cleared the log, and by all means, don't hit the brakes, or you may do some interesting acrobatic maneuvers!
  - **ROCKS.** Worse than highway potholes! Stay relaxed, let your elbows and knees absorb the shock, and always continue applying power to your pedals. Staying seated will keep the rear wheel weighted to prevent slipping, and a light front end will help you to respond quickly to each new obstacle. The slower you go, the more time your tires will have to get caught between the grooves.
    - **WATER.** Before crossing a stream or puddle, be sure to first check the depth and bottom surface. There may be an unseen hole or large rock hidden under the water that could wash you up if you're not careful. After you're sure all is safe, hit the water at a good speed, pedal steadily, and allow the bike to steer you through. Once you're across, tap the breaks to squeegee the water off the rims.
    - **LEAVES.** Be careful of wet leaves. These may look pretty, but a trail covered with leaves may cause your wheels to slip out from under you. Leaves are not nearly as unpredictable and dangerous as ice, but they do warrant your attention on a rainy day.
- **MUD.** If you must ride through mud, hit it head on and keep pedaling. You want to part the ooze with your front wheel and get across before it swallows you up. Above all, don't leave the trail to go around the mud. This just widens the path even more and leads to increased trail erosion.

Beachway Press

Urban Obstacles

- **CURBS** are fun to jump, but like with logs, be careful.
- **CURBSIDE DRAINS** are typically not a problem for bikes. Just be careful not to get a wheel caught in the grate.
- **DOGS** make great pets, but seem to have it in for bicyclists. If you think you can't outrun a dog that's chasing you, stop and walk your bike out of its territory. A loud yell to *Get!* or *Go home!* often works, as does a sharp squirt from your water bottle right between the eyes.
- **CARS** are tremendously convenient when we're in them, but dodging irate motorists in big automobiles becomes a real hazard when riding a bike. As a cyclist, you must realize most drivers aren't expecting you to be there and often wish you weren't. Stay alert and ride carefully, clearly signaling all of your intentions.
- **POTHOLES**, like grates and back-road canyons, should be avoided. Just because you're on an all-terrain bicycle doesn't mean you're indestructible. Potholes regularly damage rims, pop tires, and sometimes lift unsuspecting cyclists into a spectacular swan dive over the handlebars.

LAST-MINUTE CHECKOVER

Before a ride, it's a good idea to give your bike a once-over to make sure everything is in working order. Begin by checking the air pressure in your tires before each ride to make sure they are properly inflated. Mountain bikes require about 45 to 55 pounds per square inch of air pressure. If your tires are underinflated, there is greater likelihood that the tubes may get pinched on a bump or rock, causing the tire to flat.

Looking over your bike to make sure everything is secure and in its place is the next step. Go through the following checklist before each ride.

- *Pinch the tires to feel for proper inflation.* They should give just a little on the sides, but feel very hard on the treads. If you have a pressure gauge, use that.
- *Check your brakes.* Squeeze the rear brake and roll your bike forward. The rear tire should skid. Next, squeeze the front brake and roll your bike forward. The rear wheel should lift into the air. If this doesn't happen, then your brakes are too loose. Make sure the brake levers don't touch the handlebars when squeezed with full force.
- *Check all quick releases on your bike.* Make sure they are all securely tightened.
- *Lube up.* If your chain squeaks, apply some lubricant.
- *Check your nuts and bolts.* Check the handlebars, saddle, cranks, and pedals to make sure that each is tight and securely fastened to your bike.
- *Check your wheels.* Spin each wheel to see that they spin through the frame and between brake pads freely.
- *Have you got everything?* Make sure you have your spare tube, tire irons patch kit, frame pump, tools, food, water, and guidebook.

The Maps

Map Legend

I don't want anyone, by any means, to feel restricted to just the roads and trails that are mapped here. I hope you will have the same adventurous spirit and use these maps as a platform to dive into Vermont's backcountry and discover new routes for yourself. One of the best ways to begin this is to simply turn the map upside down and ride the course in reverse. The change in perspective is fantastic and the ride should feel quite different. With this in mind, it will be like getting two distinctly different rides on each map.

For your own purposes, you may wish to copy the directions for the course onto a small sheet to help you while riding, or photocopy the map and cue sheet to take with you. These pages can be folded into a bike bag, used with the **BarMap™** or **BarMapOTG™** *(see the* **back of the book for more info**), *or stuffed into a jersey pocket. Please remember to slow or even stop when you want to read the map.*

After a short introduction of each particular ride, there will be a profile map, followed by a cue sheet which will provide detailed directions and information about each ride.

81	Interstate Road
522	U.S. Highway Road
654	State Road
	Maintained Dirt Road
	Unmaintained Jeep Trail
	Singletrack Trail
	Highlighted Route
	Ntl. Forest/County Boundarie
	State Boundaries
	Railroad Tracks
	Power Lines
	Appalachian/Long Trails
	Rivers or Streams
★	Start of Ride
	Directional Arrows
🚲	MTB Trail or Center
	X-Country Ski Center
	School
▲	Mountain Peak
☼	Scenic View
▲	Campground
	Hiking-Only Trails
	Shelter
	Gate
	Ski Resort
△	Radio Tower

Beachway Press

Ride Location Map

Trails Location

Honorable Mentions

A. Central Vermont Trail
B. Burke Mountain Ski Area
C. Cross Vermont Rail-Trail
D. Firefly Ranch
E. Coyote Hill Farm
F. Moosalamoo
G. Blueberry Hill Ski Area
H. Cortina Inn, MTB Trails
I. Delaware & Hudson Rail-Trail
J. Grafton Ponds Ski Center
K. Prospect Mountain Touring Ctr

1. Craftsbury Singletrack
2. Wild Branch Wilderness
3. Kirby Mountain Loop
4. Underhill/Mt Mansfield Loop
5. Catamount Outdoor Center
6. Bolton Valley
7. Woodbury Mountain Loop
8. Groton State Forest
9. Cross Vermont Trail
10. Dirt Roads Of Orange
11. Waitsfield Gap
12. Mad River Valley Tour
13. Bull Run Ramble
14. Williamstown Dirt Roads
15. Connecticut Corners Loop
16. Tucker Mountain Loop
17. Mount Cushman
18. Green Mountain Touring Ctr
19. Hurricane Ridge
20. Vershire Loop
21. Coyote Hill
22. Five Corners
23. Connecticut River Amble
24. Lyme, New Hampshire, Loop
25. Downer State Forest
26. Killingtrack Singletrack Tour
27. Cloudland Loop
28. Hurricane Reservoir
29. Hartland Hill Loop
30. Kedron Valley
31. MountAscutney View
32. Putney Mountain Tour
33. Old Stratton Turnpike
34. Mount Snow MTB Center

Courses At A Glance

Courses Elevations

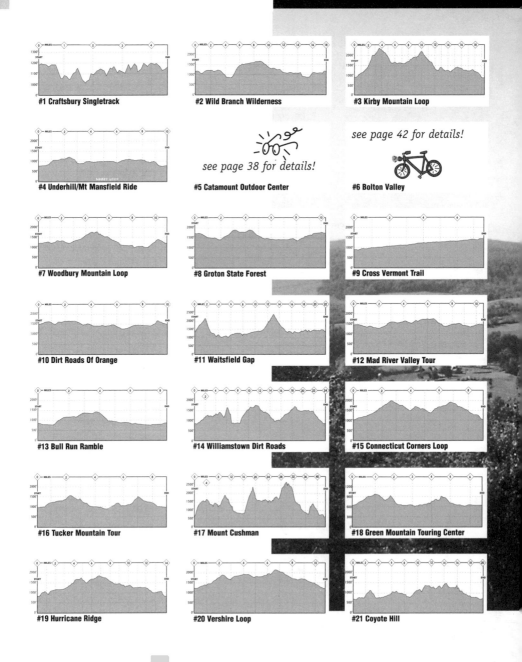

#1 Craftsbury Singletrack

#2 Wild Branch Wilderness

#3 Kirby Mountain Loop

#4 Underhill/Mt Mansfield Ride

see page 38 for details!

#5 Catamount Outdoor Center

see page 42 for details!

#6 Bolton Valley

#7 Woodbury Mountain Loop

#8 Groton State Forest

#9 Cross Vermont Trail

#10 Dirt Roads Of Orange

#11 Waitsfield Gap

#12 Mad River Valley Tour

#13 Bull Run Ramble

#14 Williamstown Dirt Roads

#15 Connecticut Corners Loop

#16 Tucker Mountain Tour

#17 Mount Cushman

#18 Green Mountain Touring Center

#19 Hurricane Ridge

#20 Vershire Loop

#21 Coyote Hill

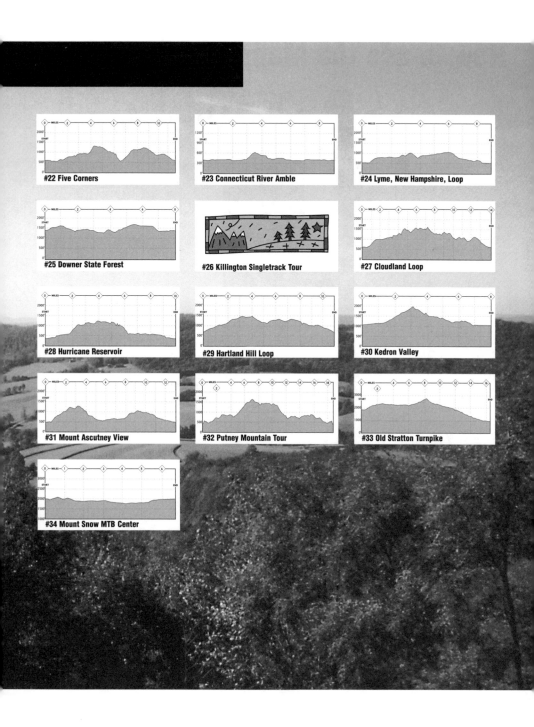

#22 Five Corners

#23 Connecticut River Amble

#24 Lyme, New Hampshire, Loop

#25 Downer State Forest

#26 Killington Singletrack Tour

#27 Cloudland Loop

#28 Hurricane Reservoir

#29 Hartland Hill Loop

#30 Kedron Valley

#31 Mount Ascutney View

#32 Putney Mountain Tour

#33 Old Stratton Turnpike

#34 Mount Snow MTB Center

How to use the Maps

1 Area Locator Map
This thumbnail relief map at the beginning of each ride shows you where the ride is within the state. The ride area is indicated with a star.

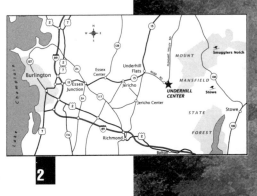

2 Location Map
This map helps you find your way to the start of each ride from the nearest sizeable town or city. Coupled with the detailed directions at the beginning of the cue, this map should visually lead you to where you need to be for each ride.

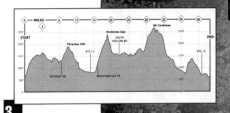

3 Profile Map
This helpful profile gives you a cross-sectional look at the ride's ups and downs. Elevation is labeled on the left, mileage is indicated on the top. Road and trail names are shown along the route with towns and points of interest labeled in bold.

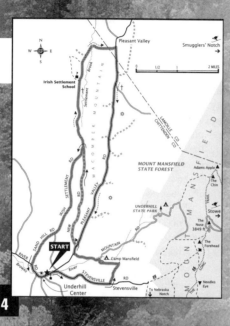

4 Route Map

This is your primary guide to each ride. It shows all of the accessible roads and trails, points of interest, water, towns, landmarks, and geographical features. It also distinguishes trails from roads, and paved roads from unpaved roads. The selected route is highlighted, and directional arrows point the way.

5 3D Surface Area Map

This three-dimensional look at the earth's surface within the area of the selected ride gives you an accurate representation of the surrounding topography and landscape. The map has been rotated for the best view and includes important roads and trails as well as distinguishable features for points of reference.

Ride Information Board (At the end of each ride section)

This is a small bulletin board with important information concerning each ride.

• The *Trail Maintenance Hotline* is the direct number for the local land managers in charge of all the trails within the selected ride. Use this hotline to *call ahead* for trail access information, or *after your visit* if you see problems with trail erosion, damage, or misuse.

• *Cost.* What money, if any, you may need to carry with you for park entrance fees or tolls.

• *Schedule.* This tells you at what times trails open and close, if on private or park land.

• *Maps.* This is a list of other maps to supplement the maps in this book. They are listed in order from most detailed to most general.

Craftsbury Singletrack

Ride Specs

Start: Craftsbury Center
Length: 4.5 miles
Approximate Riding Time: 1 hour
Rating: Moderate to Difficult
Terrain: Singletrack
Other Uses: Cross-country skiing, running

Getting There

From **Montpelier** – Take **Route 2 east** to **East Montpelier.** From here, follow **Route 14 north** to **Hardwick.** Continue through Hardwick on Route14 for another six miles until reaching a **right turn** with signs for **Craftsbury Outdoor Center.** This turn comes just after the ponds on the right. **Turn right** here and pass through the village of **Craftsbury.** Head up the hill to **Craftsbury Common.** Follow the signs for the **Craftsbury Outdoor Center** from here, passing through **Mill Village.** Once at the Center, park near the dorms and check in at the office.

C onsidered one of the most picturesque villages in all of Vermont, tiny Craftsbury sits atop high meadows in northern Vermont's Northeast Kingdom. The villages of East Craftsbury and Craftsbury Village lead uphill to the hamlet of Craftsbury Common. Still lined with a traditional rail fence, the green in the center of town was once used as communal pastureland for the residents' livestock. The family cow, goat, or sheep could graze near home with easy access. In those days, accessible grassland was a scarce commodity, since most of the land surrounding the Common was in virgin hardwood forests—and so the village "common" evolved.

Craftsbury is named after Colonel Crafts, an energetic settler from Massachusetts who owned a dozen acres or so in what is now the Mill Village area. In the late 1700s, he cleared some of his land and constructed a saw and gristmill. Upon completion, he returned south to retrieve his wife and family. Along the way, several other families joined his caravan to Vermont. After arriving in Cabot, Vermont, the group was stalled by a winter storm that dumped over four feet of snow. Determined to complete the passage to their new home, the Crafts left their horses and traveled the last 20 miles on foot, pulling their possessions and each other on hand sleds.

Today Craftsbury is known for its educational and athletic leadership. Both Craftsbury Academy and Sterling College are reputable academic institutions, with Sterling's ecology, resource management, and environmental programs

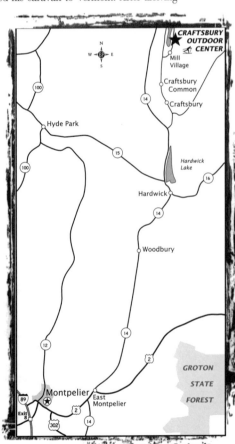

MilesDirections

0.0 START from the dining hall/office area and turn right up the dirt road toward the Nordic Touring Center. At the touring center, turn left across the playing fields to Trailhead B.

0.2 The trails begin. Bear left at the "Y" and be ready to follow the mountain bike markers, which will lead you on the best singletrack here.

0.3 Bear right at the "Y."

0.4 Quick right and then left into the singletrack. Be ready to handle a tight downhill. Pass straight through several intersections with the main ski trails, always following the narrow mountain bike singletrack.

0.8 The downhill comes to a "T" with the doubletrack ski trails. Turn left and shift down, ready to climb up a steep grassy section.

0.9 At the top of the hill, turn right on the doubletrack.

1.0 Turn left and climb up another short steep hill.

1.1 Reach a five-way intersection and turn right.

1.2 Turn right and downhill into the singletrack at a four-way intersection.

1.3 Turn left at the bottom of the gnarly downhill, and look for another quick left.

1.4 Turn left again.

1.5 Reach a "Y" intersection. Bear left on a nice singletrack section.

(continues on next page)

being some of the finest in the country. Just down the road a few miles on Lake Hosmer is the Craftsbury Center, a multi-sport training and touring center. This year-round facility offers lodging, dining, and activities for up to 90 guests. The 140 acres owned by the Center are home to a wide range of wildlife, including catamount and moose. Besides the access to wilderness trails, the Center offers lessons in sculling, canoeing, orienteering, cross-country skiing, and, of course, mountain biking.

MilesDirections (continued)

2.0 Turn right, as another trail heads straight.

2.2 Make a quick left onto the singletrack. This turn comes up fast because you are flying downhill, so it's easy to miss.

2.3 Pedal straight through a four-way intersection.

2.5 Come back out onto the main trail and turn right.

2.7 Bear left at the "Y," on the nicely mowed path.

2.8 Bear right at this intersection.

3.0 Reach a five-way intersection. Bear to the left. Be ready to look for a turn to the right in another tenth of a mile, as it is on another downhill.

3.1 Make a sharp right turn onto the singletrack, which is difficult to see as it comes up quickly. This is also a four-way intersection.

3.2 Turn left, and then left again at the next four-way intersection.

3.4 After descending, turn right and go up the short hill.

3.6 You are back at one of the original starting intersections, though you may not realize it. Take a sharp right, and then a quick left into the narrow singletrack that ducks into the forest.

(continues on next page)

CRAFTSBURY SINGLETRACK MTB TRAIL

One of the best things for off-road cyclists riding in this area of Vermont is the region's lack of pavement. A vast network of dirt roads supplies the local transportation needs—which translates to great mountain bike riding. The Craftsbury Center has recently produced a large selection of tours and rides in this pavementless area, complete with maps and cues. They offer rentals, guides, and package deals for enthusiasts able to stay more than one day.

For riders who desire the elusive Vermont singletrack ride, this tour through the hilly trails at the Center provides a showcase for the narrow goat paths that otherwise exist primarily on Vermont's private lands. Be sure to check in at the Center and pay the small trail fee—well worth it for the excellent maintenance Craftsbury's crew provides. This twisty tour appears complicated on paper but is actually well marked and easily negotiable, provided riders are headed in the right direction.

Starting at the cross-country ski center and warming hut, this ride begins on the ski trails. These wide tracks were designed for ski-skating, although they make awesome mountain bike trails as well. However, John Broadhead and his crew had other ideas in mind for knobby tires. By cutting small connector trails the width of a bike, the folks at the Center

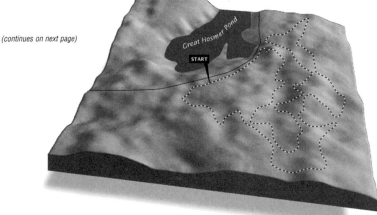

Roadway Press

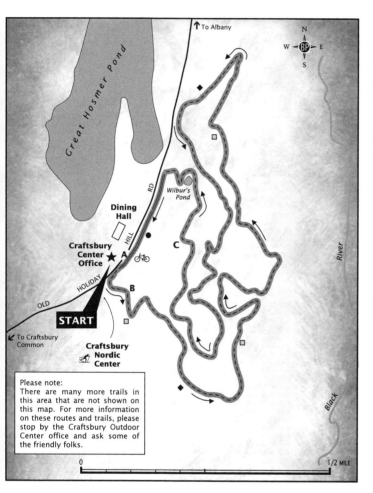

Ride Information

Trail Maintenance Hotline:
Craftsbury Outdoor Center
1-800-729-7751

Schedule:
The Craftsbury Outdoor Center is open May 23 through mid-October. Call the center for details on seasonal events and weekend tours.

Maps:
USGS maps: Craftsbury, VT
Delorme: Vermont Atlas & Gazetteer – Page 53 K-12

MilesDirections *(continued)*

3.75 Back on the main trail. Bear right and, in about 10 yards, bear right again.

3.8 Sharp left into the woods on a narrow singletrack. When it ends on the main trail, turn left.

4.0 Reach the main trail. Turn left and then right onto the singletrack again.

4.1 Turn left onto the main trail, and then go straight through the next intersection, on a partially hidden singletrack that circles the marshy area.

4.3 Turn right on the main trail. When it intersects with the dirt road in another tenth of a mile, turn left to go back to the Center.

4.5 Reach the office here on the right.

laid out a roller coaster loop of about five miles that is best experienced the second time around (after you've committed its quick turns to memory). The loop uses the ski trails to connect pieces of singletrack that dive into the thick forest and roll through the hilly terrain. The ride is technically challenging, but not exasperating, making it an enjoyable singletrack tour. Back at the Center, a dip in the lake or a hearty bowl of chili in the dining hall can complete the day.

Wild Branch Wilderness

Getting There

From **Montpelier** – Take
Route 2 east to **East
Montpelier.** From here, fol-
low **Route 14 north** to
Hardwick. Continue through
Hardwick on Route14 for
another six miles until reach-
ing a **right turn** with signs
for **Craftsbury Outdoor
Center.** This turn comes just
after the ponds on the right.
Turn right here and pass
through the village of
Craftsbury. Head up the hill
to **Craftsbury Common.**
Follow the signs for the
Craftsbury Outdoor Center
from here, passing through
Mill Village. Once at the
Center, park near the dorms
and check in at the office.

T his ride is named after the Wild Branch River,
whose headwaters begin in the Lowell
Mountains and run south through Eden,
Craftsbury, and Wolcott before joining the
Lamoille River. The river received the moniker
Wild Branch because of its habit of flooding the
banks after heavy rains and spring run-offs.

This region of the Northeast Kingdom is known for its remote
natural terrain, not to mention miles of dirt roads without an
automobile or house in sight. The route passes over a piece of the
old Bayley-Hazen military road, which used to stretch from the
Connecticut River to Canada.

The Bayley-Hazen road was designed to replace the long
tedious route which ran across Vermont from east to west, then
north to Lake Champlain and on to Canada. This tedious lake
route was used by American troops during the Revolutionary War.
It was General Jacob Bayley who suggested to General
Washington that a new route be constructed. His idea was to use
the Connecticut River
to reach Newbury,
Vermont, and then
switch back to land
along the established
Native American
trails heading north-
east to the northern
end of Lake
Champlain.

Washington
ordered a race of sorts
to be organized that
would test the speed
of the two south-to-
north paths. General
Bayley's nephew,
Frye, was coerced by
his uncle to undertake
the newly proposed
route during what
happened to be one of
the worst winters in
some time. Struggling
through five feet of
snow on foot, Frye

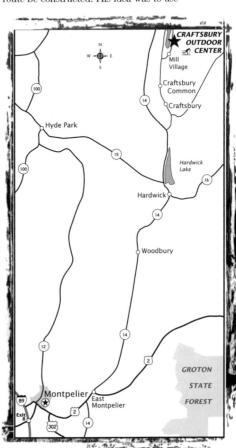

passed through the Lowell Mountains on his 18-day trip to the Missisquoi River in the northeastern corner of Vermont before moving on to Montreal. Ten days later, the other group, which had traveled by way of Lake Champlain, met them in Montreal, proving Bayley's theory correct.

Construction began in 1776 with General Hazen's help (nearby Hazen's Notch bears his name). Moses Hazen is remembered as a zealous early patriot who commandeered a group of rebels in Canada, much like Vermont's Green Mountain Boys. After the American Revolution broke out, Hazen fled Canada to help the American cause, burning his large estate before departing so the British couldn't use it. After the war, he joined General Bayley in the torturous job of hand building the road through the wilderness. Several historic accounts portray the teams of men in bare feet and ragged clothing, with swarms of bugs feasting on their skin. Moses Hazen is said to have possessed an indestructible nature, explaining why this wild area of Vermont still retains his name.

Around 1780, the Bayley-Hazen road was completed all the way to Westfield, Vermont, becoming part of the first stagecoach road from Boston to Montreal. Schools, churches, and blockhouses were built along its corridor, which continued to be well maintained through the early 1900s.

Now the road can only be followed in its entirety on foot or mountain bike. Although sections still remain as segments of dirt or even paved roads, other parts of the original route have simply faded into private farmland or overgrown thickets. In 1976, a

MilesDirections

0.0 From the Craftsbury Outdoor Center, turn right and head out along the dirt road known as Lost Nation Road.

0.5 At the "T," turn right on Mill Village Road (Town Highway #7).

3.3 Reach a four-way intersection. Turn left on Hitchcock Hill Road. Page Pond is to the right.

4.3 Turn left at the "T" on Center Hill Road and cross the bridge over the Black River.

4.7 Reach the intersection with Route 14. Turn right.

5.0 After passing the Albany Mini Mart, turn left on Lowell Road (paved). The pavement lasts for about two tenths of a mile.

5.4 At the "Y" intersection, bear to the left. The climb goes on.

6.0 At this "Y," bear left again, following East Hill Road (Route 100s) on the snowmobile system.

8.0 Cross a small stream.

8.5 Pass the logging landing on the left.

8.6 Stream crossing.

9.2 Bear left at this intersection.

10.2 Route 100s goes right. Stay straight.

10.5 Cross over a wooden bridge.

11.7 Cross the steel bridge.

12.0 Reach a "T" intersection. Turn left. This is TH #27.

13.5 Petrol King. Bear to the left after refueling.

13.6 Turn left on Branch Road (paved). You can see Craftsbury Common above.

(continues on next page)

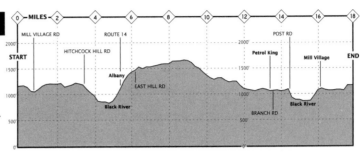

MilesDirections (continued)

14.0 Reach the intersection with Route 14. Turn left here.

14.4 After the large red barn, turn right on Post Road, and look for the Craftsbury Outdoor Center sign.

15.5 At the top of the hill, go straight across the pavement, and bear left immediately on a dirt road.

15.6 Bear right, and look for the sign to the Center on the telephone pole.

16.0 Ride downhill into Mill Village. Follow the curve in the road as it turns left.

16.7 Turn right on TH #12 and go up Murphy's Hill.

17.2 Reach the Craftsbury Outdoor Center.

group of hikers walked the entire 65-mile route, making special efforts to mark its original course. It took them nine days to reach Hazen's Notch and the junction of the now well-known Long Trail.

The Wild Branch ride begins at the Craftsbury Center and follows a loop of classic Vermont dirt roads over its 16-mile course. Descendants of the black flies and mosquitoes that tortured Bayley and Hazen over 200 years ago still permeate the landscape on hot summer days, motivating riders to keep moving. The first major climb begins after Albany, as you head up the flanks of the Lowell Mountains. Depending on how much ice cream you ate at the Albany Mini-Mart, it may pass by quickly or seem to climb endlessly.

The middle section of the ride is high along the Lowell Range, where logging roads are abundant and options for exploration exist on all sides. Aside from moose, deer, and possibly the elusive catamount, mountain bikers won't spot many other creatures out

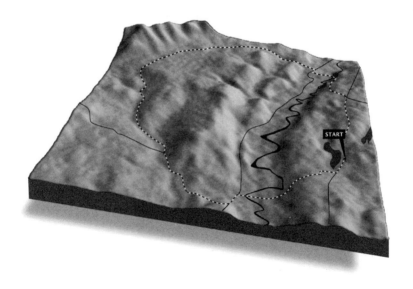

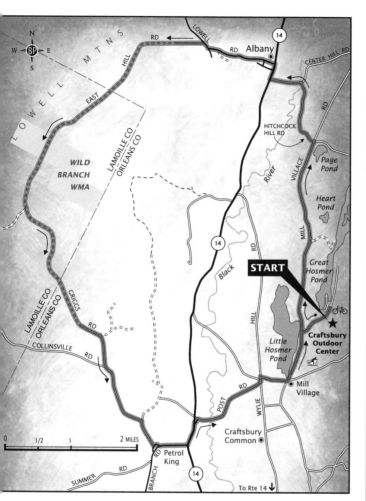

Ride Information

Trail Maintenance Hotline:
Craftsbury Outdoor Center
1-800-729-7751

Schedule:
The Craftsbury Outdoor Center is open May 23 through mid-October. Call the center for details on seasonal events and weekend tours.

Local Events/Attractions
In nearby Hardwick, VT:
Spring Festival/Carnival, 5k run
Craftsbury Chamber Players:
  every Thursday, July 10-
  August 14 at Town Hall.
Call the Hardwick Chamber of
  Commerce for more informa-
  tion on these and other events:
  (802) 472-5906
In nearby Glover, VT:
Bread & Puppet Theatre Festival
  (802) 525-3031

Maps:
USGS maps: Albany, VT;
  Craftsbury, VT
DeLorme: Vermont Atlas &
  Gazetteer – Page 53 K-12

here, unless it's deer season in November. At which time it's best to stay home and ride the indoor trainer. After traveling under Lowell Range, the ride passes through the Wild Branch Wildlife Management Area and meets the second substantial climb back toward the Center. The stepping stone villages of Craftsbury are highly regarded for their craftsmanship. Riders may wish to stop back at the Center for a hearty meal at the dining hall and check out the other rides mapped in the area.

Kirby Mountain Loop

This northern Vermont region is known to Vermonters as the Northeast Kingdom. Its name is supposedly derived from a politically fueled shouting match in the early 1900s between two men from opposite ends of the state, featuring the line: "What do you think? You live up there in your own kingdom or something?" Others speculate that the sheer beauty and wildness of the region accounts for the name.

The Northeast Kingdom is unique in that it possesses a shorter growing season than the rest of the state, as well as a variety of northern species of plants and animals not typically found in Vermont. Even the Connecticut River, which provides access to the eastern half of Vermont, isn't navigable north of Barnet, flowing eastward as if to run clear of this hilly region altogether. Native Americans utilized the land as hunting grounds, and tales are recorded of large herds of moose and deer roaming the countryside. Later, early settlers reported harrowing winters, crops frozen in August, and a scarcity of neighbors.

Lake Willoughby, with the dramatic cliffs of neighboring Mount Pisgah and nearby Mount Hor (all of which are visible from this ride), is one of the Kingdom's real treasures. Formed by a glacier cutting deep into the valley, the lake is Vermont's deepest, at over 300 feet, and its clear cold waters are a real treat on those humid July days. The lake, a National Natural Landmark, is an excellent example of glacial scouring, and its surrounding flora still includes hints of arctic times, especially on the walls of nearby cliffs and summits. Those interested in camping here should

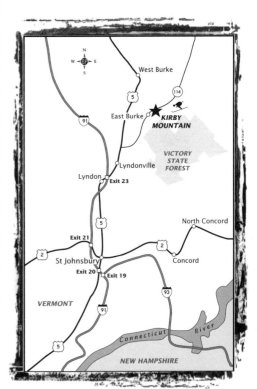

expect primitive conditions. They may get lucky, however, and spot Peregrine falcons nesting in the cliffs above.

Burke Mountain, where the first half of the ride ascends, contains exposed rock reflecting the formation of molten rock produced by heat deep in the earth's core. It is adjacent to Victory State Forest and Bog, which spans over 15,000 acres. The maze of forest roads in the Victory area are ideal for mountain biking. There is a place along the ride (mile 8.8) that connects easily to

the Victory area, where the dirt road through the bog offers easy access.

Beginning from East Burke Sports on Route 114 North, the ride ascends roughly four to five miles from the start. Groups can remedy this difficult beginning by leaving a car at the shop and shuttling another car up the access road (pavement for three miles), parking at the Burke Mountain Sugarhouse. The toll road gate would have to be open to make this work, so check with the folks at East Burke Sports first. The shop also has an excellent catalogue of rides, some of which are mapped, and its staff is always happy to help plan a ride or advise on the condition of the Kirby Mountain loop. They also offer a special Carhart section for those going back to the farm or heading home from the ride.

East Burke is a recreational and tourist-friendly town with a bevy of bed and breakfasts. There is even a town-funded mountain bike trail network in the planning stages. Bailey's General Store is just across the way, with all the trappings of a classic Vermont country store. Down the road is the town of Lyndon, which boasts Avery's Natural Foods Café and the famous Lyndon

MilesDirections

0.0 START at East Burke Sports. Turn left on Route 114 and roll through town.

0.28 Turn right at the sign for Burke Mountain/Northern Star. The road is paved and gradually uphill.

2.3 Bear right for the auto road to the summit. Pass Burke Mountain Academy on the right. Each fall, this has been the starting point for the Kingdom Classic Mountain Bike Race.

2.5 Bear left through the gate up Summit Road. This is a steep, narrow asphalt road.

3.1 Turn right at the small sign reading CCC Trail. You will pass a green water supply building and an old red shack. This trail is nice forest doubletrack. Traverse across the Burke Mountain Ski Area, following the track until it meets with the forest again.

4.5 Pass a lean-to on the left at the top of the hill. Stay straight here. Follow the sporadic blue diamond blazes. Mossy waterfalls and rocky ascents mark the climb.

5.3 Pass a lean-to on the right. Stay straight here and descend. The trail is a bit rough from horse traffic.

6.3 Reach an intersection at the bottom where several trails converge. Stay straight. Keep your eyes peeled for moose tracks.

7.5 The trail becomes a town dirt road. Go around the gate and head downhill.

(continues on next page)

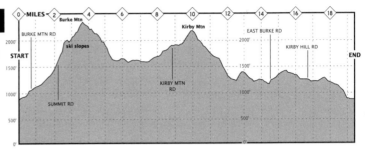

MilesDirections *(continued)*

8.8 Pass an old farm at the bottom of the hill. Turn right on Kirby Mountain Road, heading toward Kirby Mountain and Lyndonville (there's a sign on the barn). Turning left on Kirby Mountain Road toward Concord takes you to Victory State Forest and Bog.

10.8 Reach an intersection with snowmobile trails. Go straight, heading downhill.

11.95 Reach an intersection with town roads. Turn right on the dirt and prepare to descend.

13.2 Reach a three-way intersection. Turn right on Town Highway #7.

13.6 Stay to the left. Some driveways head off to the right.

14.55 Reach the end of Town Highway #7 at North Kirby. Turn right on Burke Road. This is a little busier dirt road.

(continues on next page)

town diner. Slightly further south on Route 91 is Saint Johnsbury, with the Fairbanks Museum and Planetarium (northern New England's weather center). Back in East Burke, be sure to join the Thursday night rides from East Burke Sports if you happen to be around. All the local trails, so they say, are excellent.

The Kirby Mountain Loop begins straight up the pavement toward Burke Mountain Academy (home of many U.S. Olympic skiers), and then climbs the Burke Mountain toll road. The name is a misnomer, as there is no toll, and the gate is usually open. If it's not, skirt around the gate and prepare for an ascent. The CCC trail sign that begins the wooded section is located beyond the Sugarhouse on the right. This doubletrack, used by horses, hikers, and skiers alike, winds across the face of the ski area, under the lifts, and offers incredible views of the Northeast Kingdom, Lake Willoughby area, and Caledonia County. It affords an especially dramatic view of the Willoughby Cliffs, which look as if a giant slice were taken out of the mountain range.

After skirting the side of Burke Mountain, cyclists will climb a rocky technical stretch of doubletrack, then dip downhill past West Peak through a particularly beautiful hardwood forest. The trail passes the gate at the "Wild Man's" house and heads up Kirby Mountain. A local sign points the way to the Wild Man's realm, but don't panic—mountain bikers find him harmless. At the next junc-

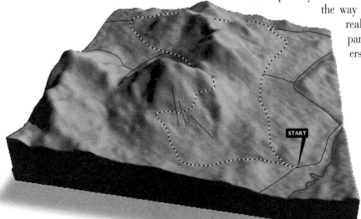

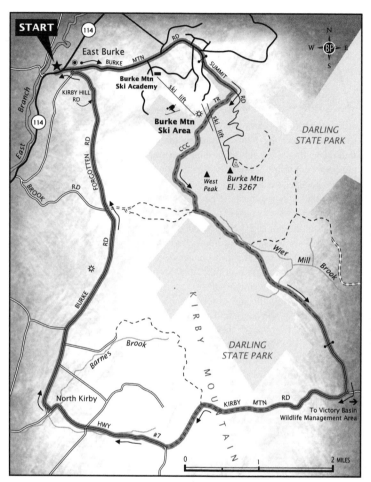

START
114
East Burke
BURKE MTN
Burke Mtn
Ski Academy
KIRBY HILL
RD
RD
SUMMIT
SKI LIFT
TR
RD
Branch
East
114
BROOK
RD
FORGOTTEN RD
Burke Mtn
Ski Area
SKI LIFT
CCC
DARLING
STATE PARK
West
Peak
Burke Mtn
El. 3267
BURKE
RD
Wier
Mill
Brook
K
I
R
B
Y
Brook
Barnes
DARLING
STATE PARK
M
O
U
N
North Kirby
HWY
#7
KIRBY
MTN
RD
T
A
I
N
To Victory Basin
Wildlife Management Area
0   1   2 MILES

N
W — BP — E
S

Ride Information

Trail Maintenance Hotline:
East Burke Sports
    (802) 626-3215
Burke Mountain Ski Area
    (802) 626-3305

Schedule:
Trails are open from late May to late
October.

Local Events/Attractions:
In St. Johnsbury:
Annual Festival of Traditional Arts
    and Crafts: (802) 748-2372

Maps:
USGS maps: Burke Mountain, VT;
    Gallup Hills, VT
DeLorme: Vermont Atlas &
    Gazetteer – Page 48 D-7

MilesDirections (continued)

15.0 Stay straight, passing a road
that forks to the left.
16.9 Travel straight through the
four-way intersection onto Kirby Hill
Road. The town news is often posted on a board here.
19.1 Turn left then roll up to the
stop sign where you must turn left
again on Route 114.
19.4 Turn right into the parking lot
at East Burke Sports.

tion, signs point the way to Victory, at which place cyclists could
connect to this region. Otherwise, take in the local scenery and
head up Kirby Mountain Road, past a cabin called Heaven. The
old, narrow dirt road intersects with snowmobile trails but finally funnels out to the town roads of Kirby, with more views of
Mount Pisgah and Mount Hor.

The remaining miles follow dirt roads in the high meadowland, an area of wide-open land, with open space, and amazing
summer wildflowers. Large farms populate the landscape, and it
can be windy on the way back to East Burke on Forgotten Road.
The dirt roads extend to the pavement on which the ride began,
so it's only a short spin to the general store for snacks.

Underhill/Mount Mansfield Ride

Ride Specs

Start: Underhill Center General Store
Length: 9.6 miles
Approximate Riding Time: 1-3 hours (depending on choice of loop)
Rating: Easy
Terrain: Doubletrack, dirt roads, paved roads
Other Uses: Automobiles

Getting There

From **Burlington** – Follow I-89 to **Route 15** east (Exit 15). Follow Route 15 east through **Essex Junction** and **Jericho.** In **Underhill Flats,** turn right on **River Road** to **Underhill Center,** where the ride begins.

As a result of trail closures in the Bolton Notch area south of Underhill and the lack of mountain bikeable terrain in the forests of Mount Mansfield, this route was designed to give cyclists a taste of the incredible beauty the area possesses regardless of the absence of single-track. Because of the extremely limited trail access, this route is ridden entirely along dirt roads, with a smattering of pavement for good measure. For those interested in local trail riding, the eastern side of the mountain near Stowe has some excellent local shops offering both guided tours and designated areas maintained exclusively for mountain biking.

Underhill is home to many national-caliber skiers who got their start on the local slopes of the Underhill Ski Bowl, then traveled around the looming bulk of Mount Mansfield to the steeper slopes of Stowe or Smuggler's Notch. It's easy to see how one's interests can be governed by the looming presence of a 4,393-foot mountain standing sentry over their small town.

Mount Mansfield, Vermont's highest peak, forms rocky ridges that have long been thought to resemble human features on an imagined profile. And so we find curious names along the ridgeline: "Forehead," "Nose," "Upper and Lower Lips," "Adam's Apple," and the highest peak "Chin." Even the ski trails that descend steeply from the mountain's summit have similar names, such as "Nosedive"—well known for its thrilling terrain.

Mount Mansfield is also home to some of New England's rarest plants. The wild columbine, bog-laurel, mountain cranberry, and highlands rush are just some of the flora found on this National Natural Landmark.

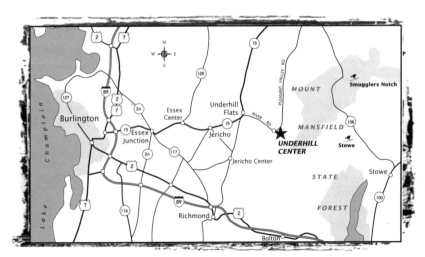

From the summit of Mansfield, the view on a clear day is stunning. Mountain bikers can only access this peak by taking the toll road from the Stowe side. The remaining trail systems on the mountain unfortunately prohibit mountain biking. Looking westward from the summit, Lake Champlain and the nearby Adirondack peaks of Whiteface and Mount Marcy are majestic sunset views. To the north lies the faint rim of the Laurentian Mountains above Montreal. Foreground views include Jay Peak, Hazen's Notch, Belvidere Mountain, and the Saint Lawrence

River. To the south lie Camel's Hump, Killington, and Middlebury's Bread Loaf. Finally, to the east rise the Presidentials in New Hampshire's White Mountains and the rocky depths of Smuggler's Notch.

Smuggler's Notch is yet another natural phenomenon worth visiting if you're in the area. Located on the northeast end of Mount Mansfield, this pass between Spruce Peak and Mansfield was once used to smuggle goods to and from Canada when the War of 1812's Embargo Act prohibited trade with Canada. Its caves and recesses along the towering cliffs and ledges served as valuable hiding places for various smuggled goods. Herds of cattle, British gold and silver, and potash were among the commonly smuggled items often stashed in the rocks until a safe time for retrieval could be found. More recently, the notch has been the starting point for the classic Stowe Road Race, a bike race that passes through the narrow cliffs, before diving down the other side at breakneck speeds.

Cycling on the Underhill side of the mountain has a decidedly different flavor than its neighbor Stowe. Though the public trails

MilesDirections

0.0 START in Underhill Center and park near the general store. Head west up Stevensville Road, past the town offices toward Mount Mansfield.

0.3 Bear right at the split in the road and continue up the pavement.

1.9 Turn left on the dirt road at Maple Leaf Farms. Stevensville Road continues up to the hiking trails through Nebraska Notch and up Mount Mansfield. Bikes are not allowed on any of these trails.

2.4 Bear left down the narrow, steep dirt road.

3.2 Bear left at the intersection with Mountain Road, continuing west toward Pleasant Valley Road. Mountain Road will take you to Underhill State Park. There are forest service roads in this area open to bikes.

3.7 Turn right on Pleasant Valley Road.

4.3 Turn left on New Road. This is a great road for mountain biking—unmaintained, gradual gradients, and miles of beaver ponds and old forests. Several areas get very wet but remain negotiable.

(continues on next page)

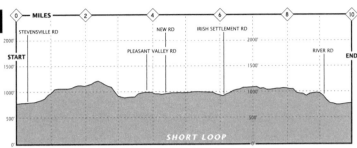

SHORT LOOP

MilesDirections (continued)

6.1 Reach the intersection with Irish Settlement Road. You now have a choice of turning left and finishing this ride in a hurry, or turning right, following a longer, more scenic route through the valley, affording some of the greatest views of Mount Mansfield from any place in Vermont. The tradeoff on this longer route is about six miles of pavement (fairly quiet roads, though).

To do the longer loop: Turn right on Irish Settlement Road, which becomes Marsh Road as it crosses into Cambridge. At mile 9.4, turn right on Pleasant Valley Road and follow it all the way back into Underhill. Total distance is 15.8 miles.

(continues on next page)

are less challenging, the quiet mountain views are equally inspiring.

Beginning in the center of Underhill, our ride follows old town roads uphill toward Nebraska Notch, a popular backcountry skiing trail network. These trails are all a part of the Green Mountain National Forest which, unfortunately, still has very limited mountain biking access in its vast acreage. These trails are not open to knobbies, but keep them in mind for winter ski tours.

After cruising downhill on a twisting narrow dirt road, the ride intersects with the road leading to Underhill State Park, on the western flank of Mount Mansfield. Apparently, the park is a well kept secret for those who enjoy camping, fishing, and hiking high above the madness below.

The paved road just beyond this junction is aptly named Pleasant Valley, as it affords a continuous view of the mountain while maintaining a subtle, rolling grade. This popular cycling route affords a view of the strange Cantilever Rock atop Mount Mansfield. This unusual rock formation is a horizontal obelisk-shaped rock, 60 feet above ground and wedged into the face of a 100-foot cliff. It extends 31 feet beyond the rock and has been estimated to weigh 75 tons!

The next section, known by locals as the "dump road," is the only portion of the ride that requires some technical skills. Depending on the weather and time of year, sections can become quite wet as the nearby beaver ponds spill over into the road. Beaver activity is common, so watch

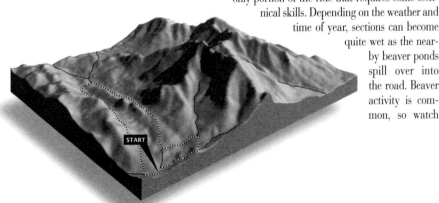

START

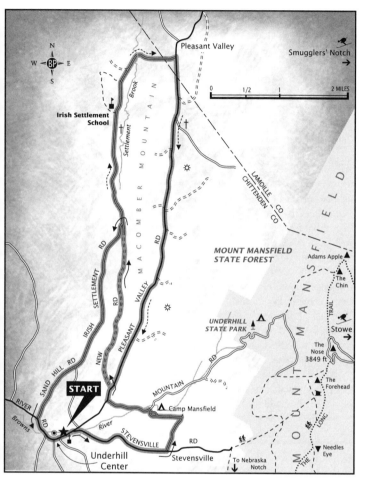

Ride Information

Schedule:
The roads for this ride are open year-round

Local Information:
The Mountain Bike Shop, Stowe, VT:
(802) 253-7919, 1-800-682-4534
• Tuesday night rides:
   (group/social), May- September.
• Rentals available

Stowe Area Chamber of
   Commerce: (802) 253-7321
   www.stoweinfo.com

Maps:
USGS maps: Underhill, VT; Mount
   Mansfield, VT
Delorme: Vermont Atlas &
   Gazetteer – Page 45 F-14

MilesDirections (continued)

To do the shorter loop: Turn left on Irish Settlement Road, which becomes Sand Hill Road, and head back to Underhill. You may come to a section of the road closed to cars, but passable on bikes. Proceed down the dirt, which turns to Sand Hill Road. Continue with the following cues:

9.1 Reach the intersection with River Road. Turn left on River Road and follow this into Underhill.
9.6 Reach the center of Underhill. Ride back to your car then visit the general store for some refreshments.

for the characteristic tail slap and underwater plunge. The remaining section of this old road winds through the forest and is surprisingly flat for Vermont.

At the intersection with Irish Settlement Road, your choice is to continue on a longer loop (about six miles with some pavement) toward Jeffersonville, or drop back down into Underhill to complete a shorter 10-mile loop. Both loops are on town-maintained roads, but the longer Pleasant Valley trek offers fantastic views of Mount Mansfield. Both rides follow roads used mainly by local traffic.

Catamount Outdoor Center

Ride Specs

Start: Catamount Center Offices

Length: Variable

Approximate Riding Time: Variable

Rating: Easy to Difficult

Terrain: Singletrack, double-track

Other Uses: Cross-country skiing, running

Getting There

From **Burlington** – Follow **I-89 south** to **Exit 12,** then head **north** on **Route 2A** to **Tafts Corners.** Turn **right** here on **Governor Chittenden Road.** Follow Governor Chittenden Road for about three miles until you reach the **Catamount Outdoor Center.** Park in their lot.

Located just southeast of Burlington (Vermont's largest town), the Catamount Outdoor Center offers a large expanse of wilderness for mountain biking that is easily accessible from town. Off-road options in Burlington are limited, and many of its parks prohibit mountain biking— with the exception of the path along Lake Champlain. The lack of riding options in town makes the Catamount Outdoor Center even more valuable.

The Catamount Outdoor Center, set on an old farm in Williston, was created as a conservation effort to restrict development that might tarnish the area's natural beauty. The spectacular views of Mount Mansfield and Camel's Hump from the fields that connect the trails to one another attract many visitors to the Center. But for our purposes, the best feature of Catamount is its well-maintained and clearly marked system of trails that challenge every level of rider. In addition, Catamount offers weekly programs just for mountain bikers. Their race-training series has traditionally been held Monday evenings on a short but sweet four kilometer loop, which is about 50 percent singletrack. Programs of different levels with varied distances are held and include fun-filled events for families. A weekly dual slalom training series was added for those aspiring to improve bike handling and downhill skills.

Besides the weekly activities, the Center has traditionally hosted a popular mountain bike race, and most recently has been part of the newly established American Mountain Bike Challenge Series. The race course, with its rolling singletrack, short, sharp

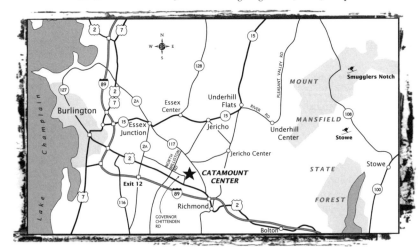

climbs, and twisting turns is worth checking out if you're looking for a great off-road loop. The race has been held on both sides of the trail system, which is split down the middle by Governor Chittenden Road, so be sure to ask about both courses. A small shop at Catamount also rents bikes and is the place to stop for a trail pass (costing $6 a day for adults—season passes available). Their schedule is also available at the farmhouse shop and includes other events such as camps for kids, races for cops, and orienteering. Trail running, triathlons, and fundraisers have also been held at this versatile farm, which, in winter months, is transformed into a full-service cross-country ski center. Now that's the definition of creative land use!

Following the Winooski River west from Catamount, back to Lake Champlain, travelers will run across the bustling town of Burlington, a personable town despite its designation as Vermont's largest city. Burlington offers an array of both indoor and outdoor activities. The 1,000-acre working Shelburne farm, the Shelburne museum, and the original farmland and homestead of Vermont hero Ethan Allen are just a few notables of this queen city, rich in both history and beauty.

Perhaps Burlington's biggest asset is Lake Champlain. Measuring 120 miles in length, Lake Champlain is the sixth largest lake in the United States. The lake is named for French explorer Samuel de Champlain, who spent 30 years traveling, mapping, and surveying this territory he claimed for New France. The French built forts along the lake to protect their settlements to the north and made mortal ene-

MilesDirections

Because Catamount Outdoor Center has so many individual trails suitable for cycling, it would be unreasonable to create a single loop. Instead, cyclists are encouraged to use the map provided and to select their own route within the center's vast network of trails. For this reason there are no directional cues and no profile map.

mies with the Iroquois Indians after Champlain killed two of their chiefs.

Even before the French, the Iroquois used the lake as an important transportation route. Its confluence runs north to Canada and south to the Hudson River area. Millions of years ago, the lake was a vast saltwater sea that receded when the land rose after glacial activity. Lake Champlain covers over 200,000 acres and is popular for fishing, swimming, boating, and camping. Mallets Bay, to the north in Colchester, is also a favorite recreational site. For road cyclists, a group in Burlington, known as the Lake Champlain Bikeways, identified principal cycling routes around the lake.

Besides the lake, which is famous for its summer sunsets over the nearby Adirondack Mountains, Burlington has a tremendous amount of municipal activity; including festivals, theaters, museums, and plenty of places to eat. Many of the town's bike shops, including the Ski Rack and Earl's Cyclery, offer weekly rides and have information on many other local riding hotspots.

At Main Street's highest point, you get a bird's-eye view of Burlington, with a clear view of the University of Vermont (provided for in Vermont's constitution written in the

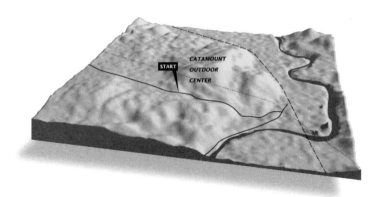

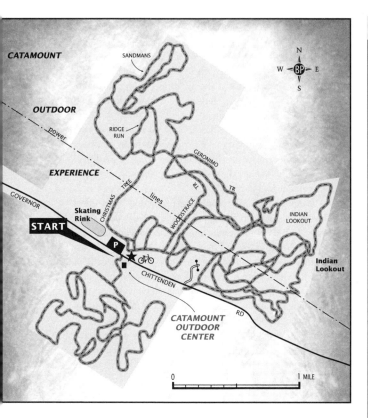

Ride Information

Trail Maintenance Hotline:
Catamount Outdoor Center
(802) 879-6001

Cost:
Trail Passes: $6

Schedule:
Call the Catamount Center for details on events including weekly races, clinics, kid's camps, orienteering course, and rentals.

Local Bike Shops:
In Burlington:
The Ski Rack
(802) 658-3313
Earl's Cyclery
(802) 864-9197
Climb High
(802) 985-5056

Local Events/Attractions
Shelburne Farms and Museum
"New England's Smithsonian"
open year-round: (802) 985-3346
Lake Champlain Balloon & Craft Festival: May 31-June 2
(802) 899-2993
Autumn Fair-Ethan Allen Homestead: October:
(802) 865-4556

Maps:
USGS maps: Essex Junction, VT
DeLorme: Vermont Atlas & Gazetteer – Page 45 H-10

late 1770s). Incidentally, Vermont's constitution was the first in America to ban slavery. UVM was opened in 1800 with one teacher and four students. Today, student enrollment is up to nearly ten thousand.

Back at Catamount, the trail system grows steadily, and the singletrack continues to flourish. Most of the riding is relatively smooth compared to some of the trademark roots and rocks found elsewhere in the state. It is a great place for families, and it sports a growing number of dedicated riders under the age of ten.

As for the name "catamount," it is derived from the "cat" known to have terrorized the early pioneers. The catamount is quite an elusive creature, and little is known about it, as it is rare today. In other parts of Vermont, the locals call it a "puma" or a "lynx." It is known to be particularly fierce, stubborn, loyal, and aggressive—which perhaps explains why modern Vermonters enjoy it as their symbol so much.

Bolton Valley

A long the spine of the western Green Mountains is a series of smaller peaks leading up to Vermont's highest mountain, Mount Mansfield. Bordering the south end of these peaks in Mount Mansfield State Forest is the 3,680-foot Bolton Mountain. Nearby are Stimson, Ricker, Woodward, and Bone Mountains.

The town of Bolton itself is just a blink on Route 2 between Richmond and Waterbury. From here, a narrow, winding access road descends between rocky cliffs and Joiner Brook. Joiner Brook flows swiftly into Bolton Valley—home to an alpine ski area and a growing mountain bike center.

The Mountain Bike/Adventure Center in Bolton Valley offers 6,000 wilderness acres to explore. The Bolton Valley trails alone cover roughly 100 miles of terrain and includes both downhill and cross-country trails in some of the more remote areas. The nearby Catamount Trail, which runs nearly the entire length of Vermont, is connected to the system. Besides having an outstanding trail system, the Center also offers rentals, guided tours, and food and lodging on-site. A trail map designed by Huntington, Vermont, cartographer Michael Early provides a clear and accurate picture of the trail network in Bolton Valley and the surrounding land. The trail-access fees are reasonable, and terrain for both novice and expert cyclists is available. A weekly training race and a challenging downhill event have been conducted here in the past, along with a host of other fun races. Contact the Center at 1-800-451-3220 for an updated schedule.

One of the most noticeable aspects of Bolton is its cliffs and

Ride Specs

Start: Bolton Mountain Bike Center
Length: Variable
Approximate Riding Time: Variable
Rating: Easy to Difficult
Terrain: Singletrack, double-track, class-4 dirt roads
Other Uses: Cross-country skiing, hiking

Getting There

From **Burlington** – Follow **I-89 south** to **Exit 11 (Richmond),** and head **south** on **Route 2.** Pass through Richmond, Jonesville, and Bolton. Once in **Bolton,** turn **left** up **Bolton Valley Road,** which winds uphill for nearly **five miles** before reaching the **Bolton Valley Ski Area.** Park in the ski area lot.

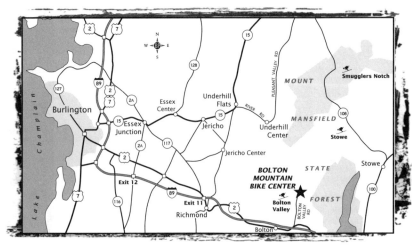

rocky overhangs in the local hills. This rocky terrain was cause for serious frustration while building the Central Vermont Railroad in the mid-1800s. The construction of the rail line through this particular section on the way to Burlington from Montpelier was estimated to cost an outrageous amount more than normal because of the impervious rocks the railroad would need to pass through. Irish settlers immigrated to the area in 1847 to tackle the job, establishing themselves in two villages: the upper, "Cork," and the lower, "Dublin," both in memory of their green isle.

It was soon apparent to these hard-working Irish settlers, however, that there was little or no money in return for their hard work. In a fashion similar to poorly treated workers in the Central Vermont Copper Mines, the Irish laborers protested loudly. They surrounded the boarding house of the job foreman and threatened to kill both him and themselves if they weren't paid. The militia from Burlington was soon called in and arrests were made. The scene was a picture of chaos. Order wasn't restored until a Catholic priest arrived to calm the masses. Work was suspended

MilesDirections

Because Bolton Valley and the Adventure Center area has so many individual trails suitable for cycling, it would be unreasonable to create a single loop. Instead, cyclists are encouraged to use the map provided and to select their own route within the center's vast network of trails. For this reason there are no directional cues and no profile map.

Amtrak to Vermont

For easy access to the Green Mountain State from points south, Amtrak has two regular routes that deliver you to the town center of places like Rutland, Brattleboro, Windsor, White River Junction, Randolph, Montpelier, Burlington and Saint Albans.

The Amtrak Vermonter runs up the eastern side of the state and then heads west to Lake Champlain. Its specially equipped baggage car can carry mountain bikes easily. The new Ethan Allan

Express runs from New York, NY, to Rutland, VT, by way of Albany, NY. From there, it is a short commute to the Killington area. Someday this line may continue north to Burlington.

For information call Amtrak at 1-800-USA-RAIL.

for two years, and sadly enough, the feisty Irish were never paid—even as 17 of them perished in the dangerous working conditions. The railroad would not open through this section until 1849.

Just down the road a piece in Richmond is another symbol of early workmanship. The 16-sided "Old Round Church" was the country's first community church. In the early 1800s, a group representing four different religions assembled with the need for a common place of worship. It is believed that 16

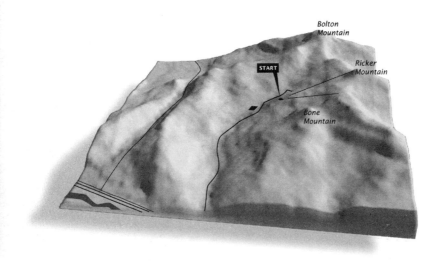

Bolton Mountain

START

Ricker Mountain

Bone Mountain

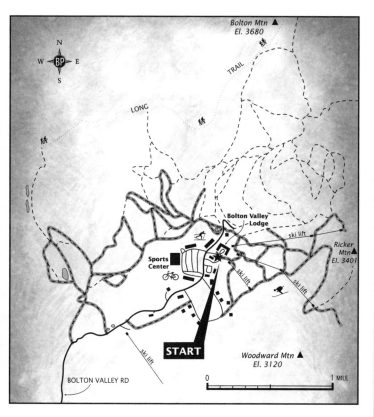

men offered to work on the now historic building, each being responsible for building one entire side. Apparently automobile mogul Henry Ford tried to buy the polygonal church, but the locals wouldn't hear of it. It still sits proudly in the town of Richmond, just down the road from the wonderful town bakery (The Daily Bread).

Back at the trails in Bolton, you'll find lots of options for rides of all length, including a trek to Stowe. After exploring the great terrain here, head over to Waterbury, just east on the interstate or Route 2, and find out why the local Ben and Jerry's factory makes it the biggest attraction in Vermont.

Woodbury Mountain Loop

Ride Specs

Start: Curtis Pond, Maple Corners
Length: 11.2 miles
Approximate Riding Time: 2 hours
Rating: Difficult
Terrain: Singletrack, double-track, dirt roads
Other Uses: Horseback riding, snowmobiles

Getting There

From **Montpelier** – Head **north** from Montpelier on **Main Street** and bear **right** at the first intersection, following **County Road** for about nine miles. Go past the **Morse Farm/Sugarbush,** and reach **Maple Corner,** officially known as **Calais.** Once in Maple Corner, turn **left** after the post office on **Worcester Road. Curtis Pond** will appear on the right. Park in the **boat access lot** on the right, just a few tenths of a mile down the road.

Montpelier, the tiny capital of Vermont, is the only state capital in the nation without a McDonalds in the city proper. It is also noted for being the nation's smallest state capital, with a population of merely 8,000. Montpelier's size serves to magnify its personality and charm with its impressive state buildings, the rushing Winooski River, and its unique businesses and restaurants.

The town is also home to one of Vermont's favorite bike shops, Onion River Sports, as well as what was once the state's only mountain bike publication, *Fat Content.* Located right on the Winooski River, Onion River Sports derives its name from the river itself—Winooski means "the wild onion river" in the native Abenaki tongue. The story follows that in the pioneer days a lost hunter was kept alive through the generosity of the Abenaki Indians who shared the only food they had—wild onions. For years the town was known as "Montpelier on the Onion," until locals lobbied to have the original Abenaki name, "Winooski," re-instituted. Not only does Onion River Sports organize some great mountain bike races, they are active in promoting local racing talent. Their one-of-a-kind Onion jerseys are easy to spot.

Just north up the road toward Woodbury, where this ride begins, is the former production site of *Fat Content* magazine. This off-the-cuff publication was widely enjoyed by both back-

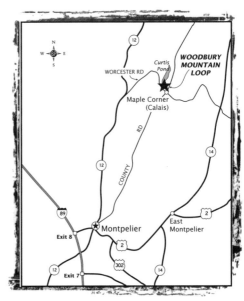

woods hermits and Lycra-clad racers because of its witty style and local intrigue. You can sample some of *Fat Content's* former style and intrigue in *The Ride*, currently New England's only full-scale cycling publication *(see the Ride Information box)*.

Before heading north to the Woodbury Mountain ride, you should stop and visit the capitol buildings in downtown Montpelier. The granite capitol building with its 14-carat gold-leaf dome and marble floors is worth a look. It shows off a variety of Vermont's indigenous stones, and some master craftsmanship. It was built in the early 1800s and rebuilt in 1859 after a massive fire destroyed all but the granite walls.

Montpelier was chosen as the capital in 1808 after several other towns had enjoyed the prestigious distinction. The arrival of the railroad after the Civil War helped Montpelier grow as a commercial center. Today its thriving downtown reflects the benefit of being the state capital. The name Montpelier is perhaps attributable to a local affection for the French who helped Americans in the Revolutionary War. Folks in this area were particularly grateful for their help as the name "Verd-Mont," (Green Mountains) might also imply.

On the way to Maple Corner (the ride's starting point) and the Woodbury Mountain area is Morse Farm—north on County Road. It is an excellent maple industry museum, with slide shows, walks, and displays that will leave you fully informed about the

MilesDirections

0.0 START from the Curtis Pond parking lot, turn left onto Worcester Road, and ride back to Maple Corner.

0.4 At the post office intersection, turn left heading north on County Road.

3.1 After a warm-up cruise on the dirt road, turn left onto the old road (Woodbury Mountain) which climbs up a rocky section. Another trail enters from the right, but stay straight. As the ride goes deeper into the woods, there are several spots where the trail diverges, but it meets itself again in a matter of yards. These spots don't all have cues, so don't panic.

4.1 Pass several turns to the left, and climb another steep rocky section.

4.3 The trail levels off for a brief respite, but prepare for more fun in the muddy, twisty turns to come.

4.6 Turn left here, as the trail splits. If you start going downhill, you know you've missed the turn, because there are still some leg-burning climbs left. Just after this turn, another trail leaves to the right, and the trail appears to split just after this. It is the first of many splits that rejoin in a few yards, so go either way.

4.97 After a lot of wet spots (unless it's a really dry spell), there is another split where you can go either way. This next section is fairly technical and quite challenging.

(continues on next page)

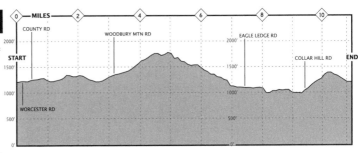

MilesDirections*(continued)*

5.2 Watch out for the nasty drop-off that appears suddenly. This is Penny's Pitch and doesn't look like much until your front wheel is over the edge.

5.5 At the left curve in the trail, another trail goes right and is marked with "No Trespassing" signs. Stay to the left.

5.9 After descending some technical sections, stay to the left.

6.0 The trees open up to a beautiful view of the Worcester area off to the right.

7.2 Pass a log cabin on the left, and stay straight as another road enters from the right.

8.0 The surface changes back to a regular class-3 dirt road (Eagle Ledge).

9.7 Cross Calais Road, and begin the grind up Collar Hill Road (known by the locals as a "short hill").

10.7 At the "T" intersection, turn right, and cruise downhill to Curtis Pond.

11.2 Reach the parking lot for Curtis Pond on the left.

maple sugaring process. They have a great selection of the sweet syrupy stuff.

Begin the ride at Curtis Pond by parking in the recreation parking area and heading north on the dirt road. The few miles of warm-up are perfect for the technical adventure ahead. Watch out for the local guide and his trusty companion as they may fly by you on their tandem—quite a sight on such a technical trail. This loop is one of their favorites. Also be prepared for some water, as this ride can be quite wet and consequently muddy—adding to the fun in the woods. Woodbury, alone, has 23 bodies of water in it, which is the most of any town in Vermont

After leaving the dirt road for the trail system, the first rocky uphill is one of the more technical climbs in the ride. After this, the trail dips up and down with surprises around almost every corner. The rolling banked turns and whoop-de-doos are like being on a carnival ride—and this ride lasts for quite some time. There are several places where the trail seems to split, but the paths eventually converge a short distance down the trail.

As you ride the unpredictable, twisting trail through this thick Vermont forest, imagine negotiating these challenges on a tandem. The day we rode this loop, our guides were on a mountain bike tandem, and they cleaned just about everything on this

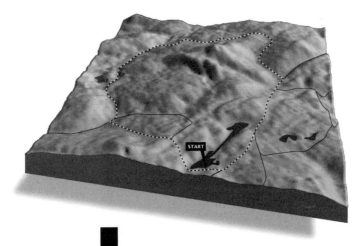

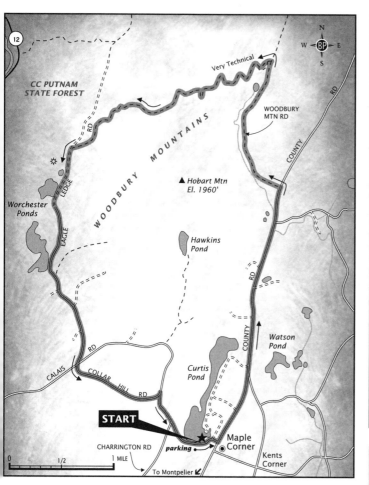

Ride Information

Schedule:
Public roads open year-round. Call the Vermont Chamber of Commerce for details on events in the Montpelier area.
 (802) 223-3443

Local Attractions/Information:
Morse Farm: 1-800-242-2740
 (802) 223-2740 (local)

The Ride:
 Woodburn, MA
 (617) 933-1808
 ridezine@aol.com

Local Bike Shop:
Onion River Sports, Montpelier
 (802) 229-9409

Maps:
USGS maps: Mount Worcester, VT
 Woodbury, VT
DeLorme: Vermont Atlas & Gazetteer – Page 47 K-9

Q: How many Vermonters does it take to change a light bulb?

A: One to change it and two to argue why the old bulb was better.

gnarly trail, including the unexpected drop-off about five miles into the ride (called Penny's Pitch by locals). It's enough of a thrill to scream down the hills after the wet woods section on your own bike. Imagine being on the back of a tandem without your own brake lever!

The last part of the ride through the Eagle's Ledge area opens up to a nice view of the Worcester Mountains, then climbs sharply uphill to connect back to the dirt roads on which you began. The last pitch downhill to Curtis Pond goes by quickly, then it's time to head back to Montpelier for a stop at the Hunger Mountain Co-op, known for its natural-food deli and great selection of healthy snacks. Or stop by any of the many unique restaurants in town.

Groton
State Forest

G roton State Forest, with its 25,000 acres, is the second largest piece of land owned by the state of Vermont. Its wilderness supports a variety of wildlife, including moose, black bear, whitetail deer, beaver, mink, otter, and both water and forest birds. The terrain features dramatic rocks and cliffs, an extensive trail network, and ponds and brooks for fishing or boating. Trails are categorized as either hiking and cross-country skiing or multi-purpose. The multi-purpose trails, which extend from the Knox Mountains to Peacham Pond, permit mountain biking on its varied terrain.

The history of Groton is primarily connected to the logging industry of the late 1800s to the 1920s, when most of the forests were harvested. The railroad that ran through the forest was built to support the local timber industry. (This railroad grade is now a multi-purpose recreational trail—*see the Cross-Vermont Trail Ride on page 54.*) The forests were partially destroyed in the early 1900s by fire, and today the maple and birch have replaced the softer evergreens that once dominated the landscape.

Both the town of Peacham and Peacham Pond (whose boundaries this ride passes along) are named for an English actress named Polly Peacham. She was popular during the early days of New Hampshire land grant settlements. The town was also the educational Mecca of many well-known lawyers, bankers, and congressmen. Thaddeus Stevens, a reputable Civil War orator, and Oliver Johnson, editor of the New York Tribune, were two of Peacham's best-known students. It is reported that Oliver Johnson rang the Peacham church bell for one hour the day John

MilesDirections

0.0 START at the New Discovery campground entrance. The cues start at the gate where fees are collected.

0.3 The campground road comes to a "T." Turn left. Heading right would take you to Osmore Pond. After turning left, the state forest road descends smoothly for a mile or so. Stay straight at any intersections, including the clearing with several trails off of it.

1.4 A major "Y" at a once-active gravel pit, now a big empty hole in the ground. Turn left here.

2.8 Intersection with the snowmobile trail, (2E) and the trail to Peacham Pond. To ride a beautiful out and back section of wilderness trail, turn right. Otherwise, skip down to when the cues return to this spot to do the Peacham Pond loop. After turning right, the trail follows signs for the snowmobile trail 2E.

3.5 A small "trail" goes off to the right. Stay to the left on the doubletrack. It is a long climb, but gradual, and with gorgeous woods on both sides.

4.2 A trail goes off to the right. Again stay to the left.

4.3 The trail appears to divide, but both turns reunite in 100 yards or so. The right side is drier.

(continues on next page)

Brown, an American abolitionist, was hanged.

Perhaps the most notable Peacham residents are Molly and Joe, the Micmac Indian couple who lived in the region during the late 1700s and were close with the white settlers. Apparently, Joe harbored great feelings of resentment toward the British after they slaughtered his tribe in Nova Scotia, prompting his relocation to Vermont. Joe was a respected scout during the war and even received a letter of commendation from President Washington. He enjoyed fishing and hunting in the same area this ride covers and had a tiny cabin somewhere near Peacham Pond. Molly was best known for herbal healing, as many settlers would seek her help in treating their sick children. She was exceptionally secretive with regards to her remedies, and equally successful with her treatment.

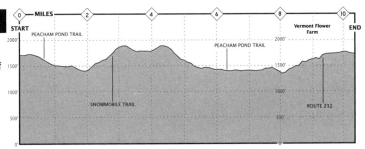

4.6 End of this section of the road. A large gate here marks the edge of the state forest. The road that goes both right and left is the old Lanesboro road. Going right goes to Peacham and eventually Groton. Going left is an old class-4 road that supposedly connects with Peacham Pond. We tried, but grew weary of bike hiking. It is marked with orange blazes. To finish this loop, turn around and head back the way you came.

5.0 Trail off to the left. Stay straight.

5.6 Another trail off to the left, but smaller. Stay straight.

6.3 Back to the original intersection for Peacham Pond and its scenic trails. Go straight past the signs for Groton (they go back to the New Discovery campground) and head for Peacham Pond.

6.7 Intersection with Peacham Pond Road. Go right around the pond, past camps on the left.

(continues on next page)

The couple eventually moved north to the Danville area, but the present-day ponds named in their memory are located close to Peacham Pond on Route 2. A memorial for Joe (as well as one of his favorite hunting caves) can also be found in the town of Newbury—giving one an idea of how much territory he covered and how many people he influenced.

These mountain bike trails begins at the New Discovery campground on Groton State Forest Road (Route 232), roughly seven miles north of the park entrance at Ricker Pond. You may have to pay the $1.50 daily use fee, depending on where you park. The park map is not very helpful for this particular ride, as it fails to include many of the turns and bends the trail features. Be sure to mark these cues when riding in Groton, as it is a large wilderness area with a multitude of trails, and it's easy to get lost. Many trails connect to private land, and others are designated for hiking only.

The early section of the ride meanders through beautiful wilderness, and sharp eyes may pick out the moose that reside here. This multi-purpose trail is rolling and enjoyable, with nothing too steep, but featuring a host of short ascents and descents. It is grassy, woodsy, and well marked, doubling as a snowmobile trail during winter, and is wide enough for two bikes in most

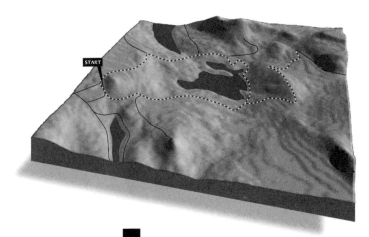

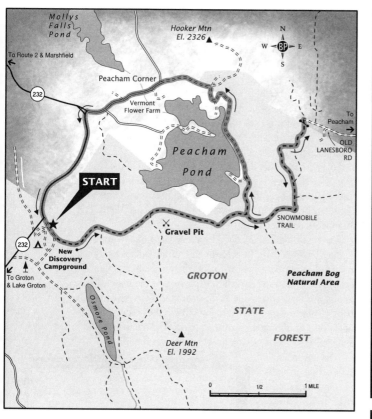

Ride Information

Trail Maintenance Hotline:
Groton State Forest
 (802) 723-4360

Costs:
Parking fee: $1.50 per car
Camping fees: $5 reservation fee,
 Campsites: $13, Lean-to: $17
New Discovery Campground:
 (802) 584-3820
Stillwater Camping at Groton:
 (802) 584-3822

Local Attractions/Events:
Groton's Annual Fall Foliage
 Festival: in late September. For
 information: (802) 748-3678

Maps:
USGS maps: Marshfield, VT;
 Barnet, VT, NH
DeLorme: Vermont Atlas &
 Gazetteer – Page 41 A-14

spots. The trail passes just north of the Peacham Bog area, a natural area of 700 acres that is home to many unusual and fragile plants and animals. The Peacham Bog hiking trail, which can be found on the area trail map, best accesses this unique preserve. Mountain bikes are not allowed on this trail.

After reaching old Lanesboro Road and the gate marking the end of the State Forest boundary, the ride returns the same way back toward the shores of Peacham Pond. The dirt roads around the pond are gentle and scenic. Summer camps surround the pond, and there is a flower farm at the end of the road, just before returning to Route 232. The last few miles cruise back on the paved state forest road, finishing at the New Discovery campground.

MilesDirections (continued)

8.4 The road comes to a "T." Turn left. There is a house here, just across the street.

9.0 Another intersection, this one at the Vermont Flower Farm. Turn right, past the farm, toward Route 232.

9.3 Intersection with the pavement Route 232, the Groton state forest road. Turn left back to the campground.

10.6 New Discovery campground. Turn left into the parking lot.

9

Cross Vermont Trail

Start: The Valley Grill on Route 302
Length: 15 miles
Approximate Riding Time: 1-2 hours
Rating: Easy
Terrain: Doubletrack, old railroad bed
Other Uses: Cross-country skiing, horseback riding, hiking, snowmobiles, four-wheelers

Getting There

From **Wells River (Exit 17 on I-91)** – Take **Route 302 west** through **South Ryegate** and **Groton.** After about nine miles, Route 232 turns **north** to **Groton State Forest. Valley Grill** is at this junction. The ride begins here.

The vision for the Cross Vermont Trail is an unbroken public access trail that extends from the Connecticut River Valley, on the eastern boundary, to the shores of Lake Champlain in western Vermont. The trail would be used for cycling, running, hiking, horseback riding, snowmobiles, cross-country skiing, and snowshoeing. The idea is presently, but slowly, being realized by the State of Vermont and the Cross Vermont Trail Coordinator. At this point, though, there are only fragmented pieces of an old railroad bed open for trail use. Besides this outlined section of the Groton State Forest, other publicly owned fragments exist east of the Valley Grill, passing through Ryegate and Newbury. Other sections can be found in the towns of Plainfield, East Montpelier, Montpelier, and Waterbury.

The transition from a railroad bed to a forest trail requires the partnership of both the local towns and private landowners. Such relationships have a tendency to get mired in detail and bureaucratic tape, unfortunately, which explains why the mapped section in this book covers only a 7.5-mile stretch (15 miles round-trip). Contacting the Cross Vermont office is the best way to stay up-to-date on the progress of the project. The number is (802) 241-3674.

The now defunct railroad was in earlier days known as the Well's River-Montpelier Railway. It was originally constructed to facilitate the transportation of timber from the vast wilderness in the Groton and Knox Mountain region. The forest has endured severe fires and intensive logging since the 1800s, changing its appearance quite dramatically. Where vast hardwoods once stood, soft-

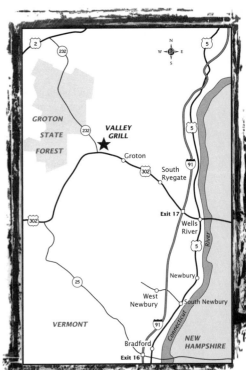

woods now reign. Today there is still controversy over how best to use the land, as it is coveted for its rich wildlife, extensive trail system, and valuable timber.

The Groton area is also rich in history, and the nearby monument to Groton native, William Scott, is only one of the many reminders. The monument is located between Groton and East Barre on Route 302. Scott's story began when he was conscripted into service during the Civil War and sent to a quiet camp in Maryland. Because this post was quiet and a good distance from any real battles, men standing sentry were often apt to fall asleep on their nightly duties. Deeming this unacceptable, a command soon came from General George McClellan, which made the offense punishable by death. Soon after the mandate, William Scott, a heretofore exemplary soldier, offered to take sentry duty for a sick comrade. Diseases such as scurvy, measles, and malaria were common at the time, and most soldiers struggled to stay healthy. After a few nights of substitute duty, Scott quite innocently succumbed to illness and fell asleep. He was caught and thrown into prison, to be executed in two days. The chaplain of his regiment heard of his situation and met with Scott to hear his story. Scott was reluctant to excuse his disgrace but eventually admitted to his poor health. The chaplain set about to obtain a pardon for the ill-fortuned Vermonter. Abraham Lincoln himself delivered the pardon personally to General McClellan. The next morning as William Scott was led to what he imagined to be his execution, he was instead read his pardon. Sadly, Scott would die months later in battle. No doubt Groton's Sleeping Sentinel would prefer to be remembered dying for his country rather than sleeping on the job, but then we'd be begrudging both ourselves and the town of Groton a good story.

The ride on the railroad bed begins on Route 302 at the Valley Grill General Store and Restaurant in Groton. On a Saturday morning in November, this can be quite an entertaining breakfast spot. While enjoying a veggie omelet and homemade muffin, you can catch the latest story of how the big buck got away. After fueling up, the ride heads north on the consistently flat surface of the old railroad bed. The surrounding

MilesDirections

0.0 START at the Valley Grill just west of Groton on Route 302. Be sure to ask the folks at the Grill if it's okay to leave a vehicle there. Head west on Route 302, taking the first right on Route 232. Head toward Groton State Forest.

0.2 Turn left on the snowmobile trail that goes uphill into the woods.

0.3 Reach a "T" intersection with the Cross Vermont Trail. This is an old railroad bed, so it should be obvious because of its consistent gradient that this is the trail. Turn right on the trail and start cruising.

(continues on next page)

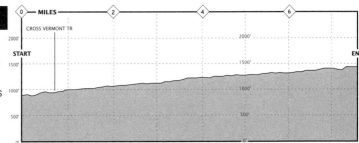

MilesDirections *(continued)*

1.75 Reach the intersection with Route 232. Go across the blacktop and find the railroad bed on the other side. A snowmobile trail goes off to the right, but is obviously uphill. Follow the flat trail along Ricker Pond (on the right).

2.3 Pass a Groton State Forest restroom on the left.

2.78 Go straight through the four-way intersection, using the red metal posts as trail markers. The next section has some beautiful rocky streams and gigantic boulders perched precariously in the forests above. Lake Groton is to the right.

5.0 Trail sign for a scenic overlook off to the left.

5.5 Cross over the pavement and head straight for the trail on the other side. The road to the right leads into the Lake Groton camping and recreation areas.

7.5 At Route 232 (paved), the public land ownership of this section of the trail ends. To complete a 15-mile loop, head back through Groton State Forest toward the Valley Grill.

Groton State Forest offers a number of sights, such as rocky granite hilltops, rushing waterfalls, and boulders strewn from glacial activity nearly 10,000 years ago. The huge rocks along the shores of Lake Groton and Ricker Pond are especially impressive.

The trail is punctuated by intersections with roads leading to campgrounds and other wilderness destinations. It runs through maple and birch forests and is marked along the way with snowmobile signs, Cross Vermont signs, and red metal posts. The friendly grade is especially nice for beginners and families wanting a pleasant Vermont trail ride, while still having opportunities to observe wildlife.

The trail finally intersects the main paved route, Route 232, where the public land ends. The route then continues toward Marshfield, where opportunities for a longer section of public trail are available. The return to the Valley Grill follows the railroad bed back again, where one may notice there has been a slight (but appreciable) incline—which, of course, provides the return trip-per an easy pedal back.

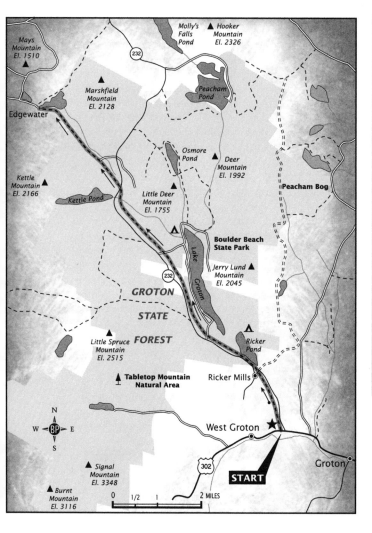

Mays Mountain El. 1510 ▲

Molly's Falls Pond

▲ Hooker Mountain El. 2326

232

Marshfield Mountain El. 2128 ▲

Peacham Pond

Edgewater

Osmore Pond

▲ Deer Mountain El. 1992

Kettle Mountain El. 2166 ▲

Little Deer Mountain El. 1755 ▲

Kettle Pond

Peacham Bog

Lake Groton

Boulder Beach State Park

Jerry Lund ▲ Mountain El. 2045

GROTON

STATE

FOREST

Little Spruce Mountain El. 2515 ▲

Ricker Pond

232

▲ Tabletop Mountain Natural Area

Ricker Mills

West Groton ★

N
W ⊕BP⊕ E
S

▲ Signal Mountain El. 3348

302

START

Groton

▲ Burnt Mountain El. 3116

0   1/2   1   2 MILES

Ride Information

Trail Maintenance Hotline:
Trail Coordinator
(802) 241-3614
Cross Vermont Trail Office
(802) 241-3674
Groton State Park
(802) 723-4360

Local Bike Shop:
Onion River Sports II, Barre, VT
(802) 476-9750

Schedule
Groton State Park is open from
mid-May to mid-October.

Maps:
USGS maps: Groton, Knox
Mountain, Marshfield, VT
DeLorme: Vermont Atlas &
Gazetteer – Page 42 E-1

Dirt Roads Of Orange

T his tour along the back roads near Orange is a small taste of the kind of riding Vermont has to offer. To start from a small Vermont village, then head out on the nearby back roads with nothing more than a mountain bike and no expectations often creates some of the greatest tours one can imagine. That's how this route was discovered, wedged in between the vast expanse of Groton State Forest and the bustling towns of Barre and Montpelier. Orange is only a few miles east of Barre and is a natural starting point for rides in the Knox and Butterfield Mountains. This dirt-road loop provides great views of the area's huge tracts of wilderness and its 3,000-foot peaks.

The highland of Orange, with its views of the Northfield Mountains and the higher peaks of the Green Mountains, was settled in the 1790s. By the mid-1800s, the town had grown to 500 strong—though meager when compared to the sheep population that had swelled to some 5,000. These days, the proportions are considerably in our favor. Just a mile east of Orange is Orange Heights, with even more spectacular views and a reputation for some fierce winters. Even years when no snow fell in the valleys, plenty lay in Orange Heights.

If you traveled west from Orange, the famous Vermont granite quarries would have been an obvious attraction. The enormous piles of rubble to the southwest in Graniteville look like small gray mountains. The Rock of Ages quarry is the world's largest granite quarry and is definitely worth a visit. Gape over the edge of this seemingly bottomless pit, now partially filled by

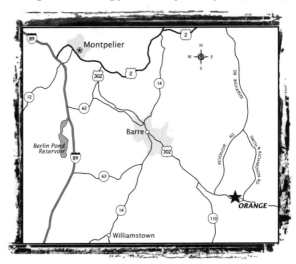

water that reflects beautifully clear shades of greens and blues. The Visitor's Center has an excellent collection of Vermont minerals and an outdoor display of the carved memorials for which the quarry is so famous.

In the 1830s, these quarries supplied the stone needed to build the capitol building in Montpelier. The stone was transported by a four-horse team that left for Montpelier every morning at 4:00 a.m., unloaded, and returned that night at 10:00 p.m. A hefty $4.00/day salary compensated these long days. Today, most of the work is mechanized, though the Graniteville quarries are still known for their superior craftsmanship.

Back in Orange, there are still colorful examples of life as it was in those early days. Recently, a local elderly couple passed away, leaving behind

MilesDirections

0.0 START from Route 302 at the center of Orange, either at the Elementary School or Church in town. Head east on 302, then take the first left called George Street. Some atlases call this Cemetery Road.

0.7 Bear right at the "Y" just past the cemetery on Bennet's Mill Road. A view of the Barre Quarries (world's largest) is off to the left.

(continues on next page)

Vermont's Dirt Roads

Dirt roads are at the heart of Vermont's rural personality. Over 50 percent of Vermont's state highways and town roads are unpaved. There are over 7,000 miles of dirt road in the state and another 1,500 miles or so of dirt "class-4" roads. Class-4 roads are categorized as such because they are not maintained by the towns they are in, but in most cases still resemble a road.

Vermonters tend to be fairly attached to their dirt roads, even though the toll on local automobiles is horrendous. These unpaved pathways provide a natural incentive to slow down and look out the window at the countryside. They also provide excellent terrain for mountain biking and often connect long stretches of land to one another with very little traffic.

As an old, native Vermonter was heard to quip: "You never know what will appear next...it could be a snapping turtle, treacherous ice, a flooded road, or those potholes we all know and love. Would I rather be on a paved road offering consistency, smoothness, and security? Not in a million years."

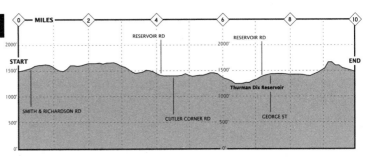

MilesDirections*(continued)*

0.9 Paved driveway goes right. Stay on the dirt road. Gradual climbing.

1.7 Cross a small bridge and begin a descent on a bumpy section of road.

3.3 Pass the first houses seen in a few miles.

4.1 Reach an intersection with the paved Reservoir Road to Plainfield. Turn right, and prepare to turn left in two tenths of a mile on Cutler Corner Road.

5.0 Pass Strong Road off to the right. Continue straight.

5.3 Reach a four-way intersection, just after the cemetery on the right. Turn left, heading toward the reservoir.

5.9 Nice view off to the left of the Knox Mountains, which are adjacent to Groton State Forest, and have acres upon acres of wilderness.

(continues on next page)

their old farm. While the estate was being settled, a cache of gold was discovered under some floorboards. Unfortunately, the money was needed to pay back taxes. The story made national news not only for the discovery of the gold, but also because the couple had maintained a rare collection of old cars in their barns. An auction was held and was attended by curious antique car collectors from around the world, all of whom were undoubtedly astonished by the humble location of these valuable treasures.

This tour begins in the town center and heads north on Cemetery Road. In less than a mile, the cemetery for which the road is named appears on your left with a fine display of stone specimens, such as granite and Vermont slate. A gradual climb along the base of Knox Mountain follows and then changes to a rough road descent. At the bottom, the dirt road intersects the paved Reservoir Road, which runs north to Plainfield. The trails to Spruce Mountain are a few miles up this road, as well as a maze of other dirt roads leading to East Montpelier, Marshfield, Plainfield, and Groton.

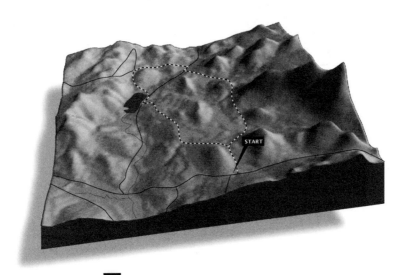

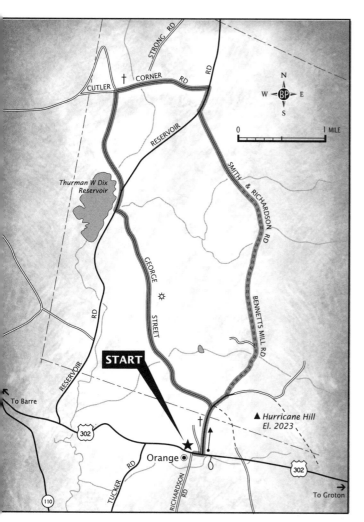

Ride Information

Local Bike Shop:
Onion River Sports II: Barre, VT
(802) 476-9750

Local Attractions/Events:
Rock Of Ages (World's Largest
    Granite Quarries: Graniteville,
    VT) Visitors Center
    (802) 476-3119

Maps:
USGS maps: Barre East, VT
DeLorme: Vermont Atlas &
    Gazetteer – Page 41 H-11

MilesDirections*(continued)*

6.1 Thurman Dix Reservoir is on the right. In the fall, there are often Canadian geese taking a break here.

7.3 Intersection with the paved Reservoir Road again. Turn right then left in another tenth of a mile onto George Street. Prepare to climb a bit.

8.0 Good vista off to the right.

8.8 Another good vista to the left of the Knox Range.

9.0 Back at the original "Y" we turned at in the beginning of the ride. Bear right, past the cemetery.

9.7 Reach the intersection with Route 302. Turn right.

10.0 Reach your car in the center of Orange.

After crossing the pavement, the ride winds along the flatter valley road past the Thurman Dix Reservoir. Nice views of the mountains are found along the way as the route heads back to Orange. Passing the cemetery once again, the loop returns to Orange center, where, like any other Vermont village, you can buy maple syrup, if nothing else.

Vermont's Farmers Markets:
Supporting Vermont's Farms

The range of products that Vermont farms produce is broader than one might think—from farm-raised trout to buffalo to emu. The state raises a variety of fish, fowl, and produce that are often organically produced without chemicals or steroids. Vegetables, fruits, cheeses, and a wide range of dairy products all bear the Green Mountain seal of approval. Maple products are probably Vermont's best known goods, but there are also Vermont oats, Vermont herbs and Vermont honey—all grown and produced here in this tiny state.

Keeping these small farms in business is essential to both the local economy and the local environment. The preservation of the pastoral landscape of Vermont is due to a combination of energies. Vermont has very strict development laws, and thankfully small family farms are still alive in the hills.

Recently there has been a resurgence of local farmer's markets, making it easier to support the local agriculture in Vermont. Most markets run from May through October and feature a colorful array of goods from the fields and homes of the Green Mountain State's rural folks.

NOTE: Many other towns also have farmers markets that may not be listed here. Please inquire at the local chambers of commerce for more information.

A list of Farmer's Markets:

Bennington Farmer's Market
Chamber grounds
Wed. and Fri., 9 – 3

Brattleboro Farmer's Market
On the Common
Wed., 10 – 2

Brandon Farmer's Market
Central Park
Fri., 9 – 2

Burlington Farmer's Market
City Hall Park
Sat., 9 – 2:30

Burlington/Old North End
Elmwood St.
Tues., 3:30 – 6:30

Caledonia Farmer's Market
Western Ave.
Wed. and Sat., 9 – 1

Deerfield Valley Market
Wilmington
Sat. and Sun., 10 – 3

Fair Haven Market
Downtown Park
Fri., 9 – 2

Hardwick Farmers Market
Hardwick, VT
Sat., June-Sept.

Londonderry/West River
Rte.11&100/Mill Tavern
Sat., 9 – 1

McIndoe Falls Farmer's Market
McIndoe Falls Academy/Rte. 5
Sat., 9 – 1

Middlebury Farmer's Market
Marbleworks
Wed. and Sat., 9 – 12

Montpelier/Capitol City Market
Courthouse Parking lot
Sat., 9 – 1

Newport Farmer's Market
Causeway/I-91
Wed. and Sat., 9 – 2

Norwich Farmer's Market
1 mile on Rte. 5
Sat., 9 – 1

Poultney Farmer's Market
Downtown
Thurs., 9 – 2

Randolph Farmer's Market
Rte. 66
Wed., 3 – 6; and Sat., 9 – 1

Richmond Farmer's Market
Volunteer Green
Fri., 3 – 6:30

Royalton Farmer's Market
On the Green
Thurs., 3 – 7

Rutland Farmer's Market
Depot Park
Tues. and Sat., 9 – 3

St.Albans/Northwest Farmer's Market
Main St./Taylor Park
Sat., 9 – 2

Waterbury Farmer's Market
Rusty Parker Park
Wed., 2 – 6

Woodstock/Mt.Tom Market
1 mile north on Rte. 12
Sat., 9 – 1

Waitsfield Gap

Ride Specs

Start: End of Union Brook Road
Length: 22.2 miles
Approximate Riding Time: 3-5 hours
Rating: Difficult
Terrain: Singletrack, double-track, paved roads, dirt roads
Other Uses: Hiking, horseback riding, snowmobiles

Getting There

From **Northfield** – Head **west** on **Union Brook Road**. Travel 4.6 miles up the pavement, then bear **left**. At miles 4.8 there is a **three-way intersection** with a small green in the center. Park at one of the many pull-offs here at the side of the road.

The interlocking ranges of Vermont always make travel from east to west through the Green Mountain state more adventurous than the valley routes laid out from north to south. Such is the case with the Waitsfield Gap ride, an especially strenuous trek from the Dog River Valley to the Mad River Valley, then back again over Roxbury Gap. The nearby peaks of Bald Mountain, Scragg Mountain, and Burnt Mountain all rise to nearly 3,000 feet—just to give you an idea of the climbs involved.

The Waitsfield Gap region was settled much later than its neighboring areas, as its elevation, rough clearings, and difficult winters made farming a challenge. Even so, the hills leading to and from the Gap are dotted with old farms. Tourists visiting Vermont are often surprised by the hilly locales of many early homesites, and although the threat of Native American attacks was often thought to be the rationale for hilltop farms, the settlers may have had other reasons in mind. Even today, if one looks closely, many hilltops are forested by the softer pines, while the lowlands are more populated with hardwoods. The hardwood was considered more difficult to clear, making the soft-pined hills more desirable for pastureland. But as the years passed, many settlers moved closer to the valley's industrial centers, such as Northfield's Factory Village, where jobs and supplies were more plentiful.

The Factory Village, as it was known in the 1800s, featured one of the first woolen mills of its type in the country. Built by Elijah Paine, a well-known Vermont pioneer, the mills produced much-needed wool during war times. It employed hun-

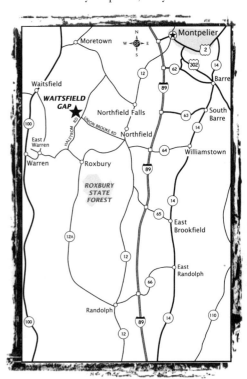

dreds, including residents from the West Hill area that today pre-cludes the Waitsfield Gap ride. Imagine negotiating these narrow dirt paths in a horse and buggy on a snow-filled day rather than on a mountain bike.

On the other side of the Scragg Mountain range, the villages of Waitsfield and Warren make up the base of this recreation-ori-

ented valley. The 4,000-foot peaks of Mount Ellen, Stark Mountain, and Mount Abe offer abundant skiing and tourist opportunities. Both Waitsfield and Waitsfield Gap were named after Colonel Benjamin Wait, an acclaimed activist for the early independence of Vermont and a member of the Green Mountain Boys. Wait is remembered as a brave soldier who was captured twice by Indians and survived conditions and treatment most could not fathom.

This loop through these two valleys is best enjoyed with ample food and water, as there are no refueling stops on the direct route. The initial ascent to Waitsfield Gap is an instant warm-up, with several rocky technical sections toward the summit. The Vermont Snow Travelers Association (VAST), whose signs mark the meet-ing of the Waitsfield and Northfield town lines at the summit, maintains most of the trail.

Descending to Waitsfield is a bit tricky. After taking in the view under the power lines, the terrain is marked by brooks, leaves, and lots of rocks. The trail finally drops you onto dirt roads lead-

MilesDirections

0.0 Head up the hill, which is to the right at the three-way intersec-tion. Prepare for some steep climbing from the start. The road begins as a town-maintained dirt road then quickly changes to some single and doubletrack.

0.63 Continue straight at the "Public Right-Of-Way" sign on the Waitsfield Gap Trail. Logging has opened up the forests considerably here, but the trail is easy to follow, especially with the snowmobile markers to guide the way.

1.55 Summit of the gap. Follow signs for 17 west, and note the beginning of the Mad River Snowmobile Club's trails. The descent tends to be tricky and especially treacherous when wet. Keep your eyes open for rocks, leaves, and slippery stuff.

2.6 Intersection with farmer's fields. Stay to the left, following the wet doubletrack, as the snow-mobile trail meanders off across the fields. Continue on this old road, staying straight. Several trails exit both to the right and left as you descend. This is called East Road (once you reach the dirt).

3.5 Bear to the left and climb a short steep hill after crossing the bridge. After the hill, bear to the right on the well-traveled dirt road leading down to Waitsfield. You are now on Long Road. Views to the left are of Scragg Mountain. Straight ahead is Mount Ellen/Sugarbush and to the right is Camel's Hump and Mount Hunger.

(continues on next page)

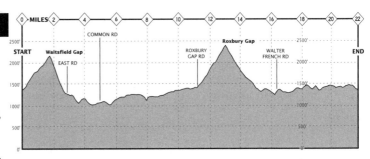

MilesDirections *(continued)*

4.97 Left on the Common Road. Straight goes to the village of Waitsfield. Stay on the Common Road as it passes the Von Trapp greenhouses and several other old, beautiful farms.

8.7 Bear left on the pavement toward East Warren. This next section of blacktop is a nice spin for the legs. A panoramic view of the Mad River Valley and the Green Mountains.

11.5 Turn left up Roxbury Gap Road. It is paved in sections and dirt in others. Be prepared for some serious climbing.

13.6 View spot on the Roxbury Gap. Definitely worth checking out the fruits of your climbing labor. At almost 2,000 feet, the valley and mountains are awesome. Get psyched to cruise down the other side.

(continues on next page)

ing to the Waitsfield Common. A spectacular view of the Green Mountains is afforded to the west.

The middle segment of the ride is comfortably rolling, with sections along East Warren Road approaching flat. This section above the Mad River Valley is a popular cycling route with numerous connections to dirt roads and local trail networks. The Mad River Bike Shop, located on Route 100 in Waitsfield, offers weekly rides through the area. The East Warren Road also passes through Morgan Horse farmland, where a slew of curious horses are liable to stare as you pedal by.

The Roxbury Gap ascent is now partially paved, but you'll still get a good leg burning with some of the nicest views of the Green Mountains waiting at the summit. Zipping down the dirt road on the other side around the sharp corners is equally rewarding. The transition from dirt to pavement is a landmark to remember because missing the turn back to Waitsfield Gap means an uphill trek in order to reconnect. Fortunately, the tiny village of Roxbury, a few miles downhill from the turn, does have a general store, should bonking be unavoidable.

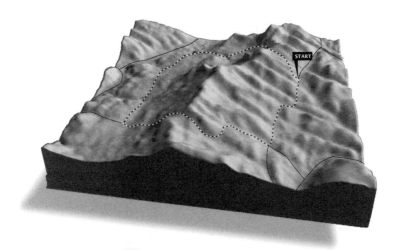

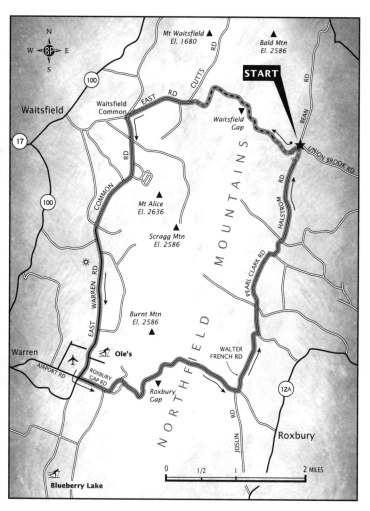

Ride Information

Local Attractions/Events:
Northfield Labor Day Observances on the town green: Fair, Running Race. Call the town offices for more information: (802) 485-5421.
Norwich Quilt Festival: mid-July

Waitsfield Area:
Sugarbush Chamber of Commerce
1-800 828-4748 o
(802) 496-3409

Maps:
USGS maps: Northfield, VT; Waitsfield, VT; Warren, VT; Roxbury, VT
DeLorme: Vermont Atlas & Gazetteer – Page 40 F-3

MilesDirections *(continued)*

16.2 Turn left on the dirt road. (This is Walter French Road, but I doubt if anyone else knows this.) Then head back on the dirt roads to the car.

17.7 Bear to the left. The right-hand turn drops down to Route 12A.

19.6 Bear to the left again after passing a small gray cape. Scragg Mountain is now to the left.

20.0 Straight through a four-way intersection and up a short hill.

22.2 Back at the parking spot.

The last few miles roll back to the parking area on a connection of dirt roads that pass farmland, hunting camps, and the base of Scragg Mountain. Epic stories of mountain bike trips over the peak of Scragg Mountain always involve lots of hiking, bike-shouldering, and endurance. This ride finishes at the junction of Union Brook Road and Halstrom Road, with a short drive back to the town of Northfield.

Mad River Valley Tour

Start: East Warren Airport
Length: Variable
Approximate Riding Time: Variable
Rating: Moderate
Terrain: Singletrack, double-track, paved roads, dirt roads
Other Uses: Cross-country skiing, hiking, horseback riding

Getting There

From **I-89** – Take **Exit 9 (Middlesex),** and follow **Route 100B south** to **Route 100.** Take **Route 100 south** to **Waitsfield** and turn **left** under the covered bridge on **East Warren Road.** Follow East Warren Road to East Warren (about six miles). At the intersection of **Roxbury Gap Road** and **East Warren Road,** turn right on **Airport Road.** From here travel about one mile following clearly marked signs to the airport and **Ole's Ski Touring Center.** Park at the airport to begin.

The Mad River Valley has become one of Vermont's more popular places to explore on a mountain bike, and it's suited for cyclists of all levels. With the potential for dramatic views in virtually any direction, this scenic cluster of villages has a lot to offer, especially if you're looking for singletrack, dirt roads, or a ride at an alpine ski area. The Valley also offers excellent cuisine, a local farmer's market in the summer, and lots of swimming holes along the rushing waters of the Mad River.

Riding possibilities in this area extend from the base of Camel's Hump in Duxbury to the Breadloaf Forest Service roads in Ripton. Besides visiting some of the cross-country ski centers (like this ride does), another good way to learn about the available riding is to visit the local Mad River Bike Shop. Ask about their group rides or get directions to other good starting points. A few other sources for riding in the area include the Tucker Hill Inn, where a small section of trail connects to other networks and dirt roads, and also Sugarbush Ski Area, where they have developed a nice system of challenging singletrack. Because of the influx of mountain bikers to this area, there has been some resistance from private landowners to keep favorite routes open for riding. The local cycling club has begun to address this issue of land access, but because of the sensitivity in this area, riding in designated areas is your best bet.

Some of the nicest legal riding areas in the Mad River Valley are the cross-country trail systems at Blueberry Lake and Ole's. Located high above the valley in East Warren, these centers sport a good selection of single-track and are easily

connected by the back roads that crisscross the area. The centers are presently run by the same organizer, Leonard Robinson, who maintains the Blueberry Lake trails throughout the entire year. Robinson is presently incorporating snowshoeing into the available activities for these trails, making it a multi-sport trail system.

You begin the tour at the East Warren airport, at the beginning of Ole's trails, where you might also get an unexpected air show. This small rural airstrip is home to several biplanes and a number of sleek gliders. On a busy July day, the trick planes will be doing loop-de-loops while the red tow plane hauls up other gliders to the thermals rising above Scragg Mountain. Be careful accessing the trails, as the runway is quite active throughout the summer.

From the East Warren airport to Blueberry Lake, you pass Roxbury Gap Road, which is also part of the Waitsfield Gap ride. *(see page 64)* This road was used extensively in the late 1800s to ship farm produce from the rich farmlands of Mad River Valley to parts of central Vermont. Cheese, butter, cattle, hogs, and vegetables were hauled tirelessly over this 2,000-foot pass. In the winter, the excessive traffic compacted the snow such that the sleds used to transport the goods often had to drag logs behind them to keep from racing uncontrollably down the slopes. Recreation has since replaced farming as the best moneymaker in the valley, though some beautiful farms still survive along the fertile Mad River floodplain.

MilesDirections

0.0 START at the Sugarbush-Warren Airport in East Warren. Turn left out of the parking lot on Airport Road.

0.5 Turn left onto the blacktop and head toward Roxbury Gap.

1.2 Turn right on the Common Road at the four corners. From this open vista point, the mountains in the foreground are awesome—Mount Ellen (Sugarbush), Molly Stark (Mad River Glen), Camel's Hump, and Mount Abe. The ski trails are often white well into May.

1.7 Turn left on Plunkton Road, following signs for Blueberry Lake Cross-Country Ski Center. This first few miles is still blacktop.

2.1 Blueberry Lake Cross-Country Ski Center on the left.

2.9 Blacktop turns to dirt road. Entering the Alpine Village, there is a maze of tiny roads, once designed for a building development. The roads are all named for trees.

4.75 Turn left on Willow Street, and watch for dogs.

4.9 Stay straight through the intersection.

5.0 Take a right at the "T."

5.1 Quick left turn at the bottom of the short hill. Going right loops back into the houses.

5.2 Another quick turn to the right. There are a few minor trails off the main doubletrack, but just stay on the traveled track.

(continues on next page)

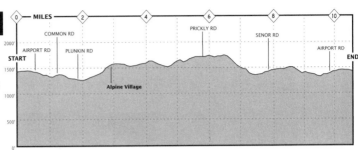

MilesDirections (continued)

5.25 The ride passes under a power line and then by a beaver pond. After this it starts to climb up a gravely section.

5.3 Sign for Mystic Road on the right. Stay to the left.

5.5 Road bears to the right past some houses and dogs on the left.

5.8 Bear left on Prickly Mountain Road. An old road goes off to the right, which often has some fresh moose tracks.

7.7 Bear right on Senor Road, after a screaming downhill on the dirt road.

9.1 Intersection with the paved Roxbury Gap Road. Turn left at the Dowdell farm here at the "T."

9.7 Go straight across the four-way intersection with the Common Road onto Airport Road.

10.4 Turn right back to the airport, still on Airport Road.

10.9 Turn right at the Sugarbush-Warren Airport sign and Ole's ski touring center.

Beyond Roxbury Gap, the road to Blueberry Lake affords an excellent view of Mount Abe, Lincoln Peak, Mount Ellen, and Stark Mountain, as well as Camel's Hump, Mount Mansfield, and Mount Hunger. Both Sugarbush and the unique Mad River Glen ski areas are located in this nearby range of the Green Mountains. Some challenging riding can be found through the Lincoln and Appalachian Gaps that cross the ridge east to west.

Blueberry Lake offers a beautifully framed reflection of the Northfield Mountains, which rise up to the east behind it. The ski trails here are gentle, with many stretches being grassy and smooth. Beyond the ski trails, the loop wanders out into Alpine Village, a failed development project that now has some nice riding on its less-traveled paths. The ride loops back to the airport on Senor Road, with some outstanding views of the mountains from a little higher elevation.

After finishing the tour, it's a good idea to visit the Warren Store down in the tiny village of Warren and sample their cookies, relax on the deck over the falls, and plan another ride in the Mad River Valley.

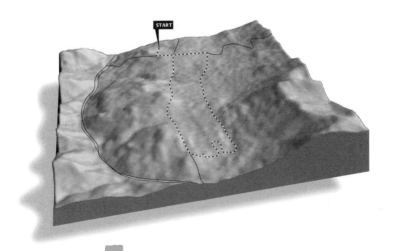

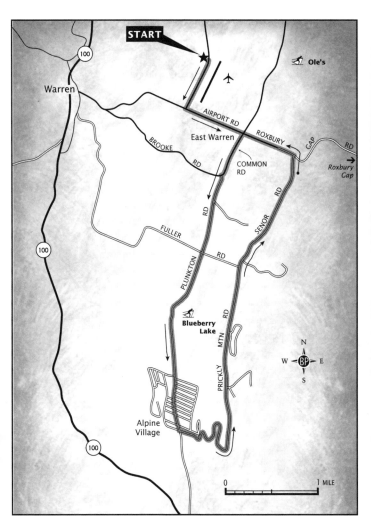

Ride Information

Local Attractions/Events:
Winter Only:
Ole's Ski Touring Center
   (802) 496-3430
Blueberry Lake Cross-Country
   Ski Center
   (802) 496-6687

Summer:
Fourth Of July Parade: Warren
Sugarbush Brewer's Festival:
   September. For more informa-
   tion: 1-800-82-VISIT.
Ben & Jerry's One World, One
   Heart Festival: 1-800-BJ-FESTS
Other Sugarbush Events:
   1-800-53-SUGAR

Local Bike Shops:
Mad River Bike Shop
   (802) 496-9500

Maps:
USGS maps: Warren, VT;
DeLorme: Vermont Atlas &
   Gazetteer – Page 40 I-1

Bull Run Ramble

Ride Specs

Start: Lover's Lane
Length: 8.7 miles
Approximate Riding Time: 1 hour
Rating: Moderate
Terrain: Doubletrack, paved roads, dirt roads
Other Uses: Horseback riding

Getting There

From **Montpelier** – Take **I-89 south** to **Exit 5** (Northfield), then follow **Route 64 west** to **South Northfield.** Park at the base of **Route 64** where it meets **Route 12** and the **South Village Grocery,** just at the start of **Lover's Lane.**

L
ike many Vermont towns, Northfield stretches along a number of tiny villages, mainly and conveniently named for their geographic locations: South Northfield, Northfield Center, Northfield (Factory Village), and Northfield Falls. The villages run from north to south along the Dog River in a valley nestled between the Northfield Mountains and the Paine Mountain range. In the 1800s, these villages were socially, geographically, and industrially independent of one another. Today, the township of Northfield is more unified, but the individual character of the four villages remains.

The Bull Run Loop begins in South Northfield, which has gone by various names over the years, such as: the "Upper Village," "Southville," and originally "Slab City" (speaking, most likely, for the road which was made of slate slabs). Today it is called South Village, or South Northfield. This once-bustling little village had seven mills and factories, according to the *Green Mountain Heritage* (a chronicle of Northfield, written by their Historical Committee). They included a gristmill, a sawmill, a blacksmith shop, a chair factory, a casket factory, a carding mill, and a sash and blind mill. There was even a large inn with a ballroom that hosted many local social events. This settlement provides the natural link between the hill farms above on Mill Hill and the fertile river valleys below. This hill area was the first settled in the Northfield region and was home to Elijah Paine, Northfield's earliest benefactor and namesake for Paine Mountain range.

The Bull Run area (a few miles south of Mill Hill) was thriving in the early 1900s. Farm families would gather together for neighborhood dances and suppers. It is now home to a summer camp called Camp Wihakowi, which offers kids and families the opportunity to learn some of the skills that the earliest settlers of the area, the Native Americans, knew well.

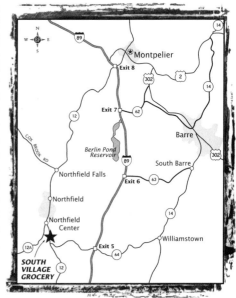

MilesDirections

0.0 START at the South Village Grocery/Mobil station in South Northfield, off Route 12. Turn right out of the Mobil station onto the dirt road called Lover's Lane. This dirt road winds along the stream, and intersects with Route 12A.

0.7 Turn left on Route 12A heading south.

0.8 Turn left up Winch Hill and prepare for the steep climb in the ride. The most difficult part is paved.

1.5 Winch Hill turns to dirt. Huge old pines line the sides of the hill, and meadows begin to open out on both sides.

(continues on next page)

The ride itself is a perfect challenge for cyclists who haven't developed tricky technical skills yet but want to explore some of Vermont's back roads and hilltop views. After leaving South Village on Lover's Lane, the ride follows Sunny Brook (which was harnessed for its water power back in the early days). The next segment up Winch Hill provides the most challenging uphill in the ride and leaves no doubt as to why Northfield has been called "the hilliest little town in Vermont." (Once you've done a few rides in the Green Mountains, you'll probably agree that a hundred towns could boast this title.) After the climb, the dirt road along the ridge in the shadow of Shaw Mountain provides a spectacular view that is well worth the effort it's taken to get there. The valley below stretches north to south, with excellent views of the town, Norwich University, and the Northfield Mountains. Just behind the first range of hills is the Green Mountain range, with Sugarbush and Mad River to the south. Camel's Hump and Hunger Mountain are in view to the north. After the high meadows, the road dives downhill steeply toward Bull Run. The narrow "S" turns provide an exciting exit.

Once on Bull Run Road, the ride turns west along Bull Run Brook. The road to the east heads toward Roxbury State Forest and a myriad of back roads. Riding west along the brook is relatively flat and shady—with some swimming holes for those hot summer days.

Mom's Northfield Refrigerator Pickles

6 cups of cold water
1/3 cup of sea salt
2 tbsp. sugar
1 cup of white vinegar
4 cloves of garlic
11/2 tbsp. mixed pickling spice
3 sprigs fresh dill

Cut cucumbers in strips. Put in large bowl and cover with the above liquid mixture. Cover the bowl and put in the refrigerator. Sample in 2-4 days. Best eating is after a week!

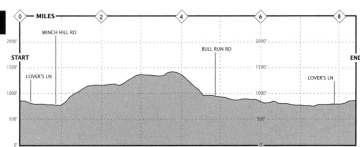

MilesDirections *(continued)*

3.1 Stop to check out the spectacular views. For the short amount of riding, it is quite a reward.

4.1 Bear right and head downhill. The downhill is steep and rocky, with narrow corners. It is not a busy road, but is passable by car.

4.9 Intersection with Bull Run. Turn right and follow the dirt road along a merry stream.

6.5 Bear right as Tucker road comes in from the left.

7.4 Intersection with Route 12A. The building across to the left is an old one-room schoolhouse. Turn right and head north toward Lover's Lane.

8.0 Turn right on Lover's Lane. Check out the pull-over spots that may help to explain this road's name.

8.7 Turn left up the entrance to South Village Grocery.

At the intersection with Route 12A, you'll want to turn right. But first, look across the road to the left and you'll see one of the many one-room schoolhouses in the area. Now a private home, the school was used for classes until the late 1970s. Northfield could not afford to build a central elementary school, so students were bused to a variety of these schoolhouses around the countryside (all within a 10-mile radius of town). Though the grades were not integrated like a traditional one-room schoolhouse, the experience was similar.

The short stretch up Route 12A is also flat, as is the final segment back on Lover's Lane. Once you reach South Village, another one-room schoolhouse is situated directly across from the South Village Grocery. They're pretty easy to spot. Even the casual explorer driving or riding further north through the Center Village, the "Factory Village," and finally Northfield Falls, will find other old schools either on hilltops or tucked away down by the rivers.

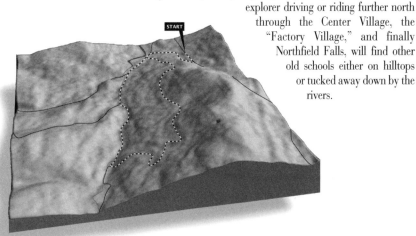

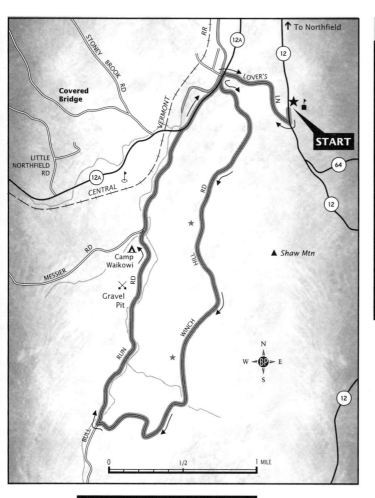

Ride Information

Local Bike Shop:
Bicycle Express, Depot Square,
  Northfield: 1-800-247-7430

Local Atractions/Events:
(see the ride info for the Waitsfield
  Gap ride)
Horse Drawn Carriage Tours: Call
  Mike MacDougal:
  (802) 485-6200

Maps:
USGS maps: Roxbury, VT;
  Northfield, VT
DeLorme: Vermont Atlas &
  Gazetteer – Page 40 H-5

In Addition...

This ride has all the elements of a basic Vermont mountain bike ride—all contained within eight short miles. It has a challenging climb, screaming downhill, magnificent views, rushing brooks, old maples, and a small family store. It's a great, accessible tour.

Williamstown Dirt Roads

Ride Specs

Start: Williamstown Downtown area

Length: 29.0 miles

Approximate Riding Time: 3-5 hours

Rating: Difficult (due to length of ride and amount of hill climbing)

Terrain: Doubletrack, paved roads, dirt roads

Other Uses: Cross-country skiing, hiking, horseback riding, snowmobiles

Getting There

From **I-89** – Take **Exit 5** and follow **Route 64 east** to **Williamstown** (about five miles). Turn **right** on **Route 14** and park in the center of Williamstown.

This 30-mile dirt road tour of Williamstown, and a bit of Washington, includes a beautiful section along old work roads through Ainsworth State Forest, as well as a dip into the Williamstown Gulf. The Gulf is a deeply incised valley that was left behind by glaciers and is home now to moose, herons, and some incredibly rocky forest walls. This lengthy tour of hilly Vermont back roads will take the better part of a day, and since there are no stores along the way, a generous supply of snacks and water is recommended.

The ride begins in downtown Williamstown at the general store, a building that has seen its share of misfortune. Back in 1839, the original Williamstown General Store burned completely to the ground. Apparently, a hogshead (an old term for a 60-150 gallon casket or drum) of rum spontaneously combusted, catching the store on fire. It seems that though losing the store was tragic, folks were more upset about the waste of good rum.

Traveling away from the general store, the ride heads east out of town toward Mount Pleasant. A steady climb up to South Hill Road brings you to a panoramic view of the Green and Northfield Mountains. The large family farms high on this hill are still struggling to make ends meet. *(See page 62.)*

After a short descent down Winchester Hill Road, the ride detours into Ainsworth State Forest and climbs steadily up a rocky utility road. The woodsy trail following this climb is one of the surprises along this ride, and the rollicking downhill it winds

MilesDirections

0.0 START at the Williamstown General Store along Route 14. Head north on Route 14 for a short distance.

0.1 Turn right on Graniteville Road. Bear right again up the hill past Lacillade's Lumber.

1.4 Turn right on Gilbert Road. This dirt-surfaced road climbs gradually above the town then meanders through farmland.

2.1 Reach the intersection with an unnamed dirt road. Stay left.

3.7 Reach the intersection with Chelsea Road. Cross the pavement and head through the right turn called Menard's Crossing.

5.3 Bear right at the intersection onto Winchester Hill Road.

5.5 Bear right again, staying on Winchester Hill Road, and descend.

6.1 The road changes from a class-3 town road to a much rougher class-4 road. At the fork, turn left and begin the climb. These roads are considered state forest highways but are little more than doubletrack trails snaking through the woods. The first mile has several turn-offs in both directions. Stay straight along the doubletrack.

6.5 Stay right at the well-traveled path marked "Private Property," which goes off to the left.

(continues on next page)

into is quite another. At the bottom, a short section of Route 14 connects you to another network of dirt roads and eventually to Staples Pond. This pond is a favorite hideout for heron and local snapping turtles (which are supposedly enormous). Just on the other side of Route 14, at the bottom of Winchester Hill Road, you can catch a glimpse of the clear blue waters of Cutter Pond—better known as Lotus Lake.

Lotus Lake is a well known family-run day camp that has been thriving since the 1950s. Local kids hunting for the elusive daddy snapper, watching beavers, shooting arrows, and splashing in the cool water have enjoyed many summers at this camp. There are several excellent raspberry patches on the roadsides here, so if you're low on snacks, you may be in luck.

Campers often hike up this section of road to pick berries, picnic, and tell stories about the legendary "Green Hand." To learn more about "Green Hand," you'll have to stop by. Sorry, but tradition says that the story is only to be told on Lotus Lake overnight camping trips. Be on the lookout for groups of giggling campers.

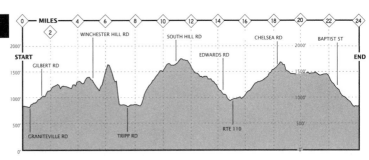

8.5 Reach the intersection with Route 14. The trail ends rather abruptly at Route 14, so be prepared. Turn left on Route 14 for a quick tour of the snapping turtle pond.

9.0 Turn right on the dirt road (Tripp Road) at the end of the pond.

9.5 Turn right on Boyce Road to complete the pond loop. Pass Pond View Farm on the left.

9.9 Reach the intersection with Route 14 again. Cross Route 14 and pass a white farmhouse on the left. Head up the hill and catch a glimpse of Lotus Lake to the left. This next climb is difficult, but rideable. Be ready to stick it in the granny gear. This hill is also known as Snapper Trail.

11.0 Bear to the left.

11.2 Back at the intersection with South Hill Road. If you've had enough already, this is a good place to backtrack to Gilbert Road and return to town. To keep going, follow South Hill Road to the right. This direction takes you on some narrow back roads, with a bit of climbing, some pavement, and, of course, great Vermont scenery. Turn right on South Hill Road.

12.2 Stay straight on South Hill Road at this split. Lighthouse Road goes right.

(continues on next page)

From the top of South Hill Road, the ride cruises downhill on the other side of the ridge toward Lighthouse Hill and Chelsea. The intersection with the pavement of Route 110 marks the end of the long descent and the beginning of another uphill. From here, the route mapped out is the most direct, but more adventurous riders may want to try some of the other dirt roads that connect back to Williamstown from Jackson Corner. A Vermont road atlas is handy to have on a long ride like this as it may provide a variety of riding options of which you may not be aware. After Jackson Corner, the ride swings downhill to Williamstown, with great views of the valley all along the way.

After finishing a tour of this hill country, you may see why Elijah Paine, the founder of both Williamstown and Northfield, wanted this village (and more particularly his home) to be the state capital. Aside from being close to the geographic center of

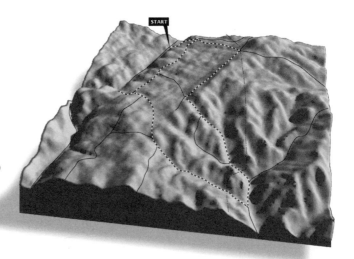

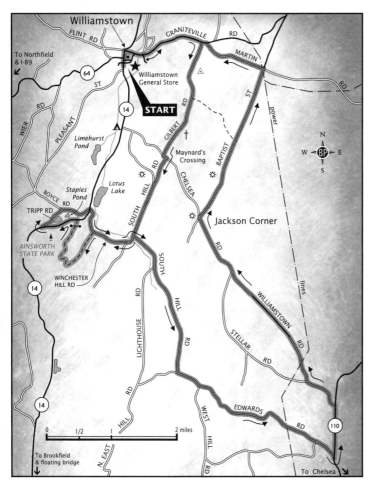

Ride Information

Local Attractions/Events:
Historic village of Chelsea:
Farmers Market: Wednesdays,
June-September, on the village
green

Maps:
USGS maps: Brookfield, VT;
Washington, VT; Barre West, VT
DeLorme: Vermont Atlas &
Gazetteer – Page 41 H-8

MilesDirections*(continued)*

14.2 The road comes to a "T." Turn left on Edwards Road.

14.7 Bear left at the split in the road, continuing to follow Edwards Road.

17.7 Turn left on Route 110. Chelsea is about three miles south of this intersection.

18.7 Turn left on Williamstown/Chelsea Road. On a clear day, Mount Mansfield and Camel's Hump can be seen from this road.

23.1 Reach Jackson Corner. Turn right on Baptist Street and head back toward town.

26.1 Turn left on Martin Road.

27.2 Turn left on Graniteville Road. Still going downhill.

28.8 The final intersection with Route 14 is in sight. Turn down the pavement to the left, heading toward the general store.

29.0 Reach the Williamstown General Store.

the state, Elijah's homestead, high on the western hillsides of Williamstown, had excellent water power to run his mills. Though Paine was an influential politician, his dreams for Williamstown floundered, chiefly because the majority of the population kept to the valleys, which made the riverside site of Montpelier more appealing. A marble likeness of the talented and outspoken Elijah Paine can be found in Montpelier today.

15

Connecticut Corners Loop

Passing through the tiny villages north of Randolph, riders may have difficulty imagining these villages were once bustling centers for farming and milling. The rarely-used roads and trails that make up this loop between West Brookfield, Roxbury, and Braintree were important everyday routes in the early 1900s, used to transport goods from the farm, to visit neighbors, or to pick up finished cream from the creamery.

Mountain biking to Connecticut Corners from West Brookfield (on the first part of this loop) follows an old mountain route used extensively by early settlers traveling from the Brookfield valley to the busy Roxbury valley. Even 20 years ago, folks who grew up in this area recall harrowing trips made on winter nights in horse-drawn sleighs. The small region is known by locals as Cram Hill, the moniker belonging to the Cram family that settled early in the area. Connecticut Corners was settled and named by emigrants from Connecticut, and nearby Mount Nevins was known as the Pumpkinshell—perhaps due to the way the light hangs orange on its slopes during the setting of the sun. In addition, West Brookfield was named Alder Meadows because of the alders (a tree or shrub in the birch family) that grew prolifically in the nearby Ayer Brook headwaters. Early settlers also nicknamed a flat piece of land in the local valley "Johnny Cake Flat" after the pancake that was commonly served as a breakfast item.

Though riders may not take notice while cycling this route, it is interesting to see how rural Vermont has changed dramatically over the course of 100 years. Many older farms

Ride Specs

Start: Near the West Brookfield Community Church
Length: 9.3 miles
Approximate Riding Time: 1-2 hours
Rating: Moderate to Difficult
Terrain: Doubletrack, dirt roads (lots of climbing)
Other Uses: Cross-country skiing

Getting There

From **Montpelier** – Travel **south** on **I-89** to **Exit 4** to **Randolph.** From **Slab City's bike shop** in Randolph, travel **north** on **Route 12.** Go through **East Braintree,** passing the **Snowsville** general store. When you come to a sign pointing toward **West Brookfield,** near a cemetery on the left (about 6.5 miles from Slab City), take the **left** going up the dirt road. Follow the dirt road until you get to the **West Brookfield Community Church** in the center of the small town. Park near here.

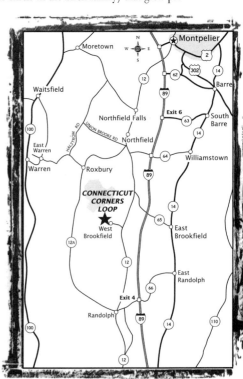

MilesDirections

0.0 START from the West Brookfield Community Church. Take the left turn on the other side of the church. Follow the trail straight, bearing to the right along the river.

0.3 At the "Bridge Closed" sign, go to the right of the bridge, crossing the river.

0.9 At the "Y" intersection, go left.

1.2 Continue to follow the river and bear right, up the main trail.

1.6 Cross over the river on the sod-covered bridge, and head straight up the hill.

2.7 At a three-way intersection go straight, and veer slightly to the left, going down the dirt road.

3.2 After going downhill, turn left at the four-way intersection on Pope Road.

3.3 After passing the buses that some folks around here live in, veer to the left and go downhill.

3.6 Pass the camp on the right, and continue to descend down the rough trail.

(continues on next page)

and homes are still maintained out on these back roads, but many are now summer homes. All of these summer homes are surrounded by roadways that have significantly altered the landscape of the area.

For people living in West Brookfield, Snowsville (now East Braintree) was the location for the main general store, offering supplies of hardware, Johnson woolens, work boots, shoes, flours, canned goods, and penny candy. The barter system was, at one

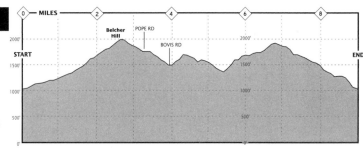

MilesDirections *(continued)*

3.9 Continue down the main road past the beige house on the right.

4.0 At the three-way intersection, turn left on Bovis Road heading uphill.

4.9 Pass the Doane's Maple Ridge Sheep Farm, and descend down the main road.

5.4 An old red school house on the left, with a sign reading "Connecticut Corners" and "Roxbury—five miles" on the building. Go left up the hill past the schoolhouse.

6.3 Pass a camp on the left after climbing up the main trail.

(continues on next page)

time, the preferred method of sale because anything grown or produced locally could be used by someone else. Sawmills, black-smiths, and the local creamery were also all located in East Braintree.

If you venture north a few miles from West Brookfield to Brookfield, you'll be at the height of land between the White and Winooski Rivers. Brookfield is also the home of the famous Floating Bridge. This 320-foot bridge crosses the beautiful Sunset Lake and is constructed entirely of barrels. Water will splash over the bridge when one crosses this seemingly large raft, giving bridge users an odd and sometimes uneasy feeling. Swimming is popular here as well in the deep, clear water; and camping up the hill at Allis State Park is also fun. Check out the fire tower at the park, which provides an excellent view of the surrounding central Vermont hills.

From the West Brookfield Community Church, this ride follows the river toward Belcher Hill. After crossing over the river for the first time, the trail begins to ascend as it passes Roxbury State

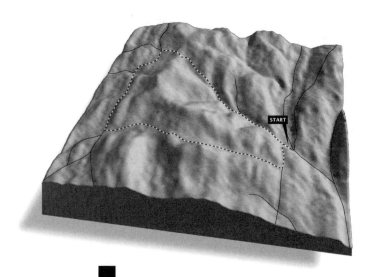

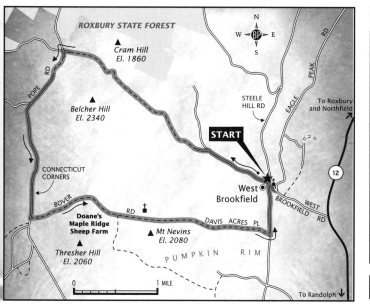

Ride Information

Trail Maintenance Hotline:
White River Valley
  Trails Association
  (802) 728-4420

Local Bike Shops:
Slab City Bike & Sport
  (802) 728-5747
Onion River Sports, Montpelier
  (802) 229-9409

Maps:
USGS maps: Roxbury, VT
DeLorme: Vermont Atlas and
  Gazetteer – Page 34, A-5

MilesDirections(continued)

Forest land. A few more passes need to be made over the river on sometimes slippery bridges before reaching what is known as Cram Hill.

Turning right at this first four-way intersection leads to Roxbury, the state forest, and its excellent network of trails. This route over Cram Hill to Roxbury was well used in the early part of the century but is better suited for mountain biking now. Riders who cycle straight ahead at the four-way will dip back down to Route 12A near the Roxbury Fish Hatchery. This loop, however, goes left toward Thresher Hill and Mount Nevins, back into Orange County and the town of Braintree. The descent from here can be a bit rough and painful.

After Cram Hill, the main dirt road rolls considerably, passing the Doane's Maple Ridge Sheep Farm. Down the hill from the farm is the old red school house with signs reading "Connecticut Corners" and "Roxbury—five miles." Be ready to climb for a bit here, as the snowmobile trail follows Bouvant Road. The last mile or so is downhill to "Davis Acres" and the West Brookfield Community Church.

6.7 Cross over the snowmobile bridge and continue straight up the trail. After cresting the hill, descend following the main trail, and pass a camp on the right. Go around the gate to the left, continuing downhill.
8.6 At the "T" intersection and main road, turn left toward the white house called Davis Acres. Pass the Davis Acres house and descend toward West Brookfield.
9.3 Bear right at the sharp corner to return to the West Brookfield Community Church.

Tucker Mountain Tour

Ride Specs

Start: Pullover at the bottom of Tucker Mountain Road
Length: 9.0 miles
Approximate Riding Time: 2 hours
Rating: Moderate
Terrain: Singletrack, double-track, old town dirt roads
Other Uses: Horseback riding, snowmobiles, four-wheelers

Getting There

From **I-91** – Take **Exit 16** (Bradford), and head **north** on **Route 5.** Just after the **Four Corners Farm** (4.5 miles north of Bradford), turn **left** in **South Newbury** onto **Snake Road.** Follow Snake Road for about three miles, staying on the paved road until reaching **West Newbury.** At this point the road changes to dirt. Continue straight uphill on the dirt road for one mile, passing **two** right turns. The **third right turn** marks the beginning of this ride. There is a place to pull over at the "Y" in the road, just at the bottom of **Tucker Mountain Road.**

The tiny town of Newbury, just north of this ride, was among the earliest towns established in Vermont, primarily due to its proximity to the Connecticut River and the valley's fertile farmland. In those early days, the river held salmon, the streams were filled with trout, and game such as moose, deer, and birds were abundant. Newbury is also the halfway point on the river between the Atlantic Ocean and Canada—the Connecticut River being the most direct link between the colonies and Canada—so it became an important trade area for the early colonists. Today there are beautiful old farms that remain in this area of the Great and Little Ox Bow—named as such for the way the river bends and curves back toward itself just north of Newbury, creating a natural meadow with water on two sides.

The Coosuck Indians of this region were responsible for another local nickname: "Coos," which was given to the land from Newbury south to Fairlee. This area had long been a favorite of the Coosuck for the same reasons the first white settlers laid claim to it. For a time, the Native Americans and white settlers lived amicably on this meadowland, much of which served as ancient burial grounds for the Coosuck. Even today some maps detail spots in Newbury where Indian caves can be found.

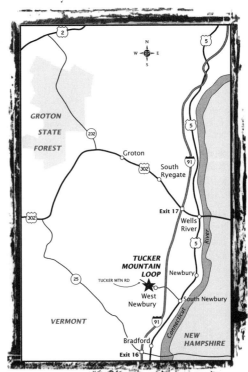

MilesDirections

0.0 START from the pullover in West Newbury at the bottom of Tucker Mountain Road. Head to the left and uphill.

1.6 Pass the turn on the right and the old red cape set back in the woods near it. Stay straight.

2.1 Straight through a four-corners after climbing a steep hill.

2.2 Swimming hole on the left, with a tiny stone building opposite on the right side of the road. A few nice apple trees and a view off to the west. Prepare for a downhill which passes a nice old cape on the left.

2.7 Just after this cape is a trail to the right. Turn here and climb briefly uphill. The downhill through the woods is great.

3.1 Cross through a clearing after the huge culvert pipe.

3.4 Intersection with Bowen Road. Turn left.

4.2 Go past the bottom of Tucker Mountain Road on the left. Stay straight on Bowen Road.

5.7 Turn left up the hill. There is a big white house right across the road from the bottom. This is called Fulton District Road.

6.4 Go straight through the three-way intersection. To the left is a red farm, and to the right is a road leading downhill. There are several trails off to the left during the next mile or so. Stay on the main trail.

(continues on next page)

Miles Directions *(continued)*

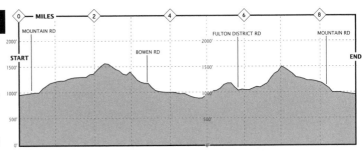

7.4 Turn left, then immediately left again, past the gate posted "No Motorized Vehicles." This is a legal trail on the Vermont State Highway maps, but there are some homes along the way, so be respectful.

7.5 Bear left, as the right turn goes to a house and small pond. Prepare for a steep uphill climb.

7.9 Bear right as another driveway goes off to the left. There is another left turn immediately following this one. Stay right again.

8.1 Go straight through the rest of the logging turns, although some of them look like great riding. The old road crests the climb, and then begins descending to Tucker Mountain Road. The descent is rough, with lots of ledgey sections and a few that drop off sharply. Keep your head up.

8.5 Intersection with Tucker Mountain Road. Turn right, and get ready to descend.

9.0 The bottom of Tucker Mountain Road and the pull-off for parking on the left.

Newbury was the location of the sawmill, gristmill, general store, and church for the early settlers of the surrounding hill country villages. Locals would carry their newly ground corn home from Newbury on their backs. The quiet Newbury commons is still graced by old churches and early brick and frame houses.

On the way to the beginning of this loop, the Four Corners farm, run by ex-Olympic skier Bob Gray and his wife Kim, is a wonderfully peaceful place to stop and pick berries, sample their recently harvested vegetables, or just chat about the local trails. Their farm stand overlooks the river and may be one of the spots the first Vermont settlers chose for farming.

From the bottom of Tucker Mountain Road in West Newbury, the beginning of the ride climbs steadily up the dirt road. It soon changes from the town-maintained class-3 to class-4 roads—the common unmaintained Vermont road, more rugged and suitable for mountain bikes. After the densely forested section of the ride between Tucker and Woodchuck

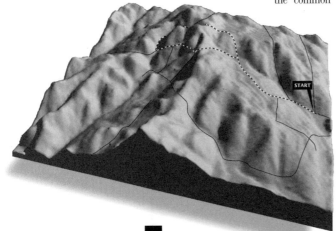

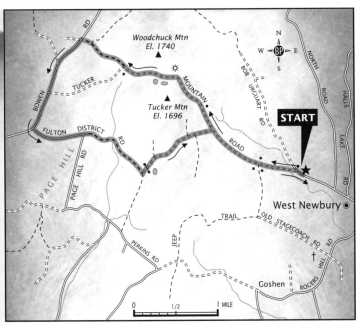

Ride Information

Local Attractions/Events:
Newbury's Annual Cracker Barrel
  Bazaar on the Common: late July.
  (802) 866-5518
Four Corners Farm: Local organic
  produce stand run by former
  Olympic cross-country skiers
  Bob and Kim Gray.
  (802) 866-3342
Wells River Chamber of
  Commerce: (802) 633-2301

Maps:
USGS maps: East Corinth, VT
DeLorme: Vermont Atlas and
  Gazetteer – Page 42 J-3

Mountains, the only landmark is an old red cape set back in the pines, thought to be well over 100 years old.

After cresting the hill, the land opens up to a beautiful view looking toward Topsham. A few ponds appear on the descent and some nearby apple trees offer a tempting respite on a hot summer day. Prolific numbers of berry bushes serve as the black bear's favorite local food. The only other house on this end of Tucker Mountain Road is the marker for the old town road that turns north and climbs to a forested doubletrack before coming back out shortly on the class-3 Bowen Road. The loop continues to follow dirt roads until making a sharp turn past a gate onto a rough doubletrack. **This road is maintained by nearby landowners,** and though it is legal to ride here, it's best to remain respectful of their property and their efforts to improve this roadway.

The top part of this grueling uphill has been logged, but the old road still winds over the top and then drops down to Tucker Mountain Road by way of a rocky, ledgey route. Use caution on this section, as a few small drop-offs may provide big surprises. The last few miles cruise downhill past some highland farms. Be sure to take in the view of the White Mountains when driving back through West Newbury to Route 5.

In 1993 the National Trust for Historic Preservation placed the entire state of Vermont on its list of endangered places. It seems Vermont is considered a national treasure.

Mount Cushman

This ride is by far the longest and most challenging in the book. With a total distance of over 40 miles, it's a full day of riding, with two major ascents that climb for several miles over the spine of the Braintree Mountains. With a good number of the miles coming from dirt roads, it doesn't take as long as one might imagine to complete this loop. It travels over the Randolph and Braintree Gaps, but the riding in the woods is fairly technical, and some of the gradients are quite challenging, both on the up and downhill sides.

For a ride closer to just 30 miles long, it's easy to shuttle one car on Route 12A and start instead at the bottom of Braintree Gap itself (16.1 miles in the cues). This removes the initial, rolling terrain of Braintree Hill but may allow the loop to be ridden in an afternoon rather than a full day. For either excursion on the Mount Cushman loop, it's helpful to check in at the Slab City Bike Shop in Randolph and ask about conditions regarding the ride. You might hear the loop referred to as the "Circus Loop," for it apparently follows the route the old circus caravans took while traveling through the hills to perform at Vermont villages.

Getting There

From **I-89** – Take **Exit 4** and follow **Route 66** downhill to the village of **Randolph.** Pass straight through the intersection for **Route 12** and bear **right** on **Route 12A.** **Slab City Bike Shop** is immediately on the left. Park here to begin the tour.

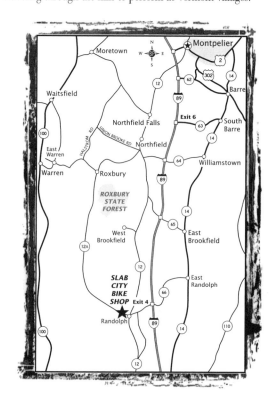

The folks at Slab City are also involved with the White River Valley Trails Association, which is an active trails advocacy group in central Vermont. This ride is one of a group of legal rides they have mapped for folks to enjoy *(see Ride #18 on page 92 for more information on this group)*.

Another way to access this ride is to start from the little village of Rochester, located on the west side of the Braintree range on historic Route 100. Route 100 runs through Vermont, north to south, along the base of the Green Mountains and is well known for its scenery. It passes through some popular ski towns (Mount Snow, Sugarbush, and Stowe), and also visits some tiny towns with fine bakeries, quaint shops, great swimming holes, and old churches on the green. Rochester is one such town in particular. It happens to have a little bike shop called Green Mountain Bikes. The folks here rent bikes, do repairs, and lead guided rides. They have an excellent handle on the incredible riding this area has to offer. Rochester's location, sandwiched between two mountain ranges, gives it challenging terrain and superb views. The last I heard, there was a possibility the state might be testing a secret singletrack trail within the nearby national forest. Soon there may be more land open for riding in the Green Mountain National Forest.

MilesDirections

0.0 START from the Slab City Bike Shop in Randolph. Head west on Route 12A.

0.1 Turn right on Brigham Hill Road at the first "Y" intersection.

0.4 At the crest of the hill, past the 30 mph signs, turn right, and go up the dirt road. Continue climbing up the dirt road until you come close to the first treeline on your right.

0.6 In the treeline on the right, turn in the grassy section that will take you to the Stagecoach Trail opening. Follow the Stagecoach Trail straight up, staying on the main trail, always veering to the left. At the top, stay to the right in the big field, along the treeline, toward the satellite dishes.

2.6 Pass the dishes to Braintree Hill Road, which travels north along the ridge toward the 35 mph signs. Look to the left and see the Braintree Mountains, which this ride eventually crosses twice.

3.3 Turn left at the Braintree Church.

4.1 After a small uphill and an "A" frame house, turn right to Mud Pond.

4.6 Turn right at the "Y" intersection.

5.2 Reach Mud Pond. There are six in Vermont! Stay on the same trail and go right at the "T."

6.2 Intersection with a main dirt road. Go left at the "T," up a slight hill.

7.9 Go straight at the four-way inter-section.

8.5 After crossing a bridge and creek, take the class-4 road (Bouvant Road) that goes left. Don't go toward the white house called Davis Acres. Stay along the creek, up the hill, always staying to the left on the main trail.

9.2 Go to the right of the gate.

9.4 A nice camp with beautiful views to the east. Go left up the grassy trail. This is still Bouvant Road (Class 4).

10.4 Pass over a snowmobile bridge, after starting to descend. Follow this main trail down, passing another camp on the right.

(continues on next page)

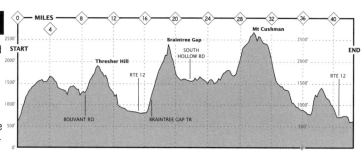

MilesDirections *(continued)*

11.6 A "T" intersection with an old red schoolhouse on the right. This is called Connecticut Corners. Go left at the "T," looking for a sharp left corner.
11.8 At the next left corner, turn right before the tree with orange ribbon. Follow this road up between the house and barn and continue straight up, following the main trail to the left at the fence-line.
12.9 At the snowmobile sign, go left, continuing downhill.
13.9 Pass a camp on the right, and go right at the next fork.
14.8 After a house on the left, pass over a white bridge and railroad tracks.
15.3 At Route 12A (pavement), turn left toward the bridge.
16.1 A white house with a large pine tree in the front lawn and "Ahearns" on the mailbox. Turn right where the legal load limit sign is. This is Braintree Gap Trail. Be prepared to climb for about three miles.
18.2 Another camp on the left. Head toward the clearing. From here, the trail continues to climb; however, it becomes rougher and more technical. Bear to the left and head for the top.
19.0 Reach the top with a small clearing. Head down the back of Braintree Gap.
20.0 At the bottom of the descent, turn left. After the gate, turn left onto the legal trail, and be ready for a rough start. Follow this trail straight to Town Line Road.
21.6 Follow Town Line Road (dirt), always taking the high road or staying left. After it turns to the North Hollow Road, look for a sharp corner with a barbed wire fence straight ahead of you.
27.0 Go straight over the fence to Randolph Gap, following the trail that goes between two treelines. There is a shed below to the right. Continue to follow the trail, and you'll pass another fenceline.

Regardless of where you start, the Mount Cushman tour makes two passes over the Braintree Mountains (seen on some maps as the Northfield Mountains), and reaches an elevation of nearly 3,000 feet each time. Both routes over the mountains are similar in that the ascent is about two to three miles of increasingly rougher terrain, and the descents run down over equally rough, rocky ground. The main difference in the two gaps is that the Randolph Gap has a sidetrip from the summit along the ridge to Mount Cushman which opens up to an expansive view of the Green Mountains and much of central Vermont. It is a favorite take-off spot for hang gliders. The sections in between the two gaps are rolling, dirt roads—sorry, no mini-marts or general stores on the direct route. It's a good idea to stock up in Rochester or Randolph before starting on this epic ride.

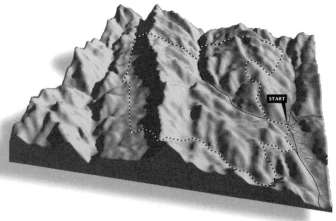

Beachway Press

(continues on next page)

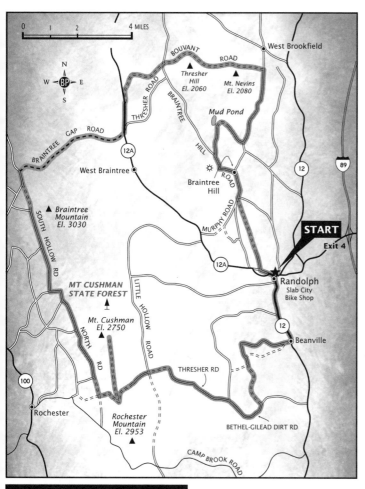

Ride Information

Trail Maintenance Hotline:
White River Valley
   Trails Association
(802) 728-4420

Bike Shops/ Trail Contacts:
Slab City Bike & Sport
(802) 728-5747

Local Events/Information:
The New England Pedros Mountain
   Bike Festival (late September):
(802) 484-5737
Randolph Chamber Of Commerce:
(802) 782-9027
Rochester Valley Chamber of
   Commerce: (802) 767-9664

Maps:
USGS maps: Roxbury, VT; Warren,
VT; Randolph, VT; Handcock, VT
DeLorme: Vermont Atlas and
   Gazetteer – Page 34 D-5

35.1 At the "Y" intersection, turn right over the bridge on Gilead Brook Road.
37.4 Turn left past the tan cape. Continue straight up the hill.
36.6 At the top of the hill, turn left at the "Y," on the class-4 road.
40.0 Bear right at the three-way intersection, following the arrows on the tree ahead.
40.2 Bear right at this intersection. Follow the main trail until you reach a nice house on the right, at the top of the hill.
40.6 At the top of the hill, turn right at the second house, on the trail that goes underneath the power line. Stay on the main trail, and descend down what turns to Spooner Road. Its condition will improve.
43.0 Descend all the way to Route 12 (paved) and turn left. Ride through the town of Randolph.
44.9 Look for Slab City on the left!

MilesDirections(continued)

27.6 At the four-way intersection, turn left up Randolph Gap.
28.0 Bear to the right at the sharp corner. Still going up!
28.5 Reach the top of the Randolph Gap. For a nice sidetrip along the top of the ridge, turn left here and follow the ridgetop trail to the first clearing where an old firetower used to be.
29.7 Reach the firetower spot. Continue along to check out the hang gliding launch area.
30.1 Reach the hang gliding clearing. Check out the view of Green

Mountain National Forest. Turn around and follow the ridge trail back to the top of the Randolph Gap.
31.7 Reach the top of the gap again. Take a left and descend down to Four Corners intersection.
33.1 At the Four Corners intersection proceed straight across to Little Hollow Road. (For a more direct, faster way back to Slab City, go left here, and then take the next right back to the shop.) Follow Little Hollow Road until it connects to the Bethel-Gilead Road.

Green Mountain Touring Center

The Three Stallion Inn, just outside Randolph village, is home to a unique network of unparalleled Vermont singletrack. Set on the hillsides above the old Green Mountain Stock Farm, this web of trails weaves through old forests and over rushing brooks, often opening up to a spectacular view of the Green Mountains. The trails are used for cross-country skiing and snowshoeing in the winter, and mountain biking from spring to fall.

In the 1800s the Inn was a working farm. Though dormant for a number of years, it has since been restored to its original appearance. With 1,300 acres available for recreation, the singletrack mapped out at the center is only the beginning of the riding possibilities in this geographic center of Vermont.

These trails are best known for their roller coaster-like ride. A short racecourse (which makes up the end of this mapped ride) on the south end of the trail system is used as a training run by Slab City, the local bike shop. Slab City also organizes other weekly events, including a time trial and group rides, both on- and off-road. The shop works closely with the local White River Valley Trails Association in creating a legal system of trails in the central Vermont region.

The White River Valley Trails Association has so far been quite successful in working with local, private landowners to connect a network of old town roads and trails for mountain biking. This work to promote responsible access for riders in Vermont has become critical in the last few years, as landowners have become stricter about opening their piece of the Green Mountains to mountain bikers. The present closure of the trails in the

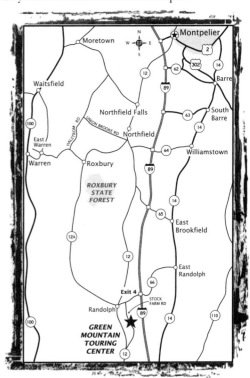

Green Mountain National Forest to mountain biking (with the exception of forest service roads and a few areas under study) also makes this kind of local trail access work important. The White River Valley Trails Association publishes a map from Royalton to Northfield with color-coded trails and the four classes of roads, covering a large section of Central Vermont. They are presently looking for similar groups to begin the same type of work in their own local regions of the state. Call the Association for information and maps at (802) 728-5747.

Besides the trails association, Randolph has another claim to mountain bike history in Vermont. For the past few years, the Pedros New England Mountain Bike Festival has been held on the same trail system that this ride utilizes. Organized to promote recreational riding and non-competitive activities on a mountain bike, the festival is an entire weekend of clinics, guided tours, food, bonfires, and live bands. The featured expo area is a great place to demo new equipment or to check out the festival's unique tricycle race. This past year, hot showers and fly-fishing were added to help please the 2,500 folks who attended. Amtrak even planned a special stop in Randolph to allow visitors living farther south the luxury of traveling by train.

MilesDirections

0.0 START at the base of Clover Hill Road, at the Three Stallion Inn. Bear left up the hill.

0.3 Trail #9 goes off to the left. Stay straight on Trail #1.

0.4 Cross over the green bridge.

0.6 Turn right onto Trail #5. There is a large wooden gate with a path around the outside and a sign marking Trail #5. At the clearing immediately following the gate, bear to the right on the singletrack.

0.9 After a downhill, turn sharply to the right as the trail comes to a "T." The right turn follows and then crosses a small stream.

1.1 Intersection with Clover Hill Road. Go left down the hill toward the green bridge.

1.3 Turn right after the bridge on Trail #3.

1.4 Reach a three-way intersection. Turn left uphill on Trail #9, climbing to a spectacular meadow.

1.5 Awesome view from the meadow. Follow the mowed path north. More climbing.

1.6 Bear left around the meadow and travel sharply downhill. There is another trail that goes straight into the woods.

1.8 At the bottom of the meadow, take a right into the woods. The meadow trail continues to the left.

2.0 A map of the trail system on a tree says we are still on Trail #9. Bear left and downhill.

2.2 Stay to the left at another fork. Everywhere you look are more trails to explore.

(continues on next page)

MilesDirections(continued)

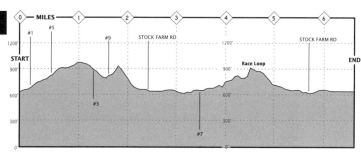

2.35 Intersection with the main Stock Farm Road that you drove in on. Turn left toward the Inn.

2.75 Pass the base of Clover Hill Road. Stay on the dirt road.

3.4 Turn left on a small dirt road heading up a sandy hill. Pass through two posts at the entrance. A field is at the top.

3.5 From the field ("start" and "finish" of the weekly race series), bear right around the meadow. A nice doubletrack follows the perimeter.

3.6 A fun trail goes off to the right. Stay in the meadow to the left.

3.8 Bear uphill into the woods to the right.

3.9 Bear quickly to the right and then the left, following the switchbacks.

4.2 Travel underneath the power lines—more sand—then curve back into a huge pine forest, almost doubling back on yourself.

4.75 Turn right, down the steep rocky descent into the woods.

4.95 Bear right, around a steep corner, and then climb a sandy uphill.

5.1 Bear left at the top of the sandy uphill. A turn goes off to the right.

5.3 After traveling along the edge of a ridge, you can look down to the left and see the main doubletrack quite a ways below. At another junction, stay to the left again.

(continues on next page)

All of this amounts to Randolph's hope of being the Northeast equivalent to a Moab, Utah—and after touring the local singletrack, you might see why they're worthy of such aspirations.

The beginning of this tour of the trail system begins at the dirt of Clover Hill Road. After one-half mile or so of warm-up terrain, the trail ducks into the woods to a maze of singletrack. It's a good idea to keep your eyes peeled for a number of intersections, as some are marked better than others are. After a quick loop on the south side of this road, the ride swings north, offering a breathtaking view of the valley below to the west. Sunsets are amazing here, and it's no wonder that a bit higher on the ridge in Randolph Center, families would walk out to Sunset Hill to see this same view at the end of a hard day's work. Now, with the addition of interstate 89, commuters get a view from their cars—but the ripples of the hills remain the same.

A quick, sharp descent back to Stock Farm Road completes the first half of the ride and gives a good break for those who need one. To get to the weekly series racecourse, the flat Stock Farm Road heading south is the route to follow. Once you've reached the field where the races are staged, it's important that you look closely for the following turns, as they'll come up on you quickly, and they tend to get missed amidst other intersections. A rapidly twisting and rolling course unfolds, with short climbs and quick

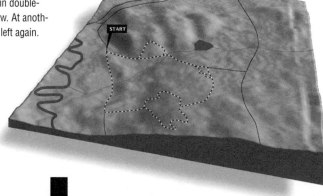

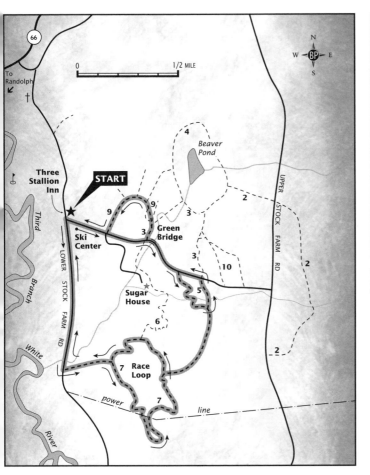

Ride Information

Trail Maintenance Hotline:
Three Stallion Inn
(802) 728-5575

Bike Shops/Trail Contacts:
Slab City Bike & Sport
(802) 728-5747
White River Valley Trails
Association: (802) 728-5747

Maps:
USGS maps: Randolph, VT
DeLorme: Vermont Atlas and
Gazetteer – Page 34 D-5

MilesDirections(continued)

5.4 After descending a rocky, technical downhill, turn left on the doubletrack. Stay on this, along the stream to the right, and notice there is a turn across the stream which takes you back to the center, through some nice singletrack.
5.7 Turn sharply to the left, uphill, back to the start/finish meadow. Stay to the right along the perimeter of the meadow, until you reach the entrance of the small dirt road on the right.
5.8 Turn right, down the dirt road back to the main Stock Farm Road.
5.9 Turn right on Stock Farm Road back to the touring center and Inn.
6.6 Reach the Three Stallion Inn and parking lot.

and sometimes rocky descents. Early in the course, a section of narrow trail winds along the edge of a sharp drop-off and provides a summit view of the trails below. The singletrack here is well groomed but challenging, with ample opportunity to let loose on the banked turns and ravine-like downhills. The course ends up paralleling a small brook, which is also the crossover point connecting to the system's other trails. A longer racecourse loop (the Galloping Gears Race), which usually has its race in midsummer, follows these trails. After returning to the staging area, where the loop began, it is worth riding again, as the second time is always more enjoyable when the turns become familiar. If you're a guest at the Inn, head back for a sauna and swim. Otherwise, like many Vermont towns, there is a fun downtown to scope out in Randolph.

Hurricane Ridge

Ride Specs

Start: Center Road in Corinth Center
Length: 14.3 miles
Approximate Riding Time: 2-3 hours
Rating: Moderate to Difficult
Terrain: Singletrack, double-track, dirt roads
Other Uses: Hiking, horse-back riding, snowmobiles

Getting There

From **Barre** – Take **Route 302 south** to **Route 25 east.** Follow Route 25 east past **Waits River.** Turn **right** after Waits River (before East Corinth) on **Brook Road,** marked **"Cookeville and Corinth Center."** It is about four to five miles along this road to the next intersection. Just before this intersection is a **dirt road** to the **right.** Pull over on the shoulder above the river just past the dirt road (called **Center Road**). Start here and ride up toward **Corinth.**

T he tiny hamlets of Corinth—East Corinth, South Corinth, Corinth Corners, West Corinth and Cookeville—are among some of Vermont's prettiest hill towns. The circuitry of dirt roads connecting them provides what one Vermonter described as, "The most beautiful stretch of road in all of Vermont." This ride passes through Corinth past some notable historical buildings, to include the old Town Meeting Hall, the Academy building, and the old Corinth church. It then climbs up through the Hurricane Ridge area, where some Revolutionary War history is still alive.

Apparently after the defeat of the British at Saratoga, New York, in the late 1770s, the North Country still needed protection by means of strategically placed forts. To connect the forts already existing on the northern route to Canada, Fort Wait was built along Hurricane Ridge. It resembled a large cabin built of rocks and stones and was surrounded by a large stone stockade. Stone walls are all that remain, some as thick as four feet or more, but nothing survives to indicate a cabin. Some conjecture that the thick walls still standing are, in fact, the cabin's foundation and not the stockade. A nearby hole reveals where the stone was quarried to build the walls. As the quarry filled with water from nearby springs, it was most probably used as the fort's water supply.

Historians still debate why this location was chosen for the fort. While it provides a good view of the valley below, it is fully exposed from above. Perhaps another lookout would have been more appropriate. The remains of Fort Wait, now just ruins in a farmer's hayfield, begin one's imagination spinning, of scouting

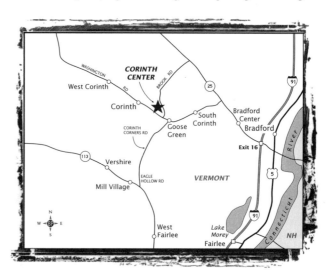

parties meeting in the cabin or of local residents hiding from Indian or British attacks.

The ride itself begins down close to the Waits River Valley. The Wait name was first used in the region in the 1770s when the Wait brothers (Ben and Joseph) became active in the Green Mountain Boys (see below). Legend has it, Captain Joseph Wait and some companions killed a deer along the river and hung what was left

from a tree along the riverbank. He then carved his name, "WAIT," in the tree so any other rangers traveling behind would know there was meat for them. And so, the river is known as Waits River. Joseph's brother Ben was the builder and commanding officer of Fort Wait on Hurricane Ridge.

After the initial climb toward Corinth, the ride passes an old white church and townhouse, and a view opens up to the south. A bit farther on Center Road, an old bridge is closed to traffic, but it is passable and safe for cyclists. At the first major intersection, the post office and old Academy buildings make up the town proper of Corinth. Here, the trail through Hurricane Ridge begins as an old cart path. One can almost see the teams of horses or oxen passing through. The terrain is rolling, with some rocky, technical sections toward the end. A spectacular view lies on the other side of the Hurricane Ridge section and looks south to Mount Ascutney with hardly a building visible. After rolling down a dirt road toward Corinth Corners, the ride turns west on the road to Washington.

To complete the loop, riders finish on the long rollicking downhill through West Corinth and pass the farms of Cook Hill. If it were a chilly day, you'd benefit from having a windbreaker for this seven-mile descent. On the way back to Route 25, it's worth driving east through Goose Green, just to say you were there. Then be sure to stop at the South Corinth General Store for some snacks.

MilesDirections

0.0 START from Brook Road east of Corinth Center. From Brook Road, turn up Center Road toward Corinth. The road climbs steadily for about one half mile to the old townhouse and church.

0.6 Pass the Corinth Church and Townhouse—beautiful old buildings, which have been well cared for. A local view off to the left.

1.2 The road splits. Bear to the left, and cross over the bridge marked "closed." It is safe and passable on a bike.

1.55 Corinth Post Office is on the right, and the old Corinth Academy is on the left. Go straight across the pavement here, as if heading to the house next to the town offices. The Hurricane Ridge Road/Trail starts here and passes in front of the yellow house as if a driveway, but then continues past it on the left.

2.3 Pass a small cabin on the left and then a marshy section on the left.

2.75 Pass an old abandoned farmhouse on the right. The doubletrack starts to get rougher and is still gradually uphill. Several less-traveled trails diverge from this main one.

4.0 Snowmobile trail goes off to the right. Stay straight.

4.5 After some rocky uphill sections, the trail levels off and comes to a "Y." Bear left and get psyched for one of the nicest views in all of Vermont.

(continues on next page)

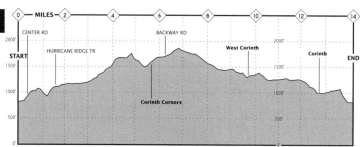

MilesDirections *(continued)*

4.6 The VIEW! After admiring the hills, roll along past the farm on the left, with rows of old sugar maples.

5.1 Mount Moosilauke is clearly visible to the left. Head downhill, and be prepared to turn sharply right in the middle of the descent.

5.7 Turn right at the flagpole. You are now back on regular dirt roads.

6.0 Bear right at the intersection (straight comes out in Chelsea). Prepare for a few miles of climbing.

7.4 Reach the beginning of a LONG downhill.

8.7 Turn right at the intersection, toward Corinth.

9.4 Pass the cemetery on the right and zip through West Corinth.

11.2 Route changes to blacktop.

12.8 Back at the Corinth Academy and Post Office. Turn left here to return to the car.

14.3 Reach the bottom of Center Road and turn right into the parking spot.

In Addition...

The Green Mountain Boys

Vermont's colorful beginnings were shaped and influenced dramatically by a group of early land owners known as the Green Mountain Boys. Disputes over the ownership of this tiny state began in the late 1700s when grants of land issued to settlers from New Hampshire were reissued to other settlers from New York. The "Yorkers," as they were then known, wanted large sums of money from the folks already working the land they had bought from New Hampshire. It was a perfect time for Robin Hood to appear. Instead, a fiery, independent named Ethan Allen took the initiative with his brothers Ira, Levi, Zimri, Heber, Heman, and their cousins Seth Warner and Remember Baker.

The name, "The Green Mountain Boys," was soon earned from the governor of New York's public promise to drive this "set of lawless people" into the Green Mountains! Relying largely on creative maneuvers, tricks, and tomfoolery, they retaliated against the encroaching New York government and their land surveyors. It is well known that they never took a life in their struggles.

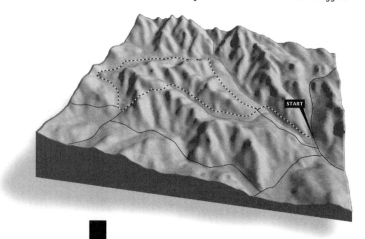

Beachway Press

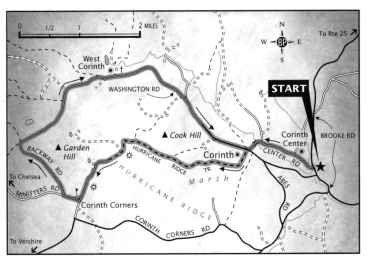

Ride Information

Local Bike Shop:
Onion River Sports II, Barre, VT
(802) 476-9750

Local Attractions/Events:
East Corinth Flea Market (mid-July)
Call the Town Offices of Corinth
(802) 439-5850

Maps:
USGS maps: West Topsham
DeLorme: Vermont Atlas and
Gazetteer – Page 35 A-14

Some of their best known jokes took place in the historic town of Bennington—where Catamount Tavern was their headquarters. The Tavern was the site chosen for the "hanging" of Dr. Adams, an outspoken "Yorker." After administering the famous "beechseal" (a swift switching on the behind with a beech branch), they tied him into a chair and hoisted him 20 feet up a post, where he sat in humiliation for some time. These acts eventually rendered New York's efforts futile and lead to Vermont's independence, which came first as their declaration as a republic. They began minting their own money and soon established a constitution in 1777 in Windsor. The first elected officials were from this core of Green Mountain Boys.

The pioneer women of this time, although not considered official "Green Mountain Boys," also contributed greatly to the independence of Vermont. One woman in particular, Ann Story, is considered a legend for her acts of bravery. A loyal follower of Ethan Allen and his gang, she built her house, farmed her land, and raised three sons alone after her husband was killed by a falling tree. Her strength was famous, and legend has it she could swing an ax better than most men could. One story tells of her return home, only to find it barred from the inside. She faced a group of approaching Yorkers and quickly figured that some of the Green Mountain Boys were hiding inside. In response to the Yorkers demand to be let in, she replied that she always entered and exited through the chimney—to keep her house safe when she was gone. Losing interest in the prospect of climbing the roof, they watched her crawl into the chimney and disappear. The Yorkers left, and Ann was greeted by a friendly gang of Green Mountain Boys inside!

Vershire Loop

Ride Specs

Start: Vershire Town Hall
Length: 11.1 miles
Approximate Riding Time: 2 hours
Rating: Moderate
Terrain: Singletrack, double-track, paved roads, class-3 and 4 dirt roads
Other Uses: Cross-country skiing, horseback riding, snowmobiles, four-wheelers

Getting There

From **I-91** – Take **Exit 14** to **Route 113.** Follow 113 **west** approximately 10 miles to the village of **Vershire.** Start close to the bottom of **Vershire Center Road.** Park in town.

E mbedded in central Vermont, Vershire is one of those villages you might miss if you blink. With just a post office, an elementary school, and a small town office, it's hard to believe this was once a booming copper mine settlement that supported over 2,000 people. The maze of back roads, snowmobile trails, and logging roads that winds through the hilly farm country is well hidden from civilization. It's easy to see why this has some of the best untapped mountain biking potential around.

This particular ride draws together both trails and dirt roads to offer a taste of what's out there in the center of Orange County. For winter enthusiasts, cross-country skiing through the old copper mines along the many snowmobile trails is one of the best ways to explore the highlands of Vershire.

The copper mines, which were once booming along the road from West Fairlee to Strafford, are now just a memory. But some historians consider their heyday in the 1850s to be one of the most colorful periods in Vermont's history. Rapid growth thrust the quiet mining village into a thriving community of no less than 50 houses with festivals, baseball games, parties, dances, and even a new school. The demise of the mines, and soon the town as well, began in the late 1890s when Smith Ely, then president of the Vermont Copper Mine Company, brought in his son Ely Ely-Goddard.

No one was more extravagant and disliked in the growing Vershire mining community than Ely Ely-Goddard; and yet, he would soon have full charge of the copper mine. He was deeply

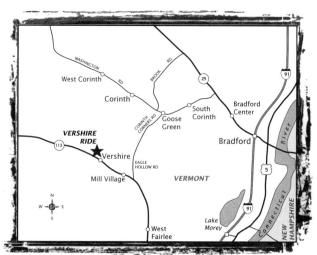

resented by locals for his unfair treatment of the miners. On his orders, the name of the town was even changed to "Ely."

Mining conditions worsened, workers became dissatisfied, and eventually money ran out. The workers, who had not been paid, organized themselves and threatened to burn the surrounding towns, blow up the mines, and even kidnap the owners. As panic ensued, the Governor called in the National Guard. A peaceful settlement was eventually reached, but it was too late to save the mines. They were auctioned off and never used as mines again. The houses and hotels vanished, with an occasional cellar hole left to mark what once was. But if you look hard, traces of copper hues can still be found staining the ground and streams. [*Word of caution: A private landowner uses much of the old mine area for a shooting range, so don't ride through without first getting the shooting schedule.*]

The name has since changed back to Vershire, and "Ely" is now, fittingly, no more than the name of a small freight station on Route 5 where copper was shipped south down the Connecticut

MilesDirections

0.0 START from the Vershire Town Hall. Park in the town offices parking lot just off Route 113. Head up Route 113 on the pavement by making a right out of the town hall.

0.35 Turn right on Durgin Hill Road. This is the bottom of a long and challenging hill climb.

0.9 Bear left at the "Y," staying on Durgin Hill Road. Rowell Brook goes off to the right. There is an incredible view a little further up Rowell Brook Road, which on a clear day shows off the highest peaks of White Mountain.

2.0 The dirt road fades into a nice doubletrack. Great farms and open meadows. About another one-half mile of climbing left.

2.9 The bottom of a tricky descent—often washed out, if rainy—and steep in sections.

3.0 Intersection with Goose Green Road (which is paved). Turn left up the hill toward Vershire Heights. At the top is the Vershire Riding school and remnants of the Vershire School, a progressive private school established in the 1970s.

3.6 Intersection with Route 113. Left goes back to the Vershire town hall, right goes to the village of Chelsea, and straight goes to the trails. Head straight on McIver Road, past Ward's garage and the lone Coke machine, for miles.

5.4 Beaver Pond. Maybe a swim if it's super hot!

continues on next page)

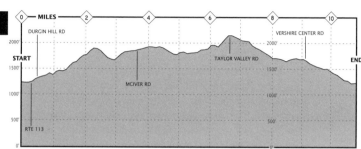

MILES · 0 · 2 · 4 · 6 · 8 · 10

DURGIN HILL RD

VERSHIRE CENTER RD

2000' · 2000'

START · TAYLOR VALLEY RD · END

1500' · 1500'

MCIVER RD

1000' · 1000'

500' · 500'

RTE 113

0'

MilesDirections*(continued)*

6.1 Turn left at the "Y," following the snowmobile signs, toward Thetford, West Fairlee, and Vershire. To the right goes to Chelsea. Prepare for a long technical climb.

6.6 Intersection with a more traveled dirt road. Turn left on Taylor Valley Road, while the snowmobile trail to Thetford and West Fairlee goes right. A gate opposite the intersection leads to private land. This downhill passes Colton Hill on the right and gorgeous views off to the left.

9.0 Turn left on Brown Road at the intersection with the Vershire Center Road. The Mountain School is just across the street, where students learn about organic farming, sugaring, and other environmentally sound topics.

10.0 Turn right, downhill. Still on the Vershire Center Road, while Brown Road goes straight.

11.0 Intersection with Route 113. Turn right heading south on the paved road.

11.1 Parking lot on the left at the town offices.

River. Today, these roads barely see the passage of cars, and as you ride through the countryside, you can almost imagine horse drawn carts of copper heading south bound for the smelting plants in Boston.

The ride starts up nearby Durgin Hill Road from the Town Office on Route 113. This dirt road eventually fades into rough doubletrack, but not without a substantial climb. Be careful as the last section can be rocky and slick, depending on the weather.

A short stint along the paved road (which, in my opinion, is one of the nicest road bike rides in the state) climbs up to Vershire Heights toward Ward's Garage. This is the only junction with refreshments of any kind, which at my last visit was a lone soda machine! The road heading northwest from here leads to the town of Chelsea, where there is a farmer's market open every Wednesday as well as some awesome local stores.

The ride continues on to the increasingly rougher surfaces of McIver Road. The beaver pond marks the real switch to a class-4 road. After a long downhill, you will come upon a junction with snowmobile signs which mark the beginning of the next substantial climb. The next section, which is visible from the snowmobile

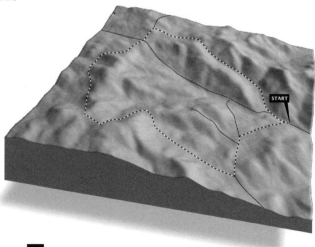

START

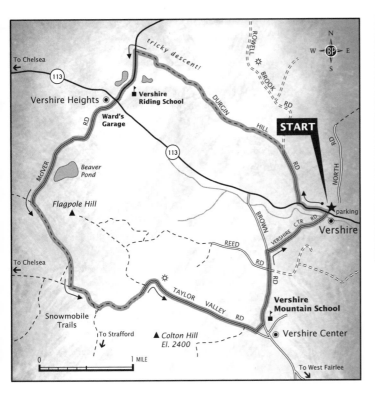

Ride Information

Local Attractions/Events:
Post Mills Airport and Balloon
  Rides: (802) 333-9254

Local Bike Shops:
Onion River Sports: Barre, VT
  (802) 476-9750

Maps:
USGS maps: Chelsea, VT;
  Vershire, VT
DeLorme: Vermont Atlas &
  Gazetteer; Page 35 C-13

signs, is somewhat difficult with rocks and washouts. If you're up for a longer day, exploring the trails leading off toward Chelsea might be fun.

The last few miles are downhill. This Taylor Valley region of Strafford and Vershire is known for its logging trail networks and great mountain biking. Remote hunting and snowmobiling camps are about all you will find in this neck of the woods. Just before pitching downhill for the final run back to Vershire, take a look through an opening in the meadows at the view of the surrounding hills.

The Vershire Mountain School marks the village of Vershire Center and the junction where you can opt to take the dirt road south to the old Ely Copper Mines. If you do decide to take that ride, be prepared for a long climb back up to the Mountain School. Looking out from the school, you should see some wonderful views of the valley and the surrounding farmland. To finish the ride, cruise down the dirt road to the town hall and head to Chelsea for some home-baked goods at the general store.

Vermont is the only state in the country that doesn't allow billboards. The law banishing them was passed in the 1960s.

Coyote Hill

Ride Specs

Start: Route 244, just before Blood Brook Road
Length: 20.2 miles
Approximate Riding Time: 3-4 hours
Rating: Difficult
Terrain: Singletrack, double-track, paved roads, class-3 and 4 dirt roads
Other Uses: Cross-country skiing, snowmobiles, four-wheelers

Getting There

From **I-91** – Exit at **Fairlee, Exit 15.** Turn off the ramp and head toward town. Turn **right** and travel **south** on **Route 5** for 2.4 miles. Turn **right** on **Route 244** toward **Lake Fairlee.** Follow Route 244 for 2.5 miles to a pull-off on the right, opposite **Lake Fairlee.** Park here.

This ride leaves from what, especially in summer months, is one of Vermont's most popular places to visit—the shores of Lake Fairlee. Bounded by rolling green hills, Lake Fairlee's clear waters are just a sampling of the endless beauty this region has to offer, explaining why so many choose to come here.

Around the south end of the lake, at the Post Mills airport, folks can find Brian Bolland's balloon rides leaving on most clear evenings. These colorful balloons rise up and cruise silently over the hilly landscape, eventually landing in a farmer's field. There's a small general store in Post Mills where you can pick up supplies for a long ride. In Fairlee, just a few miles north, there are a number of antique shops and restaurants.

While in Fairlee, don't miss Chapman's Store, a local one-stop shop, carrying everything from regional topographic maps to local history books to fishing gear. And if you head north just out of town, you'll find some truly inspiring cliffs, called the Palisades, where peregrine falcons love to nest. These birds are endangered, so they're quite a rare sight to behold. You can follow a trail on the Lake Morey side of town, near the firehouse, to the top of these cliffs.

Lake Morey is another beautiful site to visit. The paved road around its perimeter provides its best views. On the west side near the boat access area, there are more hiking trails leading toward Bald Top and its surrounding hills. For local athletes, a New England regional triathlon is held annually at the lake each July.

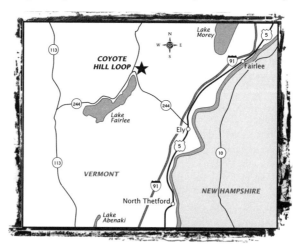

Lake Morey is named after Samuel Morey, an inventor and engineer credited with inventing the steamboat. It was Morey's steamboat that Robert Fulton—the man who crafted steamboats into a commercial success—saw sailing the Connecticut River. Fulton is said to have copied Samuel Morey's design and used it to later win himself distinction as the true pioneer of the steam-

boat. Morey was also one of the preliminary designers of an engine that predated the modern automobile engine. If credit fell into the hands of the wrong man, at least Samuel Morey's got a lake named after him.

The ride itself is a strong mix of dirt roads; gnarly, rocky trails; tricky descents; and rewarding views. At over 20 miles long, it is a fairly lengthy ride, so pack some snacks and bring extra water. This loop has some excellent technical sections followed by gentle rolling sections of old hardwood forest. There aren't any general stores along this particular route, so pack what you'll need for an afternoon of riding before heading out.

The Coyote Hill Loop starts up Blood Brook Road in West Fairlee. After a small swatch of blacktop, the route quickly switches to a dirt road. A brief warm-up on Marsh Hill Road prepares you for what's ahead on this challenging tour. The intersection at the bottom of Marsh Hill with Middlebrook Road is less than one mile from the oldest house built in West Fairlee, now known as Elmwood Farm.

The founder of West Fairlee, a preacher named Nathaniel Niles, built the cabin and is well remembered for his commitment

MilesDirections

0.0 START from the pullover parking area and turn right on Route 244.

0.1 Turn right on Blood Brook Road. This is paved for about one-half mile, providing a great warm-up for the climbs ahead.

1.5 Turn left on Marsh Hill Road. There's no sign, so look for an old mill and a big red barn just after the turn. The top part of this old road is often spongy and can be downright unrideable if the local skidder has been mucking around on it recently. After the climb there's a sharp descent past a few trailers to West Fairlee Center and Middle Brook Road.

3.5 Turn left on Middle Brook Road (paved). Then make an immediate right on Bear Notch Road at the West Fairlee Center Church. Bear Notch Road is a class-4 road used by skiers, hikers, wildlife, and recreational vehicles; including ATV's.

4.6 A snowmobile trail forks to the left. Stay to the right on Bear Notch Road. This is a slippery, technical, uphill section of rocks, offering quite a challenge before the summit. It is most rideable when dry.

6.2 Beaver Meadow Trail goes left and Bear Notch Road stays straight. Check out the rocks, cliffs, and gnarly old trees.

6.6 Reach the Notch summit. Prepare for a tricky descent.

(continues on next page)

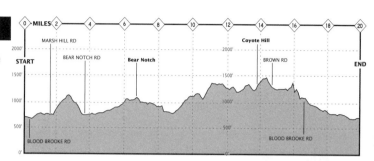

MilesDirections*(continued)*

8.5 Turn right at the bottom of the descent after crossing the bridge. Enjoy this flat section through the meadows of Corinth because the longest climb of the ride is before you! Pace yourself and enjoy the scenery.

9.2 Turn right at the "T" and continue climbing past the Wilderness Pig Farm and into the steepest part of the climb.

10.7 Reach a four-way intersection with snowmobile markers. Catch your breath and turn left for the last real climb of the ride. Check out the view above Robinson's camp.

11.3 A spectacular view is to the right, toward Mount Ascutney and the Connecticut River Valley. Pass an old homestead that hasn't been lived in for ages.

12.2 Turn right on a dirt road after a small pond on the left. Descend sharply down to Brook Road. The view here is also quite pretty. Moosilauke, the White Mountains, and Coyote Hill Mountain Bike Camp are straight across the valley.

12.6 Turn right up the hill past the white farmhouse.

13.1 Reach the height of the land and turn left up a rocky snowmobile trail. This is the end of this ride's longest climb, which totals nearly five miles!

13.8 Reach the intersection with Kidderhood Road. Coyote Hill Mountain Bike Camp is less than a half-mile down the road. Turn right on Brown Road (up the hill). Brown Road finally comes to a "T" at an old trailer.

to education and his many talents, including the ability to flush a swarm of bees out of his congregation—while preaching.

After crossing Middlebrook Road, the real nuts and bolts of this ride is on Bear Notch Road. It begins innocently enough as an old, unmaintained town dirt road. The road winds uphill through a variegated forest and rich floral display before changing near the top to characteristic Vermont slate and rock piles that often double as a trail. Local mountain bikers will tell you it's all rideable; and it is, but don't be surprised if those slippery rocks cause an unexpected dismount.

The notch itself is a slice through old cliffs, now covered in thick moss and a patch of Vermont woods. This is a good spot to reassemble if you're out with a large group. The beginning of the descent here is tricky, before funneling out to a fast dirt road. The rest of the ride follows old roads and snowmobile trails with a few diffi-

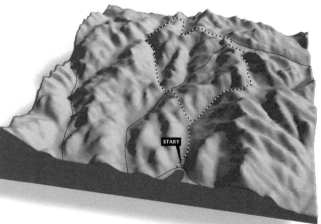

(continues on next page)

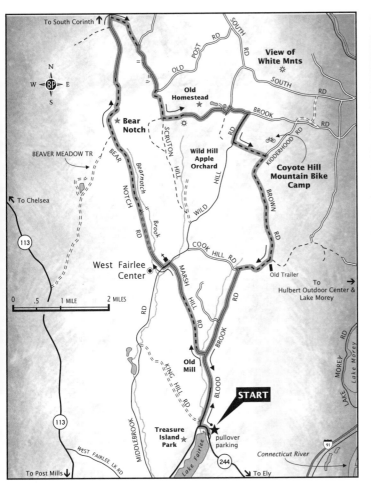

Ride Information

Local Route Information:
Coyote Hill Mountain Bike Center
(802) 222-5133

Local Bike Shops:
Hanover, New Hampshire
    Omer & Bob's
    (603) 643-3525

Local Attractions/Events:
Call Coyote Hill for information on
    races, camps, and clinics and
    accomodations at their
    Backcountry Lodge
Weekly Auctions in Bradford, VT:
    Call Ely Commission Sales: (802)
    222-5113

Maps:
USGS maps: Fairlee, VT
DeLorme: Vermont Atlas &
    Gazetteer; Page 36 E-1

MilesDirections (continued)

16.0 Turn right at the old trailer. Continue climbing up a steep rocky section and then cruise down a long descent to Blood Brook Road. The trail comes to a "T" on Blood Brook Road.

17.0 Turn left on Blood Brook Road. Descend through rolling green pastureland. This section passes several farms and lots of old maples. All downhill to the end of Blood Brook Road.

20.2 Blood Brook Road intersects with Route 244. Turn left to return to your car just around the corner.

cult climbs still to come. There are a few obvious spots to take in views of both the Green Mountains of Vermont and the White Mountains of New Hampshire. At 13.8 miles, Coyote Hill Mountain Bike Camp is located just off the trail, and you're welcome to stop and refill your water here anytime. Lodging or camping is often available at Coyote Hill if you call ahead (802) 222-5133. They are open for guided tours, camps (kids and adults), and clinics (May – November).

The ride ends on the scenic Blood Brook Road and finishes comfortably downhill at the Lake Fairlee starting point.

In Addition...

At the Back of the Pack

We rounded the corner of the trail and a steep rocky section loomed ahead. The 13 year-old boy with me slowed to a halt and mumbled something about "GU." It was time for another break at the back of the pack.

Introducing teenage boys and girls to the wonders of mountain biking is one of the goals of Coyote Hill Mountain Bike Camp. It is inevitable that every group has its slowest rider. And every slowest rider has his or her way of coping.

For instance, Ben had multiple mechanical difficulties, coupled with strange physical occurrences. For example, he might walk up the last stretch of hill and spout forth a complete history of his rear derailleur's malfunctions—which were, of course, complicated by the world's worst foot cramp. I would just nod sympathetically, and if in the mood, I'd help embellish: "Yeah, I know what you mean. I hate it when those tiny sticks creep into the cogs and screw up the shifting. No problem Ben, this isn't a race." Empathy, patience, and a good set of brake pads are imperative for coaching at the back of the pack.

Other kids are more verbal about their physical discomforts. Pete used to moan about the intense suffering our hills inflicted upon his southern quads. Even the most sincere convincing that there was always equal downhill for every uphill wouldn't dissuade him from believing that we somehow cruelly planned the rides to be much more uphill. Josh didn't like the uphills much either but decided he was just going to ride them until he got strong enough to conquer them. He was easy to encourage. With most of the stragglers, I often used a line of questioning about friends, school, family, sports, etc. to take their minds off the fact that their buddies were a mile

Beachway Press

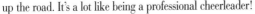

up the road. It's a lot like being a professional cheerleader!

By the end of the week, even the slowest kids would see measurable improvement. They could point across the valley and say: "I rode over that mountain." I had the back of the pack thing down pretty well. Until the last week.

Our last group of 15- to 18 year olds wanted to do a Sunday evening (first night) ride. Like a mother goose with her ducklings, I set out in the lead. (It's fun to be in front sometimes.) After the first half-mile of technical stream crossings, roots, mud, and rocks, I pulled over to wait. I turned around. And there they all were! All together in one pack of energy waiting for my next move. I re-thought my desire to lead. "Hey Tom…want to lead on this downhill?" The thought of them chomping on my wheel down the narrow trail wasn't inviting. They were off. And then I found myself at the back of the pack. Alone! Only fleeting colors in front to chase!

After that short but intense ride, I began to worry about the five days of riding left! Would I survive? Bad enough to be the only female, but I just couldn't be the slowest! I hoped that first ride had been a harsh test of egos. Sure enough, a few miles into the ride the next day, I came around the corner to about half of the group walking and struggling up a steep section. I danced by them and waited at the top. "Hey Jen, can we go a little slower? These hills are tough!" I smiled my most sympathetic smile. "No, problem guys. Now, tell me about the sports you play in school…and your pet dog…and your favorite meal at home…what?…a downhill?…sure, just up here guys!"

Five Corners

Ride Specs

Start: Thetford Village Center
Length: 11.8 miles
Approximate Riding Time:
  2 hours
Rating: Moderate
Terrain: Doubletrack, paved
  roads, class-3 and 4 dirt
  roads
Other Uses: Cross-country
  skiing, horseback riding,
  snowmobiles,
  four-wheelers

Getting There

From **I-91** – Take **Exit 14** off
I-91. Go approximately two
miles **west** on **Route 113** to
Thetford Center. Begin the
ride from the center of town.

Starting in the heart of downtown Thetford Center (a one-store town), one may not sense the colorful flavor of Thetford's historic past. But a quick stroll to the town cemetery, just behind the town hall, gives a glimpse into the lives of some of Vermont's earliest settlers. Several Thetford residents are still remembered locally for their heroic feats, but none more vividly than Richard Wallace—one of the famed Green Mountain Boys who struggled for Vermont's independence from New Hampshire and New York back in the late eighteenth century. In fact, the small brick building just south of the town hall is named in his honor.

Richard Wallace's rise to local legend occurred one cold fall evening along the shores of Lake Champlain. Colonial troops were aligned on both sides of the lake, holding ground against the enemy forces. A dilemma arose with regard to the officers' inability to coordinate and communicate plans for attack across the lake. Up stepped Richard Wallace and Ephriham Webster (from Newbury), both of whom volunteered to swim the plans across the two-mile stretch of water. Tying their clothes and the valuable papers atop their heads with rope, they began the icy crossing. They passed so close to enemy ships that they could hear the sentries' conversation. Wind and waves nearly drowned them both. At one point Ephriham's rope slipped down across his throat; but fortunately, Richard was able to rescue him and pull him to safety. The pair scrambled ashore. As they made their way to the camp, they nearly tripped over a sleeping enemy guard; but managed, once again, to avoid disaster. The plans were delivered safe-

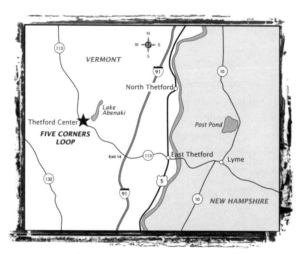

MilesDirections

0.0 START at the Thetford Center general store. Turn right on Route 113 and head northwest on the pavement.

0.9 Turn right just after the recycling station on Five Corners Road (dirt). Continue climbing up this town dirt road, passing Gillette Swamp on the left.

2.6 Encounter a steep section of uphill with a brook on the left.

3.3 Reach Five Corners. Turn right on Potato Hill Road and prepare yourself for a strenuous climb. A left down Robinson Hill Road will take you to Lake Fairlee. There are several forks and drives off this first section up Potato Hill, so stay straight.

4.15 Reach a fork in the trail. Continue to the right. Turning left leads you to a logging area.

4.28 The last steep pitch. High Peaks trail leaves to the right. Continue left.

5.0 Check out the views of the White Mountains. A scenic camp with a pond up on the left. More logging to the right. Continue straight downhill. Prepare for a screaming descent!

6.75 After a short paved section, the road comes abruptly to a four-way intersection. Turn right with the brook on your left. Gravel surface begins.

(continues on next page)

ly, and the two were forever remembered as heroes. And Wallace is just a sampling of Thetford's brave settlers.

This ride in Thetford, Vermont, combines dirt roads and old town roads (now impassable by car) for a challenging, woodsy ride, with plenty of opportunity for cooling off in fresh cold streams. The views of the White Mountains are spectacular, and the terrain is typically hilly. After the initial warm-up on Route 113, the road gradually climbs uphill for several miles to Five Corners. At Five Corners is a view of the hills surrounding Lake

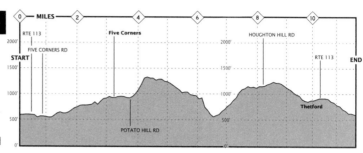

MilesDirections *(continued)*

6.9 Driveway bears off to the left. Stay straight on the snowmobile trails, following signs for Route 113 and Thetford Hill. Cross a small bridge and pass a slate quarry on the left. This is great double-track trail through an old hardwood forest that is well drained. An amazing brook races downhill as you climb. Look for some pools to cool off in.

8.03 Trail comes to a "T" with Houghton Hill Road. Turn left to complete the loop, passing a camp and ponds. Turning right takes you back to Five Corners on a pleasant, woodsy class-4 road.

(continues on next page)

Fairlee—the pavement to the left will take you to the lake. But there is more climbing to be done, and Potato Hill provides one of the more challenging uphills around. Although the ride is not technically difficult, Potato Hill is just plain steep. Pace yourself, and be thankful for that granny gear.

Once over the summit, there are some excellent views of Mount Moosilauke in the White Mountains and of the surrounding peaks of Mount Cube and Smart's Mountain. The long cruise downhill brings you almost to the Connecticut River but turns south just at the bottom and begins another long gradual climb. This incline is not nearly as steep as Potato Hill and a brook follows the trail for a while to help keep you cool.

The final miles on dirt take you down Houghton Hill to the hilltop community of Thetford Hill. Directly across the bottom of

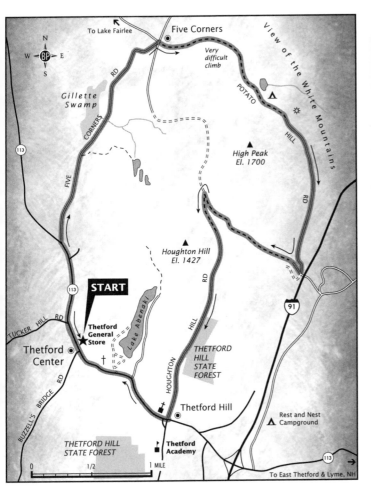

Ride Information

Local Bike Shops:
Hanover, New Hampshire
  Omer & Bob's
  (603) 643-3525
Strafford, Vermont
  The Brick Store
  (802) 765-4441

Maps:
USGS maps: Lyme, NH
DeLorme: Vermont Atlas &
  Gazetteer – Page 36 H-1

MilesDirections (continued)

10.4 Reach Thetford Hill. Turn right on Route 113 and coast downhill for 1.4 miles to the Thetford Center general store. The store will be on your right. For a more scenic tour, head straight at this intersection along Academy Road. This asphalt road is mostly downhill with awesome views of the Connecticut River Valley and New Hampshire hills.
11.8 Thetford Center general store is on your right. Back to where you parked!

Houghton Hill is Academy Road. If you ride a few hundred yards down this road, you can catch a splendid view of the surrounding countryside. Finally, cruise past Vermont Everlasting's farm stand and back to Thetford Center. For an extended tour, turn left at the bottom of the pavement and follow signs for the Union Village Dam Recreation Area. A pleasant dirt road winds along the Ompompanoosuc River with excellent swimming holes, picnic spots, and trails to explore. Back at the Thetford Center general store, you can mail your letters and stock up on some Ben and Jerry's ice cream, locally made maple syrup, or just about anything else you might need.

Connecticut River Amble

Ride Specs

Start: East Thetford Village
Length: 8.6 miles
Approximate Riding Time:
 1 hour
Rating: Easy
Terrain: Paved roads, dirt
 roads
Other Uses: Automobiles

Getting There

From **Fairlee** – Follow **I-91
south** to **Exit 14** and **Route
113 east.** Follow Route 113
east for 1.5 miles to **East
Thetford.** Park in town, possibly at the **Pioneer Plaza,**
just across the junction with
Route 5.

The 385-mile long Connecticut River has been described by travelers and writers as North America's Rhine River—or simply the "beautiful river." Its natural pathway through rolling hills and farmland provides a variety of color and life, from the great blue heron to the old white cape on the banks. Known by early Native Americans as "the long river," the Connecticut flows south from its origins in northern New Hampshire. It provides the drainage for one-third of both Vermont's and New Hampshire's rivers, and its many tributaries include the Ammonoosuc and Cold Rivers in New Hampshire, as well as the White, Wells, Waits, Ompompanoosuc, and Black Rivers in Vermont. The Connecticut River is also the modern-day boundary between Vermont and New Hampshire.

As recent as 25 years ago, the river was a common dumping ground for industrial waste. Efforts to clean up the river have been largely successful, and its waters are, once again, clear and fresh. Despite its once-tarnished state, the river remains an agricultural asset; both for its irrigation purposes and the fertile terrain for which it provides. In fact, the floodplains used for farming along the valley floors are among some of the most fertile lands in the country.

Early Native Americans once ruled the Connecticut River Valley, planting corn, pumpkins, and beans. Fish were more plentiful then, with tales of 40-pound varieties recorded. The encroaching white settlers turned the pleasant river valley into a war zone in the late 1700s, culminating in the horrific leveling of

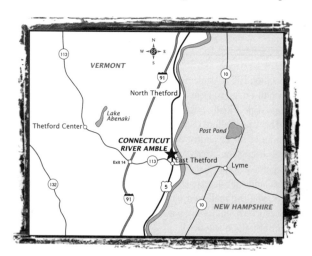

an entire Native American village in Saint Francis, Canada—burned by the renegade faction known as Roger's Rangers. Though occasionally this band of white pioneers is remembered for instances of great heroism, they are most remembered for this single, brutal act of terrorism. (The Saint Francis tribes had been targeted because they were the leading force behind the Native American resistance.)

By 1791, the white population in the Connecticut River Valley had soared to over 100,000. The surrounding land was farmed heavily, and the huge trees growing on the banks were felled for shipbuilding. Apple orchards were common, as were mills on the many waterfalls.

Today the waterfalls are no longer as prevalent, especially in the Thetford/Lyme area that this ride passes through. Large dams control the water's flow, and the section of river this ride follows is a wide and flat meandering corridor, more ideal for canoeing than waterfalls. There are several primitive campgrounds designed for canoeists along this stretch of the Connecticut. Previously, canoeists would come ashore and camp in a farmer's field or forest. Now the Upper Valley Land Trust has helped establish sites along the river specifically for camping. Scenic viewpoints, trails, and bird watching sites are often incorporated into the campsite. Most sites are on private land, and it is important to respect the landowner's generosity. Fairlee and North Thetford both have sites designed for low-impact camping.

During the riverboat era, Vermonters would often see the Connecticut River Flatboat—a long, narrow vessel that could float fully loaded in two feet of water, powered by a large square sail with one or more smaller sails in support. A large oar provided the steering, and a small cabin in the front provided shelter. These boats were used to transport cargo in the days of riverboat freighting. The canoe still served as a primary vessel, though rough ferries were often used for crossings. Some stubborn folks still crossed the river regularly by horseback, even when a boat was available. Local legend tells the story of a preacher who pre-

MilesDirections

0.0 START from the Pioneer Plaza, turn left on Route 5, heading south.

0.1 Turn left following signs for Lyme, New Hampshire. This short stretch of blacktop passes Long Wing organic tomato farm on the left, then crosses the Connecticut River. It's a beautiful view from the bridge in either direction.

0.5 Turn left on River Road. This is a four-way intersection.

1.0 Surface changes to dirt.

2.1 Surface changes back to pavement as the road cruises along the river. There are often large birds fishing in the still waters, so keep your eyes peeled!

2.6 Turn right and pass the farms and many acres of cornfields.

3.1 Turn left on Brick Hill Road, beginning the only real climb so far. This dirt road is narrow and quiet and the top affords some nice local views. Stay to the right at the one intersection in about one-half mile.

3.8 Nice local views.

4.3 Intersection with River Road. Take a quick spin to the right to check out the covered bridge just around the corner. Then head back the way you came on the dirt road, or cruise straight back on River Road (turning left), if you prefer a flat blacktop surface. River Road was the original turn made at the start of the ride after crossing the Connecticut River.

MILES

RTE 113   BRECK HILL RD   RIVER RD

START   RIVER ROAD   END

ferred his horse to the canoe for fording the river, even if it meant preaching in the church while dripping wet!

The ride along the river is the most basic and negotiable route chosen for this guide, and was picked for its scenic beauty and views of the river on quiet country roads. Beginners, kids, and visitors to the area will appreciate the relative flatness and rewarding rolling countryside and farmland.

Park on Route 5 in East Thetford, near the Pioneer Plaza. There is a pizza place here with a decent menu from which to choose when your ride is done. As you head for the East Thetford Bridge to Lyme, New Hampshire, check out the amazing greenhouses at Long Wind Farm. The early settlers probably didn't raise too many tomatoes, but these folks have the tomato down to a science. Grown organically, these beauties make it to many markets around the northeast and are prized for their quality and taste.

Don't forget to stop on the bridge, either, and take a good look up or down the river. This vantage point is often a good spot to see water birds diving and fishing in the calm waters. Sunsets are often reflected on the wide watery surface, and newly formed ice is another spectacular sight from the bridge. From here, River Road cruises along the floodplain, past old

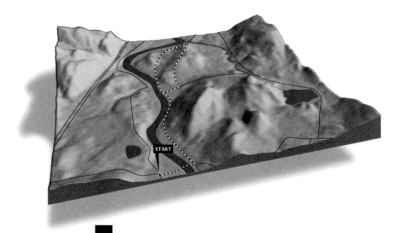

START

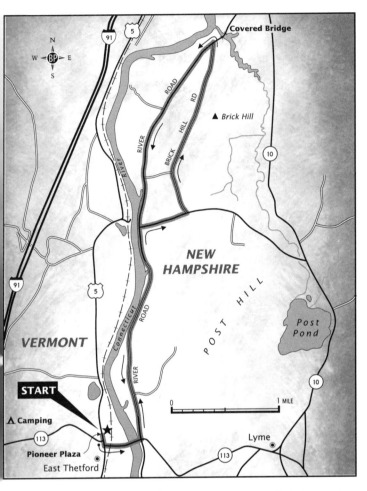

homesteads, reminding one of time's past. Early Connecticut River settlers didn't see the river as the boundary it is today. Instead, folks from both sides tried to form governments of their own, neither one being successful. The river now serves as a boundary between the two states, whose people see themselves as very different from one another.

A gradual climb on the dirt roads above the river provide the only real vertical gain, and the narrow track lined with old hardwoods is attractive enough to keep riders from noticing. On the other side of the hill, it is worth detouring a few hundred yards to check out the covered bridge over Clay Brook. The cruise back on River Road, past Post Hill and Conant Swamp, goes quickly, and the view looking south over the river reveals the hills of Thetford.

Lyme, New Hampshire, Loop

J ust across the Connecticut River from the Thetford area is the quiet town of Lyme, New Hampshire. Known for its community spirit and backroads wilderness, Lyme is a perfect place to mountain bike. This ride, combining dirt roads and trails, begins on the town green, where summer concerts and flea markets are sometimes found. Just off the common, you'll find Nichols' Hardware, which, after all these years, still sports an old-style soda fountain. The rest of the village center is comprised of the general store and a few quaint country inns. Note next to the town church the peculiar line of old red stalls. These were used by early parishioners to stall their horses during service. They've been preserved in their original state.

Like most villages in the area, just about every direction leads up, including the beginning of this ride. After a steep beginning, the dirt road levels off and runs south along the ridge between Plot and Lyme Hills. The dirt road meanders into an old, unmaintained town road, which is generally wide, but plenty challenging, with a number of rocky sections. You finally spill downhill on the other side of the ridge.

At the bottom of this rough descent, the dirt roads pick up again at an intersection with an option to head east toward Moose Mountain and the Appalachian Trail (the Moose Mountain area is excellent exploring). This ride turns north, however, toward Lyme Center, and climbs gradually on a fairly remote road. There is a section for a few miles with no houses, traveling through walls of thick forest on either side. Ride quietly and maybe you'll spot a deer or moose.

Ride Specs

Start: Lyme, New Hampshire Park & Ride lot
Length: 8.5 miles
Approximate Riding Time: 1-2 hours
Rating: Moderate
Terrain: Doubletrack, paved roads, dirt roads
Other Uses: Cross-country skiing, horseback riding, snowmobiles

Getting There

From **Fairlee** – Take **I-91 south** to **Exit 14** and **Route 113**. Follow **Route 113 east** 1.5 miles to **East Thetford**. Once in East Thetford, follow **Route 5 south** for 100 meters, then turn **left** just before the gas station following the sign for **Lyme, NH**. Cross the **Connecticut River** and follow the pavement uphill for another three miles until you reach the center of Lyme. Park here on the left in the Park & Ride Lot, just after the intersection with **Route 10**.

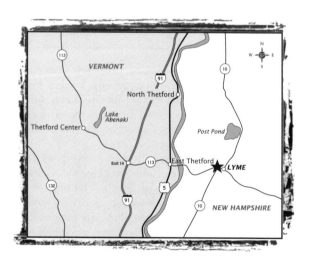

MilesDirections

0.0 START at the green in Lyme, New Hampshire, just over the border from East Thetford, Vermont. Park in the commuter spots just west of Nichols Hardware. Head north on Route 10 just past the green.

0.2 Just after the green, bear right off of Route 10, toward the Alden Country Inn. Turn right on Washburn Hill Road, in front of the Inn, and pass through a small section of houses. Prepare for a steep sudden climb, as the road turns to dirt. Stay straight on this road for the next mile, as several turns diverge.

1.7 Bear left at the split in the road and another road joins it from the right almost immediately. Just continue to the left.

(continues on next page)

At the height of land, the bulk of Smart's Mountain can be seen to the northeast, with it's fire tower just visible on top. The rest of the ride here is downhill (about 2.5 miles), so it's a good time to put on another layer if it's cool. The surface also turns to blacktop, so be prepared for some high speeds.

The next intersection is in the tiny hamlet of Lyme Center where Grant Brook (named for one of Lyme's earliest settlers) rushes west to the Connecticut River. The ride continues downhill, but take note—if you turn east here, the road leads uphill to some incredible riding around Cummins and Reservoir Ponds. These high-elevation ponds are another three to four miles up from Lyme Center, but the area around them is laced with well maintained snowmobile and logging trails, with connections all the way over to the Rumney, New Hampshire, area. The cross-coun-

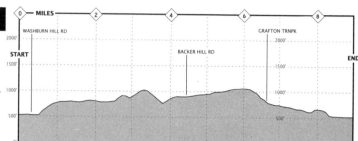

MilesDirections *(continued)*

2.5 Sharp corner to the right in the road, and the trees have just opened up providing a view off to the right. Turn left before the corner onto the old town road, which is now a nice doubletrack heading uphill. This trail climbs up for a bit and then descends a rocky section, which is rough. Stay on the main trail, as there are a few snowmobile trails that join it as it meanders on. When it heads downhill, several trails come in from the left, but you just keep descending.

3.7 Pass the old yellow farm on the left of the intersection with the main dirt road. Turn left and begin climbing. There aren't any houses in this next half-mile climb.

4.4 Two roads come in from the right; one is marked "Dead End." Stay to the left. You are riding along Backer Hill Road.

6.0 Blacktop begins, as does a rollicking descent. Look straight ahead for a quick view of Smart's Mountain.

try skiing there is superb. This road uphill from Lyme Center is also the route to Winslow Mountain, which is the site of the Dartmouth Skiway, a small alpine area with great views of the surrounding countryside, clear to the White Mountains.

Once you've reached Lyme again, it's worth the 10-mile drive south to Hanover, New Hampshire, home to Dartmouth College. This picturesque college town is great for shopping, dining, and entertainment (try Dartmouth's arts center). With the blending of a small town and an Ivy League school, you get a community that is friendly, yet elegant and upscale. There are also several bike shops in Hanover, known for their friendly and knowledgeable staffs who can give you even more ideas for places to mountain bike in the area.

(continues on next page)

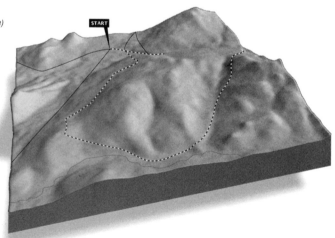

Beachway Press

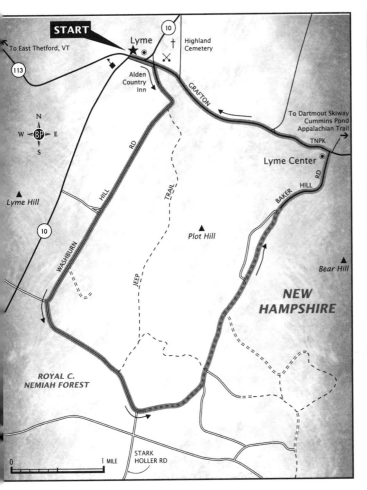

Ride Inform

Local Bike Shops:
(See Info for Connecticut River
Amble)

Local Attractions/Events:
At Dartmouth College in Hanover:
The Hopkins Performing Arts
   Center: (603) 646-2422
The Hood Museum of Art
   (603) 646-2808

In Norwich, VT:
The Moonshine Museum of
Science: (802) 649-2200

Maps:
USGS maps: Lyme, NH/VT
DeLorme: Vermont Atlas &
   Gazetteer; Page 36 H-3

MilesDirections (continued)

6.6 Reach the intersection with
Lyme Center Road and the tiny village of Lyme Center. Turn left on
Grafton Turnpike and coast downhill for almost two miles back to
the car. To the right from Lyme
Center are the Dartmouth Skiway
and Cummings and Reservoir
Ponds. There are extensive trail
networks at these upper ponds.

8.3 At the bottom of the hill, stay
to the left. You will pass the Alden
Inn on the left, and intersect Route
10. Pass the Lyme Country Store
on the right.

8.5 Reach Nichols Hardware on the
right and the parking lot.

Downner State Forest

F or a mountain biker, Downer State Forest in Sharon, Vermont, is made to order. Its wide forest trails and old growth trees create a park suited perfectly for knobby tires. The terrain is hilly, but not technically difficult, so both beginners and more experienced riders can enjoy riding here.

The forest is named for Charles Downer, a resident of Sharon in the early 1900s, who contributed these 340 acres of land to the state. Downer State Forest, reportedly the first gift to the Vermont State Forest system, lies on both sides of Downer Road, with the best off-road riding found south of the road.

To the northeast of the forest is Morrill Mountain, named for politician Justin Smith Morrill. Justin Morrill was a self-educated native of Strafford, Vermont, who, in the mid-1800s, wrote a piece of legislation establishing land grants for states to use as collateral in order to build colleges. These colleges were designed to provide educational opportunities for all classes of people. The idea was inspired in part by Morrill's own lack of educational opportunities. Morrill was also an architect, whose homestead in

Do

Downer ...

Length: 7.75 mi..

Approximate Riding ...
1-2 hours

Rating: Moderate

Terrain: Doubletrack, forest service roads, class-3 and 4 dirt roads

Other Uses: Cross-country skiing, hiking, horseback riding, snowmobiles

Getting There

From **White River Junction** – Travel **north** on **I-89** to **Exit 2.** Take Exit 2 to **Route 132 east,** following **Route 132** to **Beaver Meadow Road** on the right. Follow Beaver Meadow Road for 100 meters, then turn **left** on **Downer Road.** Follow Downer Road for two miles to the entrance and parking area for **Downer State Forest,** near CCC pond.

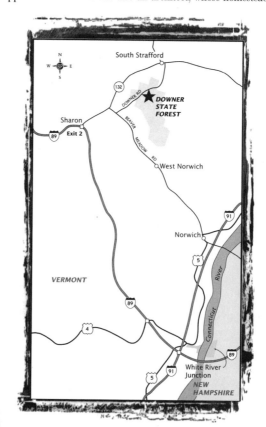

Strafford is a classic example of Roman Gothic design. His home, now owned by the state, is registered as a Vermont historic site and is open to the public.

Another famous resident of this area was Joseph Smith, founder and first leader of the Church of Jesus Christ of Latter-day Saints (more commonly referred to as the Mormon Church). Smith was born in December 1805 in Sharon, Vermont, then moved west with his family to New York where he would eventually form what was called the restoration of the original Christian faith. Sharon later honored their visionary son with a 38-foot granite monument built in his honor in the town center.

The name Sharon is taken from a town in Connecticut from which the first settlers came in 1765. It seems most towns throughout Vermont are named after places in Connecticut or Massachusetts, leaving little room for fanciful stories on how Vermont towns were named.

The Downer State Forest trails are easily accessible by driving north along Downer Road, past Crescent Lake, and parking at the CCC pond—home to the popular summer 4-H camp. From here you can see that the forest entrance is clearly marked.

The ride begins by climbing gradually up to the height of land. After about a mile, the trail takes a quick turn out of the forest and drops down past the Rootings Herb Farm to Beaver Meadow Road. This main dirt road travels all the way to Norwich—should you follow it that far—which is home to Dan and Whit's famous

MilesDirections

0.0 START from the parking area opposite the Downer 4-H Camp and the CCC pond. Head up the hill along the forest road.

0.05 Bear right at the split in the trail.

0.9 Turn right at the "T." Turning left will loop back to the car. Keep your eyes peeled along this trail for trees planted back in the early part of this century. Most are labeled with species and date.

1.2 Turn right off this forest road on another doubletrack that heads downhill past some houses.

1.3 Bear left here. Check out the waterfall.

1.8 Pass Rootings Herb Farm (an herb greenhouse that farms and produces plants used for medicinal products). Susan Root's shop is open for the public, so stop in for a visit.

2.1 Turn left on Beaver Meadow Road.

(continues on next page)

MilesDirections *(continued)*

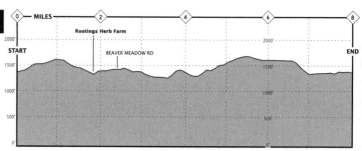

3.85 After a long downhill, turn left up the hill opposite the house with a fenced-in yard. This trail takes you back to the network of forest roads. Follow signs for 5N within the snowmobile network.

4.98 Bear to the left on the main trail, as a minor trail branches right. Prepare for a long climb. Ignore the trails off to the sides and stay on the main drag.

5.7 Reach the high point of land. At the top is a small uninhabited cabin.

6.3 Bear right at this intersection. We were here earlier, remember?

6.6 Stay right through this intersection. Prepare for a steep downhill with a sharp corner near the bottom.

7.7 Bear right at the split in the trail and cruise back to the car.

7.75 Finished! One hour. How about you?

general store. An old-time general store, it carries everything from groceries to gas lights. It's worth a stop if you're in the neighborhood.

Long before Dan and Whit's, however, the ride heads off the dirt road back along the Downer Forest trails. The trail climbs gradually, passing through a beautiful pine forest toward the top. The climb is fairly substantial, but keep in mind the downhill that follows.

At the top of the hill, a few old hunting camps mark the spot. It's all

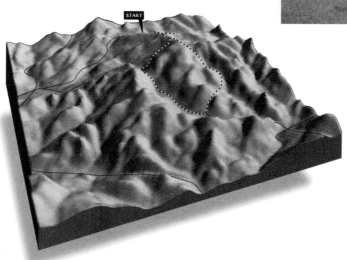

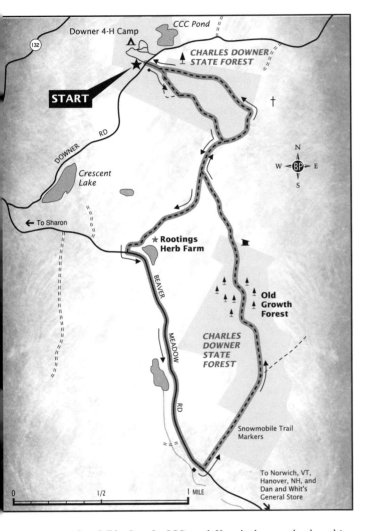

Local Atractions/Events:
Rootings Herb Farm:
  (802) 763-8156
Dan & Whit's General Store: downtown Norwich. (Check out their
  listing of local events)

Local Bike Shops:
The Brick Store
  Strafford, VT, (802) 765-4441

Maps:
USGS maps: Sharon, VT; South
  Stafford, VT
DeLorme: Vermont Atlas &
  Gazetteer; Page 35 H-11

downhill back to the CCC pond. If you're hungry, the short drive into Sharon could be rewarded with a stop at Brooksie's—a fine example of Vermont-style country cooking, with a mouthwatering assortment of homemade pies and muffins.

Killington Singletrack Tour

Start: Killington trail #17 trailhead; across from the High Ridge Condo
Length: 6 miles
Approximate Riding Time: 1-1.5 hours
Rating: Moderate to Difficult
Terrain: Singletrack
Other Uses: Alpine skiing

Getting There

From the **Killington Base Lodge** and **Mountain Bike Center** – Drive or ride down the access road and turn **right** at the **Snowshed Lodge** toward the golf course. Go past the golf course and the **Lodgings/Reservations Center,** traveling 1.5 miles to the High Ridge Condo. Directly across from the **High Ridge Condo** is a trail marked **#17.** The directions for this ride start here.

K illington has always been a popular spot for vacationers looking for a variety of outdoor recreations coupled with the natural beauty of Vermont. With the addition of over 35 miles of mountain bike trails, skiers aren't the only ones enjoying the terrain this mountain resort offers. With an excellent sampling of single-track and the option to ride the lift to access the higher trails, Killington offers challenging and exciting mountain bike adventures for cyclists of all abilities.

The full service mountain bike shop at Killington Base Lodge furnishes bike rentals, trail passes, guided tours, lessons, and maps for the Center. For the past few years, they have hosted one of the Pedros Series races and have received rave reviews about the racecourse—most likely attributed to the exciting singletrack sections, which many racecourses lack.

One account has the summit of Killington (Vermont's second highest peak by 50 feet) as the possible location for the naming of Vermont by the Reverend Sam Peters—the first Protestant clergyman to enter the state. The more likely story, however, is thought to date back to the earliest days of Vermont's history when then "republic" of Vermont was being formed. It is said that Ethan Allen (the leader of the famous Green Mountain Boys (*see page 97*) wrote a letter regarding the creation of Vermont's constitution and addressed it to the inhabitants of "Vermont," presumably borrowing from the French words "verd" (green) and "mont" (mountains).

A more definite Killington connection is to the thirtieth President of the United States. Born in the neighboring village of Plymouth, Calvin Coolidge spent his boyhood in the hills here.

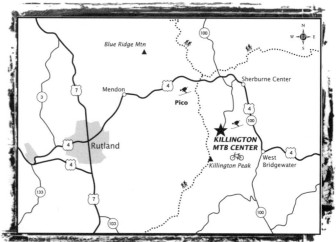

The homes of the Coolidge family—as well as the community church, the cheese factory, a one-room schoolhouse, and the general store—have all been carefully preserved, many of which retain the original furnishings. President Coolidge is buried in the town cemetery. Visitors are welcome to tour the historic village. Much of the surrounding land, including that adjoining Killington is part of the vast Coolidge State Forest. Also, don't forget to tour the wonderful Norman Rockwell museum, filled from wall to wall with paintings, sketches, and Saturday Evening Post Magazine covers that chronologically record his wonderful and successful career as one of America's most beloved character painters.

Nearby Pico Peak is also worth exploring, as it has mountain biking trails and a work road to the summit (which is rideable for

the strong at heart). The views are especially inspiring from the 3,900-foot summit of Pico—which, parenthetically, is home to the nation's first alpine ski lift, built in 1940. Across the street from Pico is the Cortina Inn, which also sports a trail system for mountain biking and has more suitable terrain for beginners than the more rugged alpine areas. The Inn offers a map, which gives an excellent layout of the surrounding dirt roads and trails.

Back at Killington, cyclists will find that some of the best riding around is within the web of singletrack below the Base Lodge, tucked in between the alpine ski trails. The ride mapped here is a taste of some of the riding you can find at Killington.

The tour begins with a steady uphill climb—which means it will end on a downhill. After reaching the first junction with sin-

MilesDirections

0.0 START at the High Ridge Condo. Follow Trail #17, which begins up a work road, passing by a trail to the left that dead ends. After passing this trail at the beginning, the work road winds through a residential section and then gradually heads up toward the mountain. The gradient is not too steep and is fairly wide to begin with. As it climbs, it becomes narrower.

0.5 Pass trails to the right that head off to some other condos. Stay straight on #17.

1.25 Turn left on #22. Be prepared for another quick left (#28).

1.33 Turn left on #28 over the snowmaking pipe. It is a short singletrack section that parallels the wider work road.

1.55 Back out onto the work road, bear to the right. The gondola is visible off to the left.

1.75 After passing a sign for #22 (the way we came up), take the next right, which is also marked #22 and goes sharply uphill into the woods. The next section is technical singletrack.

1.95 Intersection with #17. Turn left, then take an immediate right on #22. More singletrack.

2.2 #22 intersects with the main ski trails and crosses underneath several chairlifts. There is a nice view here. Head straight across and notice the sign for #16 to the right. Eventually we will loop back on that trail. #22 goes into the woods again on the other side of the ski trail. Follow signs for #22 for the next half-mile of singletrack.

(continues on next page)

MilesDirections *(continued)*

2.7 A sharp turn to the right begins #16 (there is a sign) and is also the spot to stop at the Killington Base Lodge, if needed. Trail #1 goes off to the left. Head downhill on #16, paralleling the work road and heading toward Snowshed.

3.1 Cross under the chairlifts again, and look for the trail marker on the other side, going into the woods for another nice singletrack section. Follow signs for #16.

3.75 Pass an intersection with #22 going off to the right. Continue to follow #16.

4.46 Back at the original point of meeting with #16 and #22. #22 goes into the woods to the left. Stay on the main open ski slope, and follow uphill the doubletrack on the left side of the grassy slope.

4.55 Turn left on Trail #1, a work road that is wide and smooth.

4.65 Turn left on #17 and prepare for a nice downhill cruise to the condos. Follow signs for #17 the whole way down.

6.0 Intersection with the paved golf course road and the High Ridge condos across the street. Turn left to return to Killington Base Lodge and Snowshed Lodge.

gletrack, the riding changes to a more technical terrain. Depending on the weather, this section can be muddy, but it eventually connects back to the work road. The next portion of trail is a rolling, rocky, woodsy stretch that is almost impossible to clean if the leaves are on the ground. It comes out on the alpine trails with a great view, looking north, of the Green Mountain National Forest. From here, the loop heads up to the base lodge and then swoops back down toward Snowshed. The long climb from here is a grind, but it brings you to the highest point in the ride. It is all downhill from here. There are lots of places to connect back to the other trails in the system, if you want to shorten or lengthen the ride.

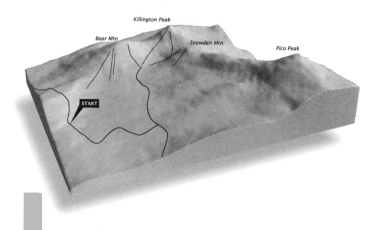

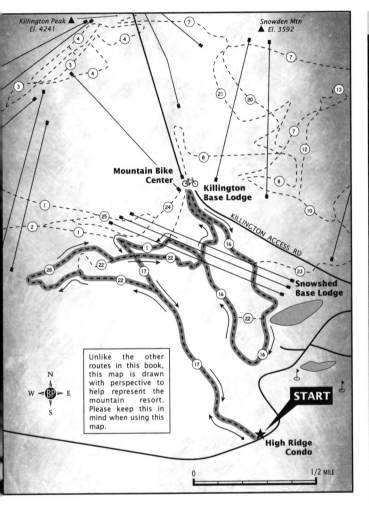

Killington Peak ▲ El. 4241

Snowden Mtn ▲ El. 3592

Mountain Bike Center

Killington Base Lodge

KILLINGTON ACCESS RD

Snowshed Base Lodge

Unlike the other routes in this book, this map is drawn with perspective to help represent the mountain resort. Please keep this in mind when using this map.

N
W E
S

START

High Ridge Condo

0   1/2 MILE

Ride Information

Trail Maintenance Hotline:
Killington Mountain Bike Center:
(802) 422-6232

Schedule:
Killington's trails are open to mountain bikes daily 9 a.m. to 6 p.m. from late May through mid-October with the chairlift operating from 9 a.m. to 4 p.m. (Call Killington for this season's exact schedule.)

Costs:
Trail access fees are from $5 to $10. Chairlift rides are around $18 for one time or $25 for a full day. (Call Killington for this season's exact prices.)

Local Attractions/Events:
The Vermont Marble Exhibit: the World's Largest Marble Museum, Proctor, VT. (802) 459-2300
Norman Rockwell Museum (802) 773-6095
Cortina Inn: 1-800-451-6108

Maps:
USGS maps: Killington Peak, VT
DeLorme: Vermont Atlas & Gazetteer; Page 30 D-2

If you are with your family or just looking for a mellow cruise, a nice dirt road can be found down Route 4 east in the town of Sherburne. Take a left off Route 4 onto River Road at the bottom of the big hill, just before the Hardware store and Physician's office. River Road is paved through to the tiny town of Sherburne; but at the town offices, it turns to a wide, smooth dirt road that winds along a beautiful river valley for 2.5 miles. The Appalachian Trail crosses River Road, and there are several logging roads that look promising. At its intersection with Route 100 (2.5 miles), you can go straight across the pavement to Colton Pond and have a picnic before you finish the return ride to Sherburne.

Cloudland Loop

Ride Specs

Start: River Road near Quechee Lake Ski Area/Golf Course

Length: 14.2 miles

Approximate Riding Time: 2 hours

Rating: Moderate

Terrain: Singletrack, double-track, paved roads, class-3 and 4 dirt roads

Other Uses: Cross-country skiing, hiking, horseback riding, snowmobiles, four-wheelers

Getting There

From **Montpelier** – Follow **I-89 south** toward **White River Junction.** Take **Exit 1** from **I-89** just before White River Junction and head **west** on **Route 4.** Follow Route 4 west for about 1/2 mile to the **Fat Hat Factory.** Turn right here on **Clubhouse Road.** Follow Clubhouse Road for one mile until you reach **Quechee Village.** Parking in town is your best bet at the large parking lot near the post office. Start your ride in town, near the ski area.

I n between the hills of Pomfret and Hartland, located on the banks of the Ottaquechee River, is the picturesque town of Quechee. The Ottaquechee is Native American for *"swift moving stream with cat-tails and rushes."* Like most Vermont rivers, the Ottaquechee is known for jamming its banks with ice in the early spring melts. Several years ago chunks of river ice pushed up on the banks so high that driving along the narrow road running east from town was like touring a glacial wall.

Like the land surrounding Quechee, there are many marshy lowlands throughout the area. Dewey's Mills is one such place, located just one mile east of Quechee Village. Once home to a bustling railroad community, little remains, except a lone brick building. The rest of the town was leveled in the 1960s as part of a flood control plan for the area dam. As it turned out, Dewey's Mills could have stayed on, right where it was, since the Ottaquechee River never reached the level engineers expected it to. It creates an eerie feeling to know that in this now desolate flatland, an entire town once thrived.

The surrounding hills provide excellent terrain for mountain biking. A good collection of snowmobile trails, class-4 roads, and barely-traveled dirt roads are found above Quechee. *Above* is the key word here, as riding from most valley villages calls for lots of climbing to reach the hill country. This ride is no exception. Views from the farm country in Pomfret and Hartford are nothing short of spectacular. Cloudland Farm is one of the better known farms in the upland, its name perfectly describing the atmosphere above the valleys.

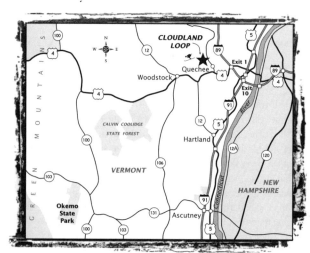

While visiting Quechee, be sure to trek on foot over to Quechee Gorge. Located at the dam in Dewey's Mills, this chasm of more than 150 feet is quite incredible, and the bridge spanning its length is equally impressive. In the late 1800s, the bridge was built for the railroad running from White River Junction to Woodstock. The original wooden bridge lasted until 1911. A more sturdy steel frame was put in its place to handle the busy railroad traffic on what today is Highway 4.

One of the more colorful stories from this era is of Philo Carpenter, a French bridge worker who loved taking risks. As the story goes, every day at noon Philo would do headstands on the trestle to thrill passers-by. On weekends, he did one better, shimmying to the top of a nearby pine tree (some 50 feet tall) to perform his gymnastics on the smooth four inch tip of the tree he had sawed off just for this purpose. Apparently, a great deal of pocket silver was lost from Philo's trousers during these escapades, so keep your eyes open for glints of 100-year-old coins!

The ride begins from the west end of town and climbs steeply in the direction of Sugarbush Farm (a maple sugaring operation), past the golf course on Hillside Road. At the first intersection with High Pastures Road is a good view of the Killington ski area from across the meadows. Follow the signs for Sugarbush Farm to keep you on track until the roads split at the two-mile marker. Here the surroundings become more remote. The dirt road narrows over the next few miles until finally it peters out into a doubletrack trail that crosses over the ridge to Cloudland Farm.

This section of doubletrack is exceptionally scenic, and not exceedingly difficult, though it does continue to climb for a bit. A

MilesDirections

0.0 START at the base of the Quechee Ski Area, across from the golf club and Quechee Inn. Turn right, following River Road west toward Woodstock.

0.3 Turn right up Hillside Road. This is a long, steep climb on pavement, but it's worth the effort once you get out on the back roads.

1.5 Turn right at the split in the road on Spaulding Lane. Follow signs for Sugarbush Farm.

2.0 Bear left, continuing on Spaulding Lane. The road to Sugarbush Farm goes downhill to the right. Sugarbush Farm is open for tours and sells maple products on the premises.

3.7 Bear left across a small stream. There are driveways on both sides of the road for the next 100 yards. Stay straight following the red wooden signs nailed to trees and poles along the road.

(continues on next page)

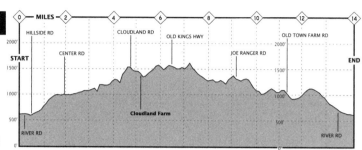

MilesDirections *(continued)*

3.95 Bear left again, while a drive goes right. The trail turns rougher and heads sharply uphill. This is a nice old doubletrack through a mature hardwood forest.

4.7 Turn right on Cloudland Road. Just after this turn Cloudland Road intersects with the Appalachian Trail. If you want to take in a great view, stash your bike in the bushes and head south on the trail for nearly one-half mile. You will be treated to a breathtaking panoramic view of the Delectable Mountains, Green Mountains, and the Connecticut River Valley—all spread out before you.

6.4 Bear right at the intersection, then right again in another tenth of a mile on Bunker Hill Road (a.k.a. the old Kings Highway). The fields to the left are often in full bloom and filled with splendid colors, as the owner sows wildflower seeds year-round.

7.3 Bear right again, past the marker for Kings Highway. Once again, you will be treated to expansive meadows and old roads lined with giant oak and maple.

7.48 Stay right, past the old stone markers. The road becomes a bit rougher and more narrow through here.

8.2 At the bottom of the hill, stay to the right, as the road curves left and down to Pomfret. One last climb.

(continues on next page)

rolling downhill, with woodsy curves and plenty of room, leads you to the dirt surface of Cloudland Road and the intersection with the Appalachian Trail. If you're up for it, stash your bike and hustle west by foot for less than a mile along this famous hiking trail to an awaiting view. From the clearing, the green hills of Vermont seem to roll endlessly to the horizon, inspiring some to agree with a common opinion around here that this area is one of Vermont's finest.

After passing the Appalachian Trail, the dirt road winds past Cloudland Farm and passes the infamous bull mulling in his steep pasture. Wave hello, then continue downhill to the intersection with the old Kings Highway. At this point, it's only a few miles downhill to the town of Pomfret. This is a good place to bail out, if necessary. Otherwise, follow this dirt road up Bunker Hill, past some of the most scenic farms in the Vermont's back-

Beachway Press

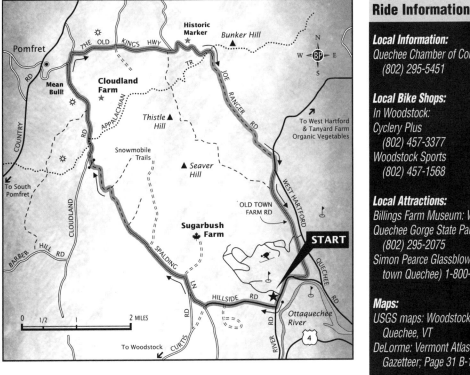

Ride Information

Local Information:
Quechee Chamber of Commerce
(802) 295-5451

Local Bike Shops:
In Woodstock:
Cyclery Plus
    (802) 457-3377
Woodstock Sports
    (802) 457-1568

Local Attractions:
Billings Farm Museum: Woodstock
Quechee Gorge State Park
    (802) 295-2075
Simon Pearce Glassblowing (down-
    town Quechee) 1-800-774-5277

Maps:
USGS maps: Woodstock, VT;
    Quechee, VT
DeLorme: Vermont Atlas &
    Gazetteer; Page 31 B-10

country. The narrow dirt roads are quiet but challenging with their undulating hills. In the spring, they are quite difficult to negotiate, so wait until they have dried out. Once over Bunker Hill, a long downhill along Joe Ranger Road awaits, crossing the Appalachian Trail once again. The ride finally spills out on West Hartford Road, leaving only a few miles back to Quechee.

Once in town, consider visiting the renowned Simon Pearce Glassware Restaurant, or take a lunch from one of the local cafés down to the banks of the Ottauquechee. From here, you can plan your next adventure—perhaps this time to the nearby Delectable Mountains.

MilesDirections (continued)

9.1 Turn right on Joe Ranger Road, at the intersection marked by a sign reading "Road Ends." You will cross the Appalachian Trail once again.

11.2 Joe Ranger Road intersects with Quechee-West Hartford Road. Turn right and head back toward town.

11.4 Turn right on Old Town Farm Road.

13.5 Reach the intersection with River Road. Turn left to return to town.

14.2 Reach Quechee Ski Area.

Hurricane Reservoir

Ride Specs

Start: Downtown White River Junction
Length: 10.6 miles
Approximate Riding Time: 2 hours
Rating: Moderate to Difficult
Terrain: Singletrack, double-track, paved roads, dirt roads
Other Uses: Hiking, horseback riding, snowmobiles, four-wheelers

Getting There

From **I-91** – Take **Exit 10**, following signs to downtown **White River Junction.** Park locally downtown (the train station is a good bet). To begin the ride, head out of town along **Main Street.**

A t one time, in the early part of this century, White River Junction was the most important railroad town in northern New England. Its location provided the link between several different railways that often switched cars here and headed for points farther north. These days, this small town, at the junction of the White and Connecticut Rivers, is making a concerted effort to revive its historic downtown area. A tasty bakery, a small family-run bike shop, a health food restaurant, a classic diner, a wonderful used book shop, and a friendly co-op food store are just a few of the downtown attractions. The downtown block is also home to an elegant, old hotel and an opera house (where you can catch performances year-round).

This is the only ride in the book that really starts in a downtown area, so there is some pavement before getting to the trails at Hurricane Reservoir. It is sometimes fun to start a ride in a more urban area, knowing that it isn't too long a ride back to food and friends. Though you might doubt it in a bustling town like White River Junction, it is typical in Vermont to hit backcountry only a mile or so out of town.

White River Junction is part of the larger town of Hartford, which also encompasses some of the other surrounding villages, like West Hartford and Quechee. It is commonplace in Vermont to live in a village that is really a part of another town—sort of like suburbs, but in a rural sense.

If you follow Route 4 west from town through these *suburbs*, you will also be following the original railroad bed of the once-

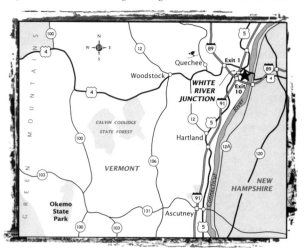

MilesDirections

0.0 START from the train station parking lot in White River Junction. Head left on Main Street out of the parking lot and take the first left on Church Street.

0.2 At the end of Church Street, turn right at the "T," and head up the steep paved hill that winds through the old houses overlooking the White River.

0.7 Turn right at the intersection.

0.9 At the end of Airport Road, turn left on Route 5, passing Evan's Expressmart. Follow Route 5, past the turns for I-91/89, the VA Hospital, and all the convenience stores and gas stations. Just after passing under the highway, look for a right turn on a road named King's Highway.

1.7 Turn right up King's Highway and prepare for a steep climb for about 3/4-mile, still on the blacktop.

2.4 The blacktop ends and a few residential streets go off to the right. A class-4 road goes straight—past signs calling it "impassable." There are some nature trails off to the left, maintained by the town of Hartford, with signs for the Hurricane Hill Nature Area. Continue straight on the class-4 road, and prepare for some rough going for the first bit.

(continues on next page)

popular Woodstock Railway. From the late 1800s to 1930s, this railroad was the main source for commuting and transportation of goods from Woodstock to White River Junction. It ran daily for over 50 years without any major accidents and often carried folks on special runs to White River for events like fairs, rodeos, and public speeches.

After parking in downtown White River Junction (there is public parking near the train station), the ride heads out of town through some hilly residential neighborhoods. Most of the enormous old houses perched up above the river valley are apartments now. It is hard to imagine one family living in (and heating) one of those homes, but they did. And some still do.

Beyond these hills, the ride passes through a brief but busy section of Route 5 before heading up King's Highway. King's

MilesDirections *(continued)*

2.8 After this gnarly uphill, the road turns back to blacktop, with a house to the right. A nice double-track trail climbs steeply up to the left and is a good sidetrip up to some weather equipment, if you'd like the extra 1/2-mile climb up and back. Otherwise, continue straight downhill on the pavement.
3.2 Turn left on Reservoir Road.
3.7 Pass straight through a clearing, with a trail off to the left. The town dirt road changes to a rough class-4 road with rocky and muddy sections ahead.
3.8 Continue straight past the reservoir on the right and a trail to the left.
4.2 A major snowmobile trail intersection. Route 5 north goes right and is actually excellent riding. Stay on Route 5 south, which is to the left. The terrain is rolling double-track through a beautiful old forest.
5.0 Another trail goes off to the left. Stay on the main trail.
5.2 The trail intersects with a driveway in front of a barn. Turn right and go to the end of the drive, then immediately left downhill. The White River Valley is spread out below.
5.4 Just as the dirt road meets the blacktop, an old class-4 road goes off to the right into the woods. It is well traveled and shouldn't be confused with the tractor trails going into the farmer's fields. The view is quite nice here. Over the next mile, there are quite a few intersections and trails leading off to both sides of this main trail. Just stay on the main trail, always heading downhill.

(continues on next page)

136

Highway climbs sharply and steeply uphill from Route 5 and gives an immediate view of the valley below. It passes the Hurricane Hill Nature Area with some walking trails and signs detailing the local flora and fauna. After this landmark, be prepared for more climbing and some technically challenging sections.

This next piece of unmaintained town road is full of rocks and can be slippery in the rain—or even with a bit of dew on it. Be careful as it's dark and shadowy in this ravine, which may cause you to pedal hurriedly out. After about one-half mile, the road changes back to residential blacktop and then dirt for another mile until reaching the trails to Hurricane Reservoir. These trails are used by snowmobiles in the winter and all-terrain vehicles in the summer, so they are well maintained and lots of fun to explore.

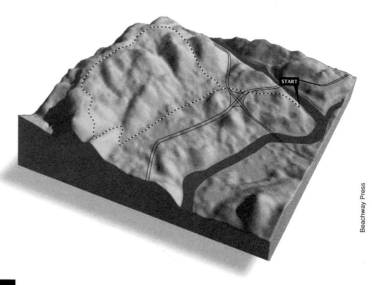

Beachway Press

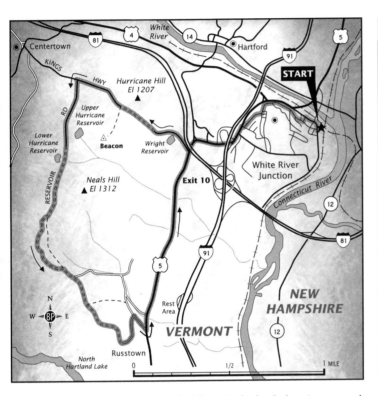

MilesDirections *(continued)*

6.3 Road changes to a class-3 road. Head down the hill past the houses on both sides.

6.6 At the "T," turn right on Rustic Road.

6.7 Intersection with Route 5—the Recycling Center with its great thrift shop is right across the street. Turn left on Route 5 and head back toward White River Junction.

8.8 Pass King's Highway on the left and pass under the interstate. Stay on Route 5.

9.6 Turn right on Airport Road at the Evan's Expressmart. Bear left as Beech Street goes right.

9.8 Turn left at the "T" and cruise downhill.

10.3 Turn left on Church Street.

10.5 Turn right to the public parking.

The route this ride follows is the legal class-4 town road through the area, but there are lots of great looking options off of it to explore by mountain bike. Many of them are marked as snowmobile trails. The riding in here is rolling and fairly smooth, with thick forests and lots of dips that fill with water. Riding is quite pleasant at this point as you reach the height of the land.

After crossing over a maintained road at five miles or so, the forests open up for a view of the valley below. From here it is all downhill on another class-4 road, then a dirt road to Route 5. Once you reach Route 5, check out the recycling thrift shop across the street for treasures not to be found anywhere else. Route 5 then winds back in its friendly, fairly flat course to White River Junction.

Hartland Hill Loop

T he Central Vermont town of Woodstock is well known for its colorful downtown streets lined with delightful shops that make up a still-thriving village center. During the Christmas season, early evenings are illuminated by the white lights of town, often blanketed with snow from the last storm.

Years ago, Woodstock was known for its publishing strengths, with five newspapers in circulation at one time. It was also home to the first ski tow in America—a rope tow set up in 1939 on Clinton Gilbert's farm outside of town. A Model T Ford engine powered the tow. An historic plaque can still be found near the old farm, north of here on Route 12 toward Barnard.

Today Woodstock, with its many local bed and breakfasts, is a favorite stop for skiers en route to Killington. In addition to the excellent skiing, the area's mountain biking terrain is nearly flawless. Access to old dirt roads and trail networks is simple and direct right from town.

This ride climbs above the town of Woodstock, on Hartland and Garvin Hills, then dips over the other side into Hartland. Hartland was formerly named "Hartfordland" after its original settlers' native home, Hartford, Connecticut. Although this ride has some substantial climbing, it's entirely on dirt roads, giving even beginner riders a chance to ride to nearby farms and witness the views this route provides. Not only is this route designed to give all levels of riders a taste of Vermont's backroads, it also features several spots to visit along the way, including a real Vermont sugarhouse and a wetland preserve—perfect for a picnic lunch ride.

First on the list of things to check out is the Eshqua Bog Area—about one mile along Garvin Hill Road. Garvin Hill is the

Ride Specs

Start: Across from 18 Carrots Natural Foods Store (near Cumberland Farms Store)
Length: 7 to 8 miles
Approximate Riding Time: 1-2 hours
Rating: Easy to Moderate
Terrain: Doubletrack, dirt roads
Other Uses: Horseback riding, automobiles

Getting There

From **White River Junction** and **I-89** – Take **Exit 1** off I-89 to **Route 4 west.** Follow Route 4 west to **Woodstock.** Park near **Cumberland Farms,** just east of Woodstock. **Hartland Hill Road** rises sharply uphill and to the right from here, so park locally, and head up the hill.

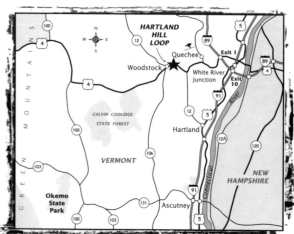

first dirt road this ride follows after ascending the paved Hartland Hill Road from town. As soon as the surface changes to dirt here, the ride takes on a whole new character. The narrow thoroughfare is reminiscent of a horse and buggy scene from the early 1800s, shaded by the huge old trees that line the edges of the road. Old pastures open up on the east side and roll away into more open space, often punctuated by round hay bales in the summer months.

Eshqua Bog is best known for the wild and unusual plants often found in this wet habitat. Leave your bike stashed in the woods, as the wetland is not open for mountain biking but is great for a short hike. A trail with 10 marked stations winds along the periphery of the fence, and plants such as lady's slipper and orchids can be spotted. A boardwalk into the center of the bog gives yet another perspective on this fragile ecosystem. There should be trail maps inside a box at the bog's trailhead. For nature enthusiasts, the Nature Conservancy in Montpelier has more information on this preserve—call (802) 229-4425.

Continuing along Garvin Hill, it might be worth tuning into the energy surrounding this woodsy, hilly byway, as local psychics believe the hill is home to some powerful crystals that emanate sources of energy. Regardless of what's underground, Garvin Hill does have a magical aura, reinforced by the view south from the height of land. After descending into old "Hartfordland," the ride takes a sharp turn back uphill on Weed Road. A Vermont atlas will reveal a junction here where back road exploring options abound. It's worth it to venture further if you have the time and a good map. Otherwise, continue up Hartland Hill and pass by the Richardson Family Farm.

MilesDirections

0.0 START near Cumberland Farms on Route 4 heading east out of Woodstock. The natural foods store called 18 Carrots is just west of here on Route 4 and is another possible starting point. Head out of the lot at Cumberland Farms and go right on Route 4.
0.1 Start up Hartland Hill Road. The bottom portion is paved.

(continues on next page)

Lee Graham's Johnny Cake

Lee was a first cousin to the Richardson's on Hartland Hill. He lived in Hartland, Vermont. This recipe turns out a cornbread that is deliciously moist and corny!

3/4 c. cornmeal
1/4 c. softened shortening
1/4 c. sugar
1 egg
dash of salt
3/4 c. white flour
1 c. sour milk
1 tsp. baking soda

Combine all ingredients and pour into a greased pie dish or 8x12 pan. Bake at 350 degrees for about 25 minutes.
-submitted by Amy Mynter Richardson

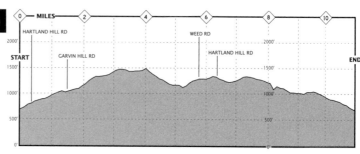

MilesDirections *(continued)*

1.5 Bear right off the pavement onto the dirt surface of Garvin Hill Road. This is a beautiful road—narrow, with big, old maples, and relatively rough for a town dirt road. The land on the right for this first section of Garvin Hill is protected and is known as the Eshqua Bog and Wildlife Preserve.

4.8 After cresting the top of Garvin Hill, the descent brings you to Appledore Farm, which is a well-established horse farm on the left. Turn left here on Weed Road.

5.3 Bear left at the "Y" on Hartland Hill Road.

6.3 Bear left again and look for the Richardson Farm Road on the left. The farm is a well-known family farm with a large maple sugaring operation in the spring months.

(continues on next page)

The Richardson farm is a local example of a dairy farm getting by thanks to creative additions to their farming skills. The 40 Jersey cows that roam the high meadows provide rich milk on a daily basis. In these days, however, this milk is not nearly enough for the local farmer to survive on. The Richardsons (now in their fifth generation on this farm) also make split rail fencing and produce some of the best maple syrup in Vermont. A visit to the Billings Farm Museum in downtown Woodstock shows off the simple elegance of the Richardson farm's wooden fences, as the posts and rails here seem to wander around the farm for miles.

The Richardson sugaring operation is no backyard rig either, but a well organized collection of hundreds of trees whose sap is boiled down into sweet gallons of Vermont's trademark syrup. On a spring day, it's worth trekking up to the farm sugarhouse to see the process, especially if the steam pouring from the cabin implies that sweet syrup is boiling at that moment.

While many of Richardson's maples are tapped by the modern method of plastic lines, they still handle hundreds of buckets the old-fashioned way. A tractor pulls a metal storage container through the usually deep spring snow and stops at centrally located spots where buckets can be retrieved and emptied, then hung back on their taps for another run. The cyclist's dilemma of typi-

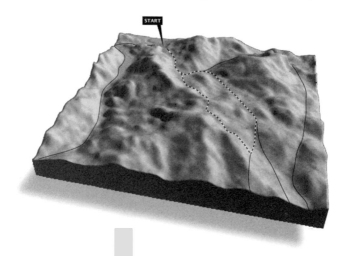

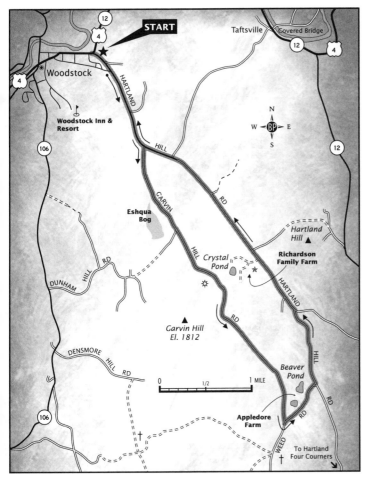

Ride Information

Local Attractions/Events:
Richardson Family Farm
  (802) 436-2246
Billings Farm & Museum
  (802) 457-2355
Sugarbush Farm
  1-800-281-1767
Nature Conservancy
  (802) 229-4425
Woodstock Chamber of Commerce
  (802) 457-3555
Eshqua Bog Nature Area: call the
  Nature Conservancy in
  Montpelier: (802) 229-4425

Local Bike Shops:
In Woodstock:
Cyclery Plus
  (802) 457-3377
Woodstock Sports
  (802) 457-1568

Maps:
USGS: Hartland, VT; Woodstock
  South, VT; Woodstock North, VT;
  Quechee, VT
DeLorme: Vermont Atlas &
  Gazetteer; Page 31 C-8

cally stronger legs than arms can be remedied by joining in on one of these bucket details. After a few hundred buckets, these sugaring folks show their fitness. Syrup can be purchased at the farm year-round, and as most of the ride is downhill from here, you could easily haul a gallon back home on your bike. *(See the **In Addition** on page 144 for more information on **maple sugaring**.)*

To finish the tour of this highland, the dirt road leads back to the original pavement you climbed when leaving Woodstock. This makes for a pleasant descent into town, with views of the Barnard and Pomfret hills to the north. Once in town, you can visit the Vermont Institute of Natural Science and Raptor Center (802) 457-2779, which is just a few miles out of town. Their living museum of over 25 species of hawks, owls, and eagles is quite unusual. Nature trails on the 77-acre preserve aren't open for biking but are great for a good walk.

MilesDirections *(continued)*

8.8 Back on the blacktop and still heading downhill.

10.6 Reach an intersection with the busy corner on Route 4 in Woodstock. Turn right toward Cumberland Farms.

10.7 Reach the finish. How much maple syrup did you haul back with you?

Kedron Valley

Kedron Valley, in which South Woodstock lies, gets its name from the tiny brook that runs through it. The name "Kedron" is derived from a stream in the Bible which is said to rise east out of Jerusalem, and the valley surrounding it is thought to be the "land of promise." This stunning valley between Woodstock and Reading is thus aptly named.

Those who visit can enjoy exploring backroads and trails of all kinds. The network of dirt roads in this area is outstanding and includes lots of junctions where many of the roads fade into unmaintained class-4 routes, perfect for mountain biking. This area is also well known for its horse farms, so be on the lookout for equines, common to these back roads and trails.

In the center of town is the Kedron Valley Inn, built in the early 1800s. It is one among a cluster of historic brick buildings in the village. The others include some from the Green Mountain Perkins Academy which was established in the mid-1800s. This educational institution functioned until the turn of the century and is now being preserved in its original state.

One of the more humorous footnotes in South Woodstock's history tells of the "Pilgrims" who lived in the area in the early nineteenth century. Apparently this particular group of settlers believed in communing with nature *naturally*—or shall we say "au natural." Being nude just happened to be one of the ways they expressed their beliefs. It appears the tradition hasn't lasted, but perhaps some Pilgrim descendants are carrying on the practice somewhere high in the hills. Be on the lookout!

Ride Specs

Start: Near the South Woodstock Fire Station
Length: 9.4 miles
Approximate Riding Time: 2 hours
Rating: Moderate
Terrain: Singletrack, double-track, paved roads, dirt roads
Other Uses: Cross-country skiing, horseback riding

Getting There

From **Woodstock** – Take **Route 106 south** to **South Woodstock** (about 5 miles). Pass through the village of South Woodstock. Turn **left** at the fire house at the bottom of **Morgan Hill Road**. Park here on the dirt parking spot. **Be sure not to park on the pavement.**

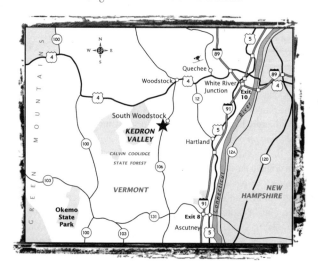

Some of the territory covered along this tour of the hills bordering Calvin Coolidge State Forest is the same as that used for the 100-mile endurance race held here each year. This 100-mile race is designed for both runners and horseback riders who compete along the gnarly tracks over hill and valley for up to 24 hours. Local residents get up at dawn to watch the courageous procession go by and are likely to be seen handing out food and water to the participants. The event raises funds for handicapped athletes.

One year, several mountain bikers from the area were invited to compete in the race. At one point, they were passed by the lead runner, even with the biker's head start. The cyclists eventually overcame the runner on the longer dirt road sections, but they were hard pressed to maintain the lead. Though it was a nice idea, the confusion of horses and runners *and* bikers, all in one race, was a little much, so nearby Ascutney now hosts a 50-mile race just for mountain bikers.

This short ride of under 10 miles can easily be made longer by connecting some of the local back roads or by exploring some of the class-4 roads along the way. To begin, park at the Firehouse on the gravel side of the lot. Head out Route 106, keeping your eyes peeled for Noah Woods Road. From Noah Woods Road, it's a steady uphill on a surface that becomes progressively less maintained. Some technical rocky sections next to the rushing brook are fun. There are a few intersections with snowmobile trails and some private trails as well. The ride stays on old abandoned town roads and, in a few miles, rejoins the town-maintained Long Hill Road—just below Old Baldy Mountain and Fletcher Hill.

A long roaring downhill reinforces the notion that the ride has been all uphill so far. It's important to be looking for the intersections, as they tend to come up on you rather quickly. The dirt road that turns to rough doubletrack at about the seven-mile marker is especially hard to recognize, as it is not well marked and is at the bottom of a long downhill. (If you miss it, Town Highway #36 will

MilesDirections

0.0 START from the South Woodstock Firehouse parking lot. (Be sure to park on the gravel side near the brook, not on the asphalt.) Turn left out of the lot on Route 106 south. The surface is paved for about one mile.

1.3 Turn right on Noah Woods Road. This is a town dirt road, paralleled by a bubbling stream for the duration of the fairly lengthy climb.

1.8 Reach a split in the road. Bear right, past a house.

3.0 Bear right at the "T."

3.7 After a short steep descent, the trail dumps out onto a regular dirt road, Long Hill Road. Prepare for a long downhill through horse country. There are often equestrian riders on these roads and trails, so be alert.

4.4 Bear left at the split in the road after the fast downhill, passing an old house on the left.

5.4 Bear right, continuing downhill.

5.8 Turn left just past the Michael J. Fox estate (careful, the turn is not marked). His home is the one surrounded by the quaint, but strong looking white fence, with enough shrubbery in the summer to hide a good view. Travel up this road to the left and climb the short steep hill, keeping your eyes out for the next right turn.

(continues on next page)

MilesDirections *(continued)*

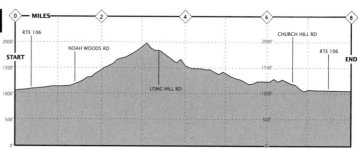

6.2 Turn right up a sharp steep hill on an old town route used by farmers and equestrians. It's often messy if it has recently rained. Stay straight on this road.

6.8 Reach an intersection at the top of the climb. Turn right on Church Hill Road and head downhill past several old farms. Enjoy the view of Kedron Valley.

7.3 Reach Route 106. Turn right past the Kedron Valley Inn and the South Woodstock general store. This little village is exceptionally picturesque with its collection of old brick houses.

7.8 Turn left at the firehouse into the parking lot. You're back!

still bring you right back to South Woodstock.) This trail connects to Church Hill Road which is only a few miles, as the crow flies, from the Vermont Institute of Natural Science. The institute (better known as VINS) is famous for its raptor center for birds of prey, some of which are recovering from injuries. It's definitely worth a visit.

The ride ends in South Woodstock village, where the general store is a fun place to stop for snacks and good conversation. If you're lucky, you could sit in on some of the great stories of the mud season.

In Addition...

Maple Sugaring

The first white settlers in Vermont learned from the Native Americans the craft of collecting sap from the plentiful sugar maples, and then boiling it down to sweet syrup. This renewable forest resource was crucial to the survival of the early pioneers, and was sometimes the chief article of food in times of hardship.

Today, Vermont's pure maple syrup is one of its most popular

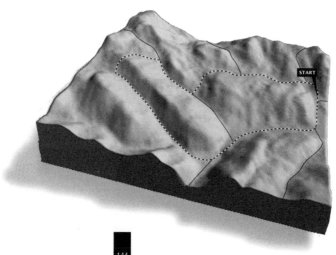

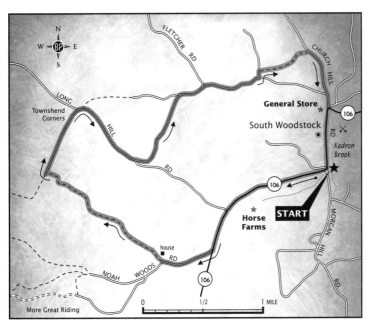

Ride Information

Local Attractions:
Vermont Institute of Natural
    Science: Raptor Center (birds of
    prey) and walking trails
    (802) 457-2779
Woodstock Chamber of Commerce
    (802) 457-3555

Local Bike Shops:
In Woodstock:
Cyclery Plus
    (802) 457-3377
Woodstock Sports
    (802) 457-1568

Maps:
USGS: Woodstock South, VT;
    Hartland, VT
DeLorme: Vermont Atlas &
    Gazetteer; Page 31 E-8

products on the market, and is produced in the state with much pride, and often by farming families who have sugared for generations. The Indians knew to begin tapping the maple trees in March when the crows first appeared and began their raucous cawing. These days it's a more delicate balance between cold nights and warm days that lets folks know the sap is running.

Maple trees are long lived, and an old tree that is cut down may show the succession of taps in the built in history of its growth rings. Slash marks from early settler's axes are found deep inside. Next are the large holes used for older wooden spouts, and finally the more exact drill marks of modern times.

The sap itself is clear when it runs from the tree, and has a slightly sweet taste. Sugar makers collect and boil about 35 gallons of sap to make one gallon of syrup. Taste and quality of sap varies widely from tree to tree and from area to area. Moisture, temperature, and the tree's heredity are all thought to play a role in the taste that eventually emerges.

Although Vermont is not the only state to produce maple syrup, folks consider the sweet stuff produced here in the Green Mountains to be of exceptional quality, and to perhaps have some of the mystical wonder added to it that seems to come from these hills. There are many small local sugarbushes around the state, so be sure to visit one when the steam is pouring out the sugarhouse smokestack, because that means the sap is a' runnin'.

Mount Ascutney View

Ride Specs

Start: Park & Ride lot at
Route 131 (Exit 8 from I-91)
Length: 12.6 miles
Approximate Riding Time:
1-2 hours
Rating: Moderate
Terrain: Paved roads, dirt
roads

Getting There

From **White River Junction** –
Take **I-91 south** to **Exit 8** and
take **Route 131** for about 100
meters. Park in the **Park &
Ride** lot immediately after
the exit ramp.

The peak of Mount Ascutney is a distinctive feature in southeastern Vermont. The summit looms some 2,000 feet above the surrounding terrain and is visible for miles around. Ascutney is a "monadnock" (meaning it is a single hill of resistant rock standing in the middle of a plain) made up largely of quartz syenite rock, which withstood the glaciation and erosion that wore away the surrounding softer rock. Mountain biking in the region around Mount Ascutney provides awesome views of the peak and the nearby Connecticut River Valley. This dirt road tour which starts in Weathersfield, explores some easily accessed backcountry byways that climb to heights with excellent vantage in all directions.

Mount Ascutney is located between three towns—Weathersfield, Windsor, and West Windsor. The village of Brownsville, in West Windsor, is where the alpine ski area and mountain bike center are located. (Not to confuse you, it is typical of Vermont to have villages located within larger towns of different names.) The Ascutney Mountain Bike Center is but a few years old and already has promoted some popular races. They also rent bikes and charge a nominal fee to ride on their cross-country ski trail network. There is also excellent riding on the surrounding dirt roads. A challenging climb to the summit of Mount Ascutney can be made on the paved road. This road was built with the help of the Civilian Conservation Corps soon after the 1,500-acre Ascutney State Park was instituted in 1933.

On the east side of Mount Ascutney is an old quarry, which

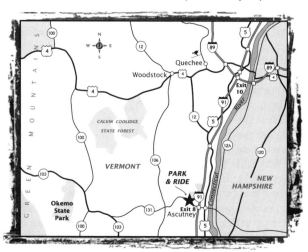

furnished "Windsor" granite (this has a dark green color, as opposed to the traditional gray). Stones were quarried here for the Columbia University library and a bank in Montreal.

This ride conveniently begins just off the interstate and immediately ascends up Goulden Ridge Road. The views up above are sometimes worth the climb. The fields begin to open up on each side after about the first mile and a half, and the Connecticut River Valley stretches clearly below. The ride then passes Pinnacle Rock on the right, and the first glimpse of Mount Ascutney is to the north.

At the intersection with the paved Weathersfield Center Road, the ride goes down Cady Hill Road. But first take a right on the pavement. It is worth traveling the extra half-mile up the blacktop to see the panoramic view from near Pikes Peak. The Green Mountains to the west include Okemo Mountain and Terrible Mountain. This view also looks toward Ludlow and Lake Rescue.

Apparently Lake Rescue was so named for an incident that

MilesDirections

0.0 START from the Park & Ride at the "Claremont/Ludlow" exit off I-91, just to the west of the interstate on Route 131. Head west on Route 131, looking for Goulden Ridge Road, which is the first left after the Vermont Public Service buildings.

0.3 Turn left on Goulden Ridge Road, and be prepared to climb for the first mile or so.

1.3 At the "Y," bear to the right.

1.7 Be sure to turn around and check out the view to the east of the lower Connecticut River Valley. Stay straight on this road, as several other roads intersect along the way. Look for the first view of Mount Ascutney off to the right.

2.4 A bit of rest from the uphill.

3.0 Steep uphill section. Again there is a great view looking back to the east.

3.2 Views of Mount Ascutney to the north.

3.6 After a steep descent, there is an intersection with the paved Weathersfield Center Road. The ride goes straight across, past an old farm and down the steep Cady Hill Road. To the left is Weathersfield Center, and to the right is an excellent vista of the Green Mountains, including Okemo. After the view, be prepared for a gnarly descent on the narrow, twisty, rough Cady Hill.

4.2 Pass Perkins Hill Road.

(continues on next page)

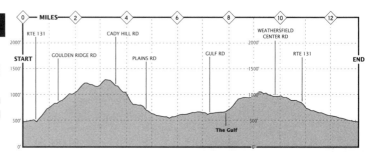

MilesDirections (continued)

4.9 Intersection with the paved Reservoir Basin Road. Turn right, and take the next immediate right on Plains Road. Stay to the right through the next intersection. The Plains Road winds along through flatter valley farmland for the next few miles.

5.4 Pass a large farm. Off to the left, an old cemetery with stone walls is visible across the field.

7.3 Four-way intersection at Nelson's Corners. Turn right and head up to the Gulf.

7.9 Pass through the Gulf, a narrow channel through steep walls of rock on each side.

8.4 At the four corners, Mount Ascutney is in view directly ahead. Turn right on Gravelin Road. This road is up high and passes through open meadows and some nice farms.

9.0 Pass Beaver Pond Road off to the left.

9.7 Intersection with the paved Weathersfield Center Road again. Turn left and roll downhill to Route 131.

10.8 Turn right on Route 131.

12.2 Pass Goulden Ridge Road where the ride started.

12.6 Reach the Park & Ride parking lot.

occurred along its shores. A farmer crossing the lake in the winter on horseback had nearly reached the far side when he broke through the ice. The horse managed to get out, but the farmer was trapped and getting cold quickly. The horse then backed up to the farmer on command, allowing him to grab hold of its tail and pull himself safely to shore. Had the farmer cut off the horse's tail, as was the custom in those days (it tended to get in the way of plows, harness furrows, and things of the like), he wouldn't have been so lucky.

After you take in the view, the ride heads down the rough Cady Hill Road and begins the loop back through the

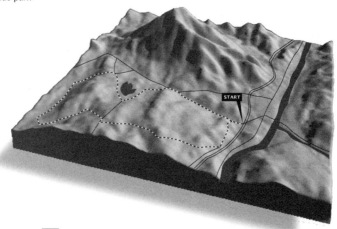

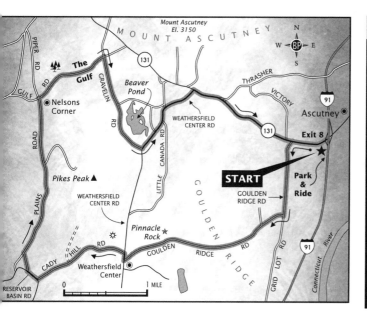

Ride Information

Local Information:
Mount Ascutney Region Chamber
   of Commerce:
   (802) 674-5910

Local Attractions/Events:
Mount Ascutney Mountain Bike
   Center: Brownsville, VT
   (802) 484-7711
In early October: Annual 50-mile
   Mountain Bike Race. Call VASS
   (802) 484-3525.

Maps:
USGS maps: Ascutney, VT
DeLorme: Vermont Atlas &
   Gazetteer; Page 31 K-11

farmland on Plains Road, passes through Nelson's Corners, and finally climbs up to the "Gulf." The Gulf is a narrow channel through the rocks with just enough room for a dirt road. The road is dark and shadowy through here. Since the path leads nowhere particularly important, you can't help but wonder why it was ever constructed, considering the labor involved. After the Gulf, another quick view of Ascutney is seen before the final downhill back to the main road.

After finishing your ride, a visit to nearby Windsor is interesting. Windsor boasts the Old Constitution House, where the Vermont constitution was born. It is also the location of a rather awesome covered bridge, which spans the entire breadth of the Connecticut River to neighboring Cornish, New Hampshire. It's quite a sight.

Town Meeting Day

The first Tuesday of each March is Town Meeting Day in Vermont. Each town holds a meeting (usually in the town hall) where issues are raised, debated, and voted on. This trademark of New England town government is alive and well in Vermont, and is especially entertaining when an issue like deer hunting comes to the floor. This hallmark of early democracy was apparently taken from the early American Indian tribes who held similar tribal meetings to decide on major issues.

Putney Mountain Tour

P utney is one of a collection of southern Vermont towns which were chartered early (in Putney's case 1753) and settled by enthusiastic pioneers who appreciated the combination of fertile lands from the nearby Connecticut River valley and the pristine hill country above. Today, Putney is a favorite stop for many cyclists for a variety of reasons. Most obvious is the unique bike shop just off the main drag called the West Hill Shop. A friend from New York City once told me he refused to stop by because he was afraid it would pale to the image he'd gotten from their web page (http://www.putney.net/westhill/clubhous.htm). He envisioned a small, homey, friendly place with a surprising array of both useful and hard to find cycling parts and gear. His description was so accurate that I was quick to put an end to his worries.

Besides the West Hill Shop (which hosts an incredible mountain bike race over almost entirely singletrack terrain), Putney has a lot to offer the visiting explorer. You'll find the Putney Co-op (Vermont's oldest), the Putney Inn (a true classic), a general store, sugarhouses, a bakery, apple orchards, and high up on the hill, the Putney School (a well-known private high school). But perhaps the most valuable asset for those of us on knobby tires is the Putney area's terrain.

With a solid community of enthusiastic cyclists and cross-country skiers, the trails and back roads in Putney, Brookline, and surrounding Newfane are incredible. Rolling apple orchards often open up to a spectacular view of the Connecticut River Valley

Ride Specs

Start: West Hill Shop
Length: 18.8 miles
Approximate Riding Time:
 3 hours
Rating: Moderate to Difficult
Terrain: Singletrack, double-track, dirt roads
Other Uses: Cross-country skiing, hiking, horseback riding

Getting There

From **Brattleboro** – Take **I-91 north** to **Exit 4** to **Putney.** Park at the **West Hill Shop,** which is within eyesight of the exit ramp.

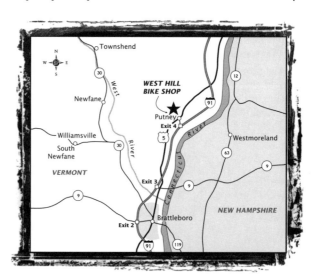

below, and the undulating hills are challenging for all levels. Group rides often leave from the shop, so be sure to check their schedule.

Putney is the home to many talented craftspeople, who produce a range of products, from drums to baskets to pottery and jewelry. In the mid-nineteenth century, it was also the home to a Utopian commune, founded by J. H. Noyes. More traditional townsfolk frowned on some of its progressive practices, so the group relocated to Oneida, New York.

One of the more comical tales coming out of Putney took place in the late 1700s. At that time, a law stated that bankrupt estates (of which there were many) would float with a widow to her next marriage—should she marry again. This would mean that her previous husband's debt would become her new husband's debt. Major Moses Joy of Putney was determined to avoid this complication when marrying a widow from Newfane. He discovered that if the marriage took place with the widow completely stripped of possessions, she would be free of any encumbrances (including the bankrupt estate). The ceremony took place in 1789, with the widow and her witness in a closet with the widow's hand extending through a hole cut in the door. An understanding parson presided over the union. After the ceremony, the naked widow was given some clothes purchased by Moses Joy himself (passed through the door, of course). The widow then emerged completely absolved of any previous debts and was the new Mrs. Joy. I'm fairly certain such extremes are no longer necessary in Putney.

The Putney Mountain Tour starts from town and climbs gradually but steadily up dirt roads to the Putney School. The school is the site of the annual West Hill Mountain Bike Race and shows off a panoramic view of the lands north in Westminster. A short piece of pavement connects the ride to the Putney Mountain Road and more uphill is in store. For riders wanting a shorter loop, the school or the bottom of Putney Mountain Road would serve well as starting points.

MilesDirections

0.0 START from the West Hill Bike Shop. Head past the elderhousing on the left on Carol Brown Way, a short connector to old Route 5.

0.2 Turn left on the paved old Route 5.

0.8 Turn right on Houghton Brook Road, still paved. Prepare for a gradual uphill that leads up to the Putney School.

1.2 Pass straight through the four corners, and continue on Houghton Brook. The pavement changes to dirt.

2.5 Watt Pond Road forks off to the left, stay to the right on Houghton Brook.

3.2 Pass the Putney School on the right. One could start from here to make the loop shorter. The view of the valley and orchards below is great from these high meadows and playing fields. The steep downhill after the school is paved. Be prepared for a sharp left at the bottom.

3.6 Turn left on West Hill Road. It is paved for the next mile or so. Pass the first right turn for Aiken and Orchard Hill Roads, but make a note that this is where the loop will intersect on the other end.

4.5 Turn right on Putney Mountain Road, and stay to the right as Holland Hill Road immediately forks left. This narrow dirt road climbs steadily to the trails for Putney Mountain.

5.3 Pass through a four-way intersection.

6.1 Stay to the left on Putney Mountain Road, as Banning Road goes right. This is the road we will eventually come back to. It will complete the loop after the out and back trip up Putney Mountain.

(continues on next page)

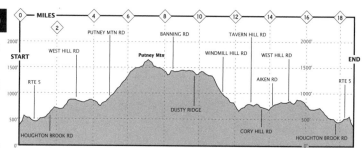

MilesDirections (continued)

6.5 Turn right into the parking area for the Putney Mountain trails. Be aware and respectful of the many hikers that frequent this area. Head up the trail and turn left at the first fire pit (about one tenth of a mile from the parking lot).

6.65 After turning at the fire pit, make an immediate right, and head up the singletrack to the summit. There are several routes to choose from depending on your technical abilities, as the trails meet at the summit.

7.2 Reach the top of Putney Mountain for an awesome 360 degree view of the New Hampshire and Vermont hills and peaks. After exploring the summit, head back down to Putney Mountain Road.

7.9 Turn left on Putney Mountain Road.

8.3 Turn left onto Banning Road. It is a town-maintained dirt road that will eventually lead to the Windmill Hill area trails.

9.4 At the "Y," bear to the right, as a private road goes off to the left. Nice stone walls surround the adjacent farm.

9.7 The town-maintained road turns into an old class-4 road. It cruises downhill through beautiful hardwood forests. Be on alert for runners and hikers.

9.9 At the "T," go left on what is known as Dusty Ridge. Down the trail to the right are some boroughs, locally thought to be Celtic or Indian.

10.6 Intersection marked with an array of signposts for faraway places and some for local spots also. Follow the sign for "Putney, the long way," to the right. Taking a left leads to the town of Brookline.

11.1 After descending a series of dips and gullies, pass a steel gate off to the left—tricky riding when leaves are on the ground.

(continues on next page)

The Putney Mountain Road climbs past thick forests on each side. Notice that many of the maples are hooked up with plastic lines to sap collection tanks. At the parking lot to Putney Mountain, the terrain and riding surfaces change dramatically. Here, roots and rocks can be found in abundance, providing technical challenges on every corner. The trails on Putney Mountain look confusing, but follow the route uphill and they'll join at the summit. Be on the lookout for folks walking, running, or hiking—and be sure to ride cautiously around them. The best etiquette is to stop riding completely and let those on foot pass by, or simply walk your bike around them. The hikers in this area are largely responsible for the trail maintenance, so proper manners are essential.

The summit of Putney Mountain is wide open and rocky, explaining why it once stood as a barrier for travel westward. The town of Brookline is nearby. Most of the west half of the mountain is located in Brookline. Descend carefully and head out toward the second half of the ride in the Windmill Hill area.

Because of the large climb you just made, the trails in the Dusty Ridge and Windmill Hill areas are full of downhill fun. Be careful if the leaves have fallen, as they can disguise roots and

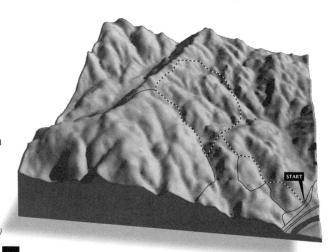

Beachway Press

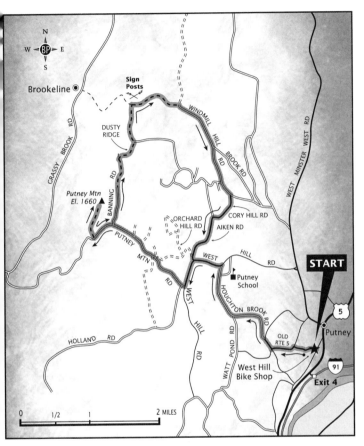

Ride Information

Local Route Information:
Brattleboro Area Chamber of
  Commerce: (802) 254-4565

Local Bike Shops:
West Hill Bike Shop
  (802) 387-5718

Maps:
USGS maps: Newfane, VT; Saxtons
  River, VT
DeLorme: Vermont Atlas &
  Gazetteer; Page 23 D-9

MilesDirections (continued)

11.4 Turn left on the dirt road, and then in another tenth of a mile, turn right at the "T," onto Windmill Hill Road. Prepare for a rollicking downhill.

12.3 Pass the turn for Brook Road, and go straight across on Windmill Hill Road.

13.1 Turn left down Tavern Hill Road, and look for the next right.

13.4 Turn right on Cory Hill Road. Pass the apple orchards on the left and then fly down the steep curves to the intersection with the pavement of Aiken Road.

14.0 Turn left on Aiken Road.

14.9 Turn left on West Hill Road. This is the intersection noted earlier in the ride, on the way to Putney Mountain Road. Cruise downhill, taking in the views on the way to the turn for the Putney School.

15.4 Turn rigm of Houghton Brook Road, turn left on old Route 5.

18.6 Turn right on Carol Brown Way.

18.8 Reach the West Hill Shop.ht up the hill to the Putney School. The uphill is paved.

15.6 Pass the Putney School to the left. It's all downhill from here to town.

18.0 At the bottom of Houghton Brook Road, turn left on old Route 5.

18.6 Turn right on Carol Brown Way.

18.8 Reach the West Hill Shop.

rocks. The long downhill intersects the dirt roads after passing through a well marked intersection of humorous signposts for both local and distant destinations (in case you're headed to Los Angeles). Once on the dirt roads, more downhill is in store, but be sure to catch the views east through the apple orchards.

Once back on the pavement of West Hill, there is only one uphill left on the road back to town. It is a steep, sharp climb, which leads to the Putney School and was once part of the cyclocross course held in these high meadows. The last miles are all downhill, and may call for a windbreaker if the weather is cool. Back in town, check out the the Putney Bakery, and maybe cruise south a few miles to Brattleboro to visit one of their many wonderful restaurants.

Old Stratton Turnpike

Ride Specs

Start: Stratton Village
Length: 16.5 miles
Approximate Riding Time:
2-3 hours
Rating: Moderate
Terrain: Doubletrack, dirt
roads
Other Uses: Cross-country
skiing, snowmobiles

Getting There

From **Wilmington** – Head
north on **Route 100** through
West Dover, past **Mount
Snow,** heading toward **West
Wardsboro.** Turn **left** on
Stratton-Arlington Road at
West Wardsboro. Follow
Stratton-Arlington Road for
about three miles until
reaching the tiny town of
Stratton. Park here and
begin the ride.

his route called the Old Stratton Turnpike used
to be the route for stagecoaches over the Green
Mountains to the Connecticut River Valley and
Brattleboro area. Because of its long history of
use, it has some landmarks and interesting stories that make the trip come alive. Since most of
the route is now in the Green Mountain National
Forest, you get a feeling of timelessness, which helps take your
imagination back to when Daniel Webster gave a famous speech
to a crowd of 15,000 in a clearing on the side of the road. A monument to the orator's visit can be found in the early part of this
route, soon after the Grout Pond excursion. It is thought, however, that the 15,000 head-count may be a little padded, as it was
made during the heat of the "hard cider campaign;" and under-
standably, as the "bowl was flowing," "heads" tended to multiply.

The Grout Pond area is not open to mountain biking but is an
excellent sidetrip, as it may someday have its trails open for biking. The National Forest is very strict about its "No Mountain
Biking" rules, so take heed. There are several experimental trail
networks open in the western part of the state, and it seems only
a matter of time before we see them spread. But for now, the
Grout Pond trails are great for hiking and wilderness camping.

Along the turnpike—it's difficult to notice these days—most of
the region used to be farming country before being overtaken by
forests. Scattered throughout the woods are the remains of the old
farms, sometimes with only an apple tree or lilac bush left to mark
the site.

The route crosses the Appalachian and Long Trails, both of
which offer a hike to the nearby peak of Stratton Mountain (with
gorgeous views). The height of the pass is also the site of an old

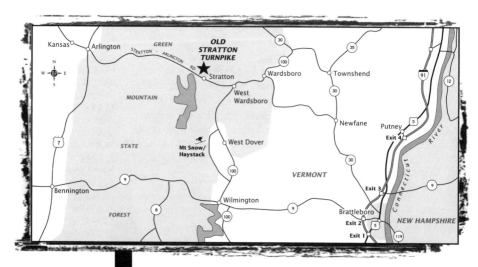

tragedy. In 1821, a man, his wife, and infant daughter started across this pass from Arlington. Misjudging the snow depth, they made it halfway when the horse could go no further. The man struck out for the town of Stratton, hoping to get help for his stranded family, but he collapsed in the snow from fatigue before getting there. In the morning, he was found frozen but alive. His wife did not survive, but the baby, wrapped in blankets and cloaks, "looked up and smiled," according to a poem written later about the tale. The poem was set to music and was known to bring a tear to the eye of even the hardiest of men.

Before the terrain changes to cliffs and roaring brooks, there is a site called Kelley Stand. It's also the place where the present day Lye Brook wilderness trails begin. Kelley Stand was once a stagecoach stop that served as an inn, music hall, and ballroom. The

top floor was the ballroom, complete with a high arching ceiling and a stand for fiddlers. Festive parties from the valleys would travel up to the tavern to dance and eat trout. In the book, *This is Vermont*, Walter and Margaret Hard write a descriptive poem about Kelley Stand. Their story of dancing and romancing stirs a wealth of images, including singing fiddlers, noisy parties, and square dance calls.

The westernmost town on the old turnpike is curiously named Kansas, in one of the most dramatically mountainous areas of Vermont. Apparently, as the story goes, an early settler of the region wanted to join the westward movement of the time to Kansas. Each year he would say: "This is the year I'm going." And invariably, he would not go. Years went by and he finally died, still in Vermont, never having made the journey. Some kinfolk, who were concerned he might be remembered as a liar, named the area Kansas.

MilesDirections

0.0 START from the tiny town of Stratton. Head west on the road toward Arlington. It begins as pavement.

2.8 For a nice side trip, turn here on Forest Road #262, toward Grout Pond.

4.0 Reach Grout Pond and the trailhead for lots of wilderness hiking and camping. At present, mountain biking isn't allowed on these trails in the Green Mountain National Forest, but may be sometime in the future. Check with the ranger on duty or read the information boards to see where the forest service roads go, because those are legal to ride. Head back out to the main road after a picnic or swim in the pond. Turn left again on the old turnpike.

5.4 Surface changes to dirt.

5.5 Pass the monument where Daniel Webster spoke to a supposed 15,000 people.

6.0 Cross over the east branch of the Deerfield River and pass the trailheads for both Appalachian and Long Trails.

7.0 The Stratton Pond Trail goes off to the right. Recreational Road #71 goes off to the left and runs south through Somerset to Searsburg. It passes near the Somerset Reservoir and through New England Power Company land—which is open for mountain biking. The riding here is supposedly excellent. Check at Mount Snow for more info. Continue straight on the turnpike.

(continues on next page)

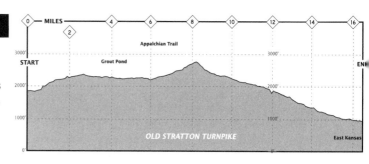

MilesDirections *(continued)*

8.3 Reach the height of the land. A nice overlook facing Mount Equinox and the surrounding peaks in the Arlington/Manchester region. Prepare for a LONG downhill. A good spot to put on an extra layer of clothing if it's chilly.

9.6 Beaver ponds off to the left.

10.1 Kelley Stand and the turn for Lye Brook Wilderness to the right. The next few miles have some unique topography as the road narrows and Whetstone Bluff's cliffs close in. The Roaring Branch River can be quite a sight with spring melt or fall rains, as it winds downhill with the rough road.

14.7 The first houses of East Kansas.

16.5 Intersection with the paved North Road. Turn left to go to Kansas and Route 7, or right to go toward Sunderland. This is the natural stopping or turning around point in the ride.

The ride's terrain is typical of any route over a gap. It climbs steadily upwards for about seven miles—which is why the side trip to Grout Pond is a nice break. The surface is dirt, fairly narrow in sections, and a bit rougher and rockier than many town dirt roads—partially due to the fact that most of the turnpike is closed to traffic (but not skiing) in the winter. From the height of land, look west to Mount Equinox and the surrounding Green Mountains. Most of the ride is wilderness, so come prepared with water and snacks. After descending through Kelley Stand, the most dramatic part of the ride is the twisty mileage that parallels the Roaring Branch River under Whetstone Bluff. The high cliffs close in on both sides, leaving room only for single lane bridges and a darkened narrow dirt road below. At times, it seems the road will vanish along the rocky river from lack of space, but somehow the walls left room for the turnpike to pass.

It would be best to do the ride as a point to point trip, rather than out and back—but a round-trip can be done with adequate preparation for the long climbs and lengthy miles.

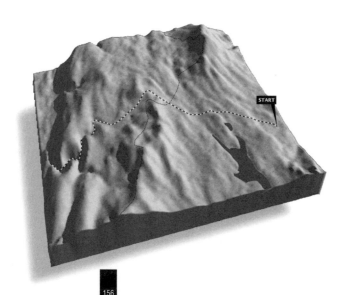

Beachway Press

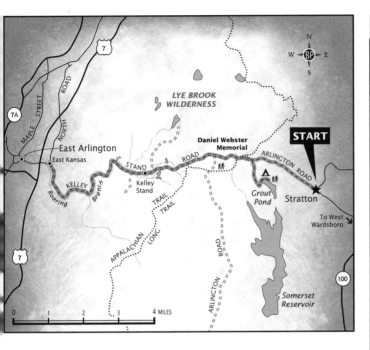

Ride Information

Local Route Information:
Green Mountain National Forest
(802) 886-2215

Schedule:
Road closed in winter months

Local Attractions:
Stratton Mountain Resort
1-800-STRATTON
Arlington Chamber of Commerce:
(802) 375-2800
Manchester and the Mountains
Chamber of Commerce
(802) 362-2100

Maps:
USGS Maps: Sunderland, VT
Stratton Mountain, VT
DeLorme maps: Vermont Atlas
and Gazetteer page 21, A-13

Dorset Bat Caves

Just north of Arlington, where the Old Stratton Turnpike ends, is the small town of Dorset. Dorset has a colorful past as a center for marble quarrying. It supplied the nation with marble in the nineteenth century. These days, the quiet village is better known for its scenery and access to the Green Mountains, including nearby Mount Aeolus.

The highlands of Mount Aeolus are home to a large cave, which has long been a favorite hibernation spot for a variety of bats, including the rare and endangered Indiana bats. These strange creatures flock yearly to the Dorset caves for their perfect winter weather conditions—40 degrees Fahrenheit and 80 percent humidity. These conditions enable them to sink into a state of torpor (similar to hibernation) and survive the winter.

Although bats may not seem like the most exciting animals, their disappearance would be noticed by most of us, as one bat eats up to 1,200 biting bugs per day! They also disperse seeds and pollinate countless flowers.

The Mount Aeolus bat caves are owned by the Vermont chapter of the Nature Conservancy and are open from May to September. For information on the annual trek to the caves each May, contact Bob West at the Manchester Historical Society: (802) 362-1577.

Mount Snow MTB Center

Ride Specs

Start: Crosstown Trailhead
Length: 6.5 miles
Approximate Riding Time: 1 hour
Rating: Moderate
Terrain: Singletrack, double-track
Other Uses: Cross-country skiing

Getting There

From **Wilmington** – Travel **north** on **Route100** to **West Dover.** Look for the signs in West Dover directing you to **Mount Snow** (they should be fairly obvious). Follow the Mount Snow access road to the **main base lodge.** Park here for tickets, then ask for directions to the **Crosstown trails.**

For the past few years, Mount Snow and the small town of West Dover have been home to hundreds of mountain bike racers, riders, and enthusiasts for one week in June when the World Cup Mountain Bike circuit comes to town. Known worldwide as technically challenging, the race here is one of the favorites on the circuit because of its thrilling sections that descend through gnarly Vermont woods over rocks, roots, and mud. It is well worth the trip to watch or race in the event as it sports one of the largest mountain bike expos in the region. There are plenty of real-life cycling heroes and heroines hanging about to meet as well.

Perhaps the hottest event at this World Cup week is the "Naked Criterium," which has truly become a Mount Snow original. The evening race is put together by a club from New York City who not only knows how to keep things interesting, but also how to keep them safe for the lightly clad racers. For those visiting the United States, especially the Europeans, this typically American event, which encircles a tiny dirt parking lot, is hard to fathom.

Besides the World Cup race, Mount Snow also offers mountain bikers a chance to attend the well known Mountain Bike School and Mountain Bike Center. 140 miles of trails are accessible from Mount Snow, with the surrounding Somerset Reservoir area contributing countless more trails. Tours are offered by the Center for two to seven hours—with experienced guides and rental bikes available. The chairlift to the 3,600-foot summit provides easy access to the trails on the mountain and is especially nice for prac-

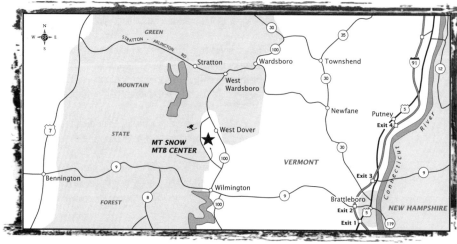

tice on the singletrack descents that are so well known here. Climbing to the summit on your bike is challenging, but the access road provides some breaks along the way up and lots of opportunities to check out the views of the southern hills and mountains of Vermont and New Hampshire.

Lots of events are on the schedule for mountain bikers, including a dual slalom series, some on-snow bike events, and several festivals. Nearby Haystack Mountain also has trails to explore, making the network here very impressive.

On the way to Haystack, cyclists will find a small trail system called Crosstown. This gentle, but technically challenging group of trails requires a trail pass and is well worth the side trip to check out.

Without the daunting, trademark climbs of most Vermont singletrack, the Crosstown trails weave in and out of a relatively flat valley with plenty of roots, rocks, and mud to give you the authentic feeling of riding in Vermont. There are also some smooth, faster trails that wind through these woods, so it can be a nice place for beginners as well.

After parking in the pullover off of Handle Road, the Crosstown trails lead east past the pond. Take a glance back at the peaks of Haystack and Mount Snow. The view is especially beautiful in the fall after the leaves are gone. The main Crosstown Trail runs down the middle of the network and is rather wide compared to the goat paths that run off from it into the forests. It's a good reference point, as some of the side trails can be confusing, but they all seem to dump back out onto this main trail sooner or later.

The first turn onto the singletrack leads you into a completely different environment than the main Crosstown Trail, as it is quite wooded and the narrow trail rolls and turns with the terrain. The singletrack winds around for a bit and ends up back on the Crosstown Trail heading again toward the golf course and airport. The ride eventually leaves the Crosstown Trail for the Airport Loop, accessed through the gate across the end of the trail.

MilesDirections

0.0 START from the Crosstown area pullover, south of Mount Snow on Handle Road. Head out on the Crosstown Trail, past the beaver pond on the right.

0.2 Beaver Trail goes off to the right. This is where the loop will reconnect at the end. Stay straight on Crosstown Trail.

0.3 Turn left into the singletrack.

0.4 Reach a three-way intersection with Berry Interesting, Fruit Loop, and the Suntec Trails. Turn left on the Suntec Trail. Typical Vermont singletrack ahead.

0.6 At this "T," turn right. Turning left takes you to the nearby condos.

0.8 The trail appears to curve to the left, but a small singletrack marked "to Berry Interesting" heads right. Turn right, and follow the narrow trail through the forest. Keep your head up as it twists and turns quickly.

1.3 Turn left at the intersection here, and in less than a tenth of a mile, turn left again, back out on Crosstown Road (the main trail). There is often a wet area next, depending on the amount of recent rain.

1.65 Pass around the gate and onto the paved Golf Course Road. The golf course is off to the right. Great views of Haystack and Mount Snow to the west.

(continues on next page)

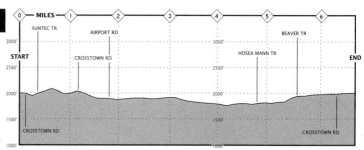

MilesDirections *(continued)*

1.85 Turn right on the gravel road just past the Mount Snow Clubhouse. Follow this gravel road down into the Partridge Condos, heading toward the airport.

2.45 Turn left on an unmarked road just before the airport entrance. This road goes on to some more condos and skirts around the back of the tennis courts and airport terminal.

2.8 Just after the tennis courts and just before the airport hangers, turn left on a trail heading into the woods running parallel with the first few hangers. It then turns more to the left and becomes a winding singletrack.

3.0 Pass through an intersection and the sign for Airport Loop.

3.7 At the "T," turn right. The trail is now a doubletrack and gradual downhill.

4.7 Turn right on the trail marked "Wetland Gap." The first section is quite rooty and then passes through a marshy area, across a stream, and past signs for the Hermitage. Proceed straight across the stream, under the power lines, and continue on the singletrack heading back to Crosstown.

5.2 Cross over the long bridge that spans some of the wetlands. Good place to look for wildlife. After the bridge is a wet area, where a singletrack diverges to the right. That is the Sugar Mama Trail, which will eventually lead back to Crosstown as well. Stay to the left and soon the sign for Hosea Mann will appear.

(continues on next page)

Keep your eyes open for the turns through the condos and around the airport, as they are not as well marked as some of the other turns. If you end up at the airport, you've gone a bit too far because the trail system skirts around it and heads south. This airport loop is doubletrack, from which a lot of smaller trails lead. Refer to the Mount Snow trail map to see which of these are open for exploring, as some may be closed or re-routed. Continue on the smooth downhill trail until the junction with the Wetland Gap Trail. This is just as it sounds, a trek across some marshy land to rejoin the Crosstown trails. Although it can be wet here, the bridges and overland routes are pretty good. There is one steep climb on the other side of the wetland.

After connecting back to the Crosstown singletrack, it is a flat trip back to the main trail. Lots of smaller trails diverge, allowing opportunities to explore and extend your ride. When you finally meet the familiar main Crosstown Trail, the beaver pond will be on your left, with a view of Mount Snow and Haystack in the background.

After your ride, you could head south on Route 100 for Wilmington where there are some interesting shops and good places to eat. North toward Jamaica and Londonderry is a

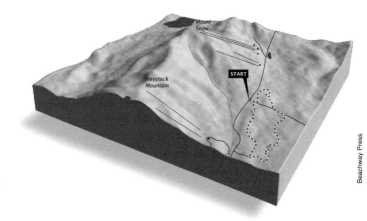

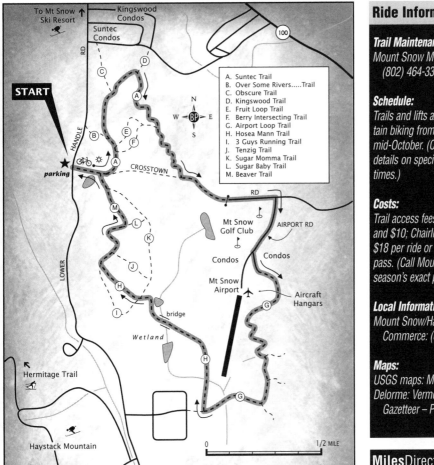

Ride Information

Trail Maintenance Hotline:
Mount Snow Mountain Bike Center
(802) 464-3333

Schedule:
Trails and lifts are open for mountain biking from late May through mid-October. (Call Mount Snow for details on specific dates and times.)

Costs:
Trail access fees are between $5 and $10; Chairlift rides are around $18 per ride or $28 for an all-day pass. (Call Mount Snow for this season's exact prices.)

Local Information:
Mount Snow/Haystack Chamber of Commerce: (802) 464-8092

Maps:
USGS maps: Mount Snow, VT
Delorme: Vermont Atlas & Gazetteer – Page 21 F-14

MilesDirections (continued)

5.4 Three Guys Running goes off to the left. Stay straight and climb up the sharp steep section ahead.
5.5 Turn right on the Beaver Trail. Over the next mile, the Tenzig Trail and then Sugar Baby Trail will intersect from the right. Stay straight on the gnarly Beaver Trail.
6.4 Intersection with Crosstown Trail. To return to the parking area, turn left. Pass Beaver Pond on the left.
6.55 Back at the parking area on Handle Road.

favorite route to travel for its natural beauty and classic Vermont towns along the way. Another option is to check out the overland route between Dover and Newfane, as it is well known for flea markets and fairs in the summer. The dirt roads on this route make excellent mountain bike riding terrain, and the views are outstanding.

Honorable Mentions

I t would be tough to map every one of Vermont's off-road bicycle rides into a single guidebook. There are far too many. Therefore, it is necessary to chart only the best bike rides the state has to offer, relegating other popular places for mountain biking to Honorable Mention status. And still, somehow, only a mere fraction of the state's rides are included. Compiled below is an index of great rides that did not make the A-list this time around, but deserve recognition. Check them out and let us know what you think. You may decide one or more of these rides deserves higher status in future editions or, perhaps, you may have a ride of you own that merits some attention.

A. The Central Vermont Rail Trail:

The Central Vermont Rail-Trail begins near the north end of the city of St. Albans, at the junction of Route 105 and Route 7. There is no organized parking. The first 10 miles travels from St. Albans to Sheldon Junction. The next 17 miles runs next to the Missisquoi River to Sheldon, continuing for a total of 27 miles. The trail passes through Sheldon Springs, North Sheldon, South Franklin, Enosburg Falls, East Berkshire, and Richford Village, ending at the Canadian border. Like most rail-trails, this one has a gentle grade and a uniform surface, excellent for beginners and those seeking the beauty of Franklin County. For more information, contact the Franklin/Grand Isle Regional Planning and Development Commission, 140 South Main, Saint Albans, VT 05478. (802) 524-5958.

B. Burke Mountain Cross-County Ski Area:

Run by long-time cyclist Stan Swain, this network of over 40 miles of trails has a good portion open to mountain biking in the summer months. Vermont Life Magazine called Burke's miles of trails "some of the prettiest and least tamed woodlands and hillsides in the Northeast Kingdom." Be sure to ride only on the trails open to mountain biking, as the ones closed are fairly wet in the off-season. Call 1-800-786-8338. The center is located in East Burke.

C. Cross Vermont Rail-Trail:

At present, the Cross-Vermont trail begins in South Ryegate, at the community ballfield on Route 302. It runs through Groton State Forest before ending in Marshfield Depot. It has about 20 miles of flat railbed with a gravel surface and reported sightings of moose and bear. Parking is also available in the Groton State Forest at Ricker or Kettle Ponds, with easy access to the trail. On the Marshfield end, the popular spot to begin or end is Rainbow Sweets, a bakery/café. Long-term plans for this trail call for a complete traverse of the state from east to west, eventually ending in Burlington. For more information, call the Vermont Agency of Natural Resources in Montpelier and talk to the Trail Coordinator—(802) 241-3614. See the Cross-Vermont Trail Trail on page 54 for a guided tour of a section of this railway.

D. Firefly Ranch:

Located in Bristol, this bed and breakfast has outlined some of the nicest backcountry rides in the Green Mountains. A vast network of dirt roads is the main system used here. Riders should expect to bring their own bikes and ask for help in planning a tour. PO Box 152, Bristol, VT 05443. (802) 453-2223

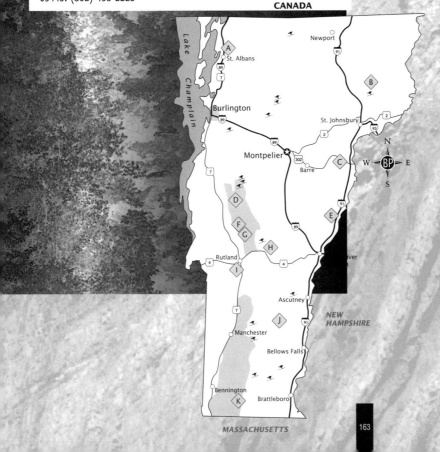

Honorable Mentions(Continued)

E. Coyote Hill Farm:

Located in the West Fairlee/Bradford area, this mountain bike camp has an excellent network of local trails, ranging from beginner to advanced. Tours are available, as is a full schedule of mountain bike camps and clinics. Rides to both Lake Fairlee and Lake Morey are possible from here. Call ahead for information and expect to bring your own bike. Lodging includes a secluded backcountry cabin located right on the trail system. Coyote Hill Farm is perfect for mountain bike getaways. Contact Coyote Hill, Box 312, Fairlee, VT 05045. (802) 222-5133. Coyote.Hill@connriver.net.

F. Moosalamoo:

This is a tract of 20,000 acres in the Green Mountain National Forest, located near the town of Middlebury on the western side of the state. Moosalamoo is an Abenaki word for "he trails the moose." If you're lucky you may even spot one yourself. This was also the summer home of poet Robert Frost. There are three trails open to mountain bikes in this region of the National Forest—Minnie Baker Trail, Leicester Hollow Trail, and the Silver Lake Trail. These trails are most easily accessed from Route 53, which runs along Lake Dunmore in Salisbury and Leicester. They are easily connected to the many forest service roads in the area, also legal for mountain bikes. For information, call the Middlebury Ranger District at (802) 388-4362. Other forest service districts with legal off-road trails are the Rochester District (802) 767-4362 and the Manchester District (802) 363-1251.

G.Blueberry Hill Cross-Country Ski Area:

Nearby to Moosalamoo is the Blueberry Hill trail network, which connects to the Breadloaf Wilderness Area and the trails described in the Moosalamoo Area. Blueberry Hill Inn, located in Goshen, is the center for these trails, and is well known for its fine fare and lodging. The best bet is to check in here and find out what's open for riding, as much of the land is privately owned. There is excellent riding north from the Inn on Forest Service Road #32, which runs right past the Moosalamoo Campground. Nearby Hogback and Romance provide plenty of challenging terrain. Call them at (802) 247-6735.

H. Cortina Inn Mountain Bike Trails:

Located off Route 4 in Killington, just one mile west of Pico Ski Area. The Cortina Center rents bikes and offers a map with local routes laid out in different colors for different levels of ability. This map offers a good overview of the local riding. Most of the riding is on old town roads, logging roads, and some singletrack trails. Several trips are planned for you in the Inn's brochure. Each of these rides include waterfalls, spectacular views, and of course, hills. Most of the trails at the Inn are geared for beginners, but just up the road, Killington's Mountain Bike Center offers more advanced riding. For more information about the Cortina Inn write HCR 34, Box 33, Killington, VT 05751. (802) 773-3331.

I. Delaware and Hudson Rail-Trail:

This trail runs northeast to southwest in the Rutland area, passing through Castleton, Poultney, West Pawlet, and West Rupert. Parking at Castleton State College provides access to the first section, which connects Castleton to Poultney. The next Vermont section may eventually connect to the Castleton section when the section of trail running through New York is completed and connected to these two Vermont trails. The second section runs from West Pawlet to West Rupert with public parking in Poultney and West Pawlet. These Vermont sections total 20 miles of scenic farmland, forests, and gravel railbeds. For more information, contact the Agency of Natural Resources, Department of Forest, Parks, and Recreation, RR2, Box 261, Pittsford, VT 05763. (802) 483-2314

J. Grafton Ponds Cross-Country Ski Area:

This ski center in the town of Grafton has plans for a mountain bike center, and already has a great selection of wilderness singletrack that is quite enjoyable. Several races over the last several years have been successfully run on these trails, and it seems the organizers at the center are excited about mountain biking. Colin Lawson is the person to talk to about available trails for riding. Call him at (802) 843-2400. The town of Grafton is well known for its production of excellent cheddar cheese and its historic Old Tavern.

K. Prospect Mountain Touring Center:

This popular cross-country ski touring center located off Route 9 in Woodford accesses some of Southern Vermont's most marvelous back-country wilderness. The trail system borders the George Aiken Wilderness and Stamford Meadows. Call (802) 442-2575.

Ski Resorts
[...for mountain biking?]

Ski resorts offer a great alternative to local trail riding. During the spring, summer, and fall, many resorts will open their trails for mountain biking and, just like during ski season, sell lift tickets to take you and your bike to the top of the mountain. Lodging is also available for the weekend mountain bike junkies, and rates are often discounted from the normal ski-season prices. Some resorts will even rent bikes and lead guided mountain bike tours. Call ahead to find out just what each resort offers in the way of mountain bike riding, and pick the one that best suits your fancy.

The following is a list of many of the ski resorts in Vermont that say yes! to mountain biking when the weather turns too warm for skiing.

Ascutney Mountain
Brownsville, VT
(802) 484-7711

Bolton Valley/Mountain Bike and Adventure Center
Bolton Valley, VT
(802) 434-4303

Burke Mountain
East Burke, VT
(802) 626-3305

Jay Peak
Jay, VT
1-800-451-4449

Killington Mountain Bike Center
Killington, VT
(802) 422-3333

Mount Snow Mountain Bike Center
West Dover, VT
(802) 464-3333

Stowe
Stowe, VT
(802) 253-7919
1-800-682-4534

Stratton Mountain
Stratton, VT
(802) 297-4139

Sugarbush
Warren, VT
(802) 583-2381

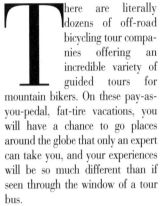

Fat Tire Vacations
[Bicycle Touring Companies]

There are literally dozens of off-road bicycling tour companies offering an incredible variety of guided tours for mountain bikers. On these pay-as-you-pedal, fat-tire vacations, you will have a chance to go places around the globe that only an expert can take you, and your experiences will be so much different than if seen through the window of a tour bus.

From Hut to Hut in the Colorado Rockies or Inn to Inn through Vermont's Green Mountains, there is a tour company for you. Whether you want hardcore singletrack during the day and camping at night, or you want scenic trails followed by a bottle of wine at night and a mint on each pillow, someone out there offers what you're looking for. The tours are well organized and fully supported with expert guides, bike mechanics, and "sag wagons" which carry gear, food, and tired bodies. Prices range from $100-$500 for a weekend to more than $2000 for two-week-long trips to far-off lands such as New Zealand or Ireland. Each of these companies will gladly send you their free literature to whet your appetite with breathtaking photography and titillating stories of each of their tours.

Selected Touring Companies

Elk River Touring Center
Slatyfork, WV
(304) 572-3771

Vermont Bicycling Touring
Bristol, VT
1-800-245-3868

Backroads
Berkley, CA
1-800-BIKE TRIP

Timberline Bicycle Tours
Denver, CO
(303) 759-3804

Roads Less Traveled
Longmont, CO
(303) 678-8750

Blackwater Bikes
Davis, WV
(304) 259-5286

Bicycle Adventures
Olympia, WA
1-800-443-6060

Trails Unlimited, Inc.
Nashville, IN
(812) 988-6232

Appendix:Repair and Maintenance

FIXING A FLAT

TOOLS YOU WILL NEED

- Two tire irons
- Pump (either a floor pump or a frame pump)
- No screwdrivers!!! (This can puncture the tube)

REMOVING THE WHEEL

The front wheel is easy. Simply open the quick release mechanism or undo the bolts with the proper sized wrench, then remove the wheel from the bike.

The rear wheel is a little more tricky. Before you loosen the wheel from the frame, shift the chain into the smallest gear on the freewheel (the cluster of gears in the back). Once you've done this, removing and installing the wheel, like the front, is much easier.

REMOVING THE TIRE

Step one: Insert a tire iron under the bead of the tire and pry the tire over the lip of the rim. Be careful not to pinch the tube when you do this.

Step two: Hold the first tire iron in place. With the second tire iron, repeat step one, three or four inches down the rim. Alternate tire irons, pulling the bead of the tire over the rim, section by section, until one side of the tire bead is completely off the rim.

Step three: Remove the rest of the tire and tube from the rim. This can be done by hand. It's easiest to remove the valve stem last. Once the tire is off the rim, pull the tube out of the tire.

CLEAN AND SAFETY CHECK

Step four: Using a rag, wipe the inside of the tire to clean out any dirt, sand, glass, thorns, etc. These may cause the tube to puncture. The inside of a tire should feel smooth. Any pricks or bumps could mean that you have found the culprit responsible for your flat tire.

Step five Wipe the rim clean, then check the rim strip, making sure it covers the spoke nipples properly on the inside of the rim. If a spoke is poking through the rim strip, it could cause a puncture.

Step six: At this point, you can do one of two things: replace the punctured tube with a new one, or patch the hole. It's easiest to just replace the tube with a new tube when you're out

on the trails. Roll up the old tube and take it home to repair later that night in front of the TV. Directions on patching a tube are usually included with the patch kit itself.

INSTALLING THE TIRE AND TUBE *(This can be done entirely by hand)*

Step seven: Inflate the new or repaired tube with enough air to give it shape, then tuck it back into the tire.

Step eight: To put the tire and tube back on the rim, begin by putting the valve in the valve hole. The valve must be straight. Then use your hands to push the beaded edge of the tire onto the rim all the way around so that one side of your tire is on the rim.

Step nine: Let most of the air out of the tube to allow room for the rest of the tire.

Step ten: Beginning opposite the valve, use your thumbs to push

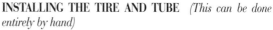

the other side of the tire onto the rim. Be careful not to pinch the tube in between the tire and the rim. The last few inches may be difficult, and you may need the tire iron to pry the tire onto the rim. If so, just be careful not to puncture the tube.

BEFORE INFLATING COMPLETELY

Step eleven: Check to make sure the tire is seated properly and that the tube is not caught between the tire and the rim. Do this by adding about 5 to 10 pounds of air, and watch closely that the tube does not bulge out of the tire.

Step twelve: Once you're sure the tire and tube are properly seated, put the wheel back on the bike, then fill the tire with air. It's easier squeezing the wheel through the brake shoes if the tire is still flat.

Step thirteen: Now fill the tire with the proper amount of air, and check constantly to make sure the tube doesn't bulge from the rim. If the tube does appear to bulge out, release all the air as quickly as possible, or you could be in for a big bang.

• *When installing the rear wheel*, place the chain back onto the smallest cog (furthest gear on the right), and pull the derailleur out of the way. Your wheel should slide right on.

LUBRICATION AVOIDS DETERIORATION

Lubrication is crucial to maintaining your bike. Dry spots will be eliminated. Creaks, squeaks, grinding, and binding will be gone. The chain will run quietly, and the gears will shift smoothly. The brakes will grip quicker, and your bike may last longer with fewer repairs. Need I say more? Well, yes. Without knowing where to put the lubrication, what good is it?

THINGS YOU WILL NEED

• One can of bicycle lubricant, found at any bike store.
• A clean rag (to wipe excess lubricant away).

WHAT GETS LUBRICATED

• Front derailleur
• Rear derailleur

- Shift levers
- Front brake
- Rear brake
- Both brake levers
- Chain

WHERE TO LUBRICATE

To make it easy, simply spray a little lubricant on all the pivot points of your bike. If you're using a squeeze bottle, use just a drop or two. Put a few drops on each point wherever metal moves against metal, for instance, at the center of the brake calipers. Then let the lube sink in.

Once you have applied the lubricant to the derailleurs, shift the gears a few times, working the derailleurs back and forth. This allows the lubricant to work itself into the tiny cracks and spaces it must occupy to do its job. Work the brakes a few times as well.

LUBING THE CHAIN

Lubricating the chain should be done after the chain has been wiped clean of most road grime. Do this by spinning the pedals counterclockwise while gripping the chain with a clean rag. As you add the lubricant, be sure to get some in between each link. With an aerosol spray, just spray the chain while pedalling backwards (counterclockwise) until the chain is fully lubricat-
ed. Let the lubricant soak in for a few seconds before wiping the excess away. Chains will collect dirt much faster if they're loaded with too much lubrication.

Vermont Bicycle Clubs and Trail Groups

Brattleboro Velo Club:
Laurent Holt, Pres., c/o Brattleboro
Bike Shop, 178 Main Street,
Brattleboro, VT, 05301,
(802) 254-8644

Dog River Cycling Club:
c/o Bicycle Express, Depot Square,
Northfield, VT 05663,
(802) 485-7430

Green Mountain Bike Club:
Ben Haydock, Pres., PO Box 492,
Williston, VT, 05495,
(802) 985-8232

Killington-Pico Cycling Club:
Jack Nuber, Pres., PO Box 522,
Pittsfield, VT, 05762,
(802) 746-8076

Kingdom Riders Mountain Bike Club:
Jeff Hale, Pres., E. Burke Sports, PO
Box 189, E. Burke, VT, 05832,
(802) 626-3215

Mad River Riders (primarily mtn. biking):
Carl Lobel, Pres., PO Box 1172,
Waitsfield, VT, 05673, 802-496-8999
(recording May-October) or
(802) 496-9500
(Mad River Bike Shop)

Middlebury Cycling Club:
David Tier, Pres., 74 Main Street,
Middlebury, VT, 05753,
(802) 388-6666

Mountain Bikers of Vermont:
Leigh Higgins, Pres., RD 1, Box 1450,
Waterbury, VT, 05676,
(802) 244-5067

Putney Bike Club:
Emanuel Betz, Pres., c/o West Hill
Shop, RR 4, Box 35, Putney, VT,
05346,
(802) 387-5718

Randolph Wheel Club:
John and Anne Kaplan, Co-Pres., PO
Box 284, Randolph, VT, 05060,
(802) 728-5747

Stowe Bike Club:
Bill Cannon, Pres., 890 West Hill
Road, Stowe, VT, 05672,
(802) 253-4368

Sunapee/Mowatt Bike Club (New Hampshire/Vermont Upper Valley):
Nelson Aldrich, Pres., 162 N. Main
St., Newport, New Hampshire, 03773,
(603) 863-3371

Index

Meet the Author

Jen's story is as unique and interesting as Vermont itself. A native of this Green Mountain state, Jen has been mountain bike racing and touring for nearly 10 years, spending several successful years on the NORBA and World Cup racing circuits. Several years ago, she and another riding companion hopped on their bikes and didn't stop until they had completed a 10,000 mile journey (by bike) through India, Nepal, Thailand, Malaysia, Singapore, Indonesia, Australia, and New Zealand! Her occupations now focus her energy on massage therapy, sports massage, alternative/natural medicine, and cooking—not to mention running and managing Coyote Hill Farm Mountain Bike Camp with husband Tom. Her other interests lie in Organic gardening, dogs, riding tandem with Tom, alpine, backcountry and cross-country skiing, and writing for regional publications such as *The Ride* and *Fat Content*. Stop by her farm if you're thirsty or hungry. Maybe she'll bake you one of her world famous "Jenergy" Bars and take you out on a ride.

Author

Now Available From Beachway Press
The Perfect Guidebook Companions

While *Mountain Bike Vermont* may be the quickest way for mountain bikers to learn the area; lugging it along on a ride will get old fast—pages will get dirty, the cover will bend, and this book will never look good on your bookshelf again. Enter the **BarMap**™ and **BarMap OTG**™. These two wonderfully designed mapcase systems by CycoActive Products make the perfect compliment to the Beachway Press **Mountain Bike America**™ Guidebook. Simply photocopy the route map and ride cues, slip them into your BarMap™ or BarMap OTG™ and you're ready to roll!

The BarMap OTG (Of The Gods) attaches to the bar and stem with three velcro loops. This compact carrying case shows an entire 8.5"x11" map inside, yet folds to a compact 5"x6" on the stem, slightly larger than a wallet. There's a 4"x5" clear pocket on the outside for route instructions or map. Inside is a mesh pocket for keys or money, and another pocket for energy bars, tools, and stuff. Sewn of Cordura and clear vinyl, with nylon borders. **$19.95**

Call Now To Order:
1-888-BEACHWAY

The BarMap mapcase is a simple, lightweight solution to this age-old problem many guidebook owners often experience. Its soft, clear mapcase velcros easily to the handlebar. Those days of digging maps out of your fanny pack, unfolding, refolding, and stuffing them back in, are forever in the past. Get the loop right the first time and leave the book in the car!
$7.95

The Perfect Mountain Biking Companion

The Forest Hump™
by CycoActive Products

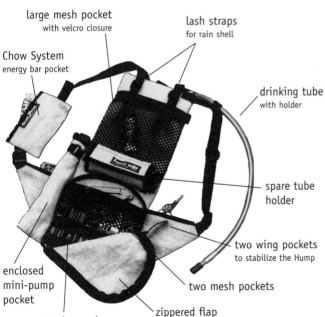

large mesh pocket
with velcro closure

lash straps
for rain shell

Chow System
energy bar pocket

drinking tube
with holder

spare tube
holder

two wing pockets
to stabilize the Hump

two mesh pockets

enclosed
mini-pump
pocket

zippered flap

tool organizer

This is not your ordinary, run-of-the-mill bladder bag. **The Forest Hump™** is the water and tool pack specifically designed with the mountain biker in mind! This incredibly light-weight pack not only carries everything you need, it also keeps it amazingly well organized—so you don't waste time fishing around. And it all stays secure on your back—even on your most insane downhill abuse sessions. You'll almost forget it's there! Available with 76 oz taste-free urethane bladder with extra-fat drinking tube.

grey/green or black	$53
with bladder	$70
Also Available:	
Forest HEmp	$63
with bladder	$80

Call Now To Order:
1-888-BEACHWAY

About the Beachway Press

MOUNTAIN BIKE AMERICA

guidebook series

The Mountain Bike America guidebook series is the cornerstone of Beachway Press' product line. This series of off-road bicycling guidebooks captures the heart and soul of one of the world's newest and most popular sports with its innovative style, casual manner, comprehensive information, and highly accurate maps using the latest in digital technology. The combination of these attributes makes each book within the series not only the preferred source of information on where to ride in each area, but also the hallmark of guidebooks on this subject.

Give us a buzz or visit us on the web to learn about other current and upcoming titles in this exciting and unique series.

... Enjoy Your World...

1-888-BEACHWAY